DANIEL

A READER'S GUIDE

WILLIAM H. SHEA

Pacific Press® Publishing Association
Nampa, Idaho
Oshawa, Ontario, Canada
www.pacificpress.com

Designed by Dennis Ferree
Cover illustration by Joe Maniscalco

Unless otherwise noted, all Scripture quotations are from the New International Version.

Additional copies of this book are available by calling
toll-free 1-800-765-6955 or
visiting http://www.adventistbookcenter.com

Library of congress Cataloging-in-Publication Data

Shea, William H.
Daniel : a reader's guide / William H. Shea.
p. cm.
ISBN 13: 978-0-8163-2077-6
ISBN 10: 0-8163-2077-2
1. Bible. O.T. Daniel—Commentaries. I. Title.

BS1555.53.S54 2005
224'.507—dc22 2004060242

12 13 14 • 5 4 3

To Karen

and to

Josie, Ted, and Becky

Table of Contents

Preface 7

Introduction to the Book of Daniel 11

1. Interpreting History 17

2. Exiled *(Daniel 1:1–21)* 32

3. Fallen Kings *(Daniel 4:1–5:31)* 45

4. Kingly Persecution *(Daniel 3:1–30; 6:1–28)* 69

5. Fallen Kingdoms *(Daniel 2:1–49; 7:1–28)* 93

6. Interpreting Prophecy 130

7. Christ as Sacrifice *(Daniel 9:1–27)* 142

8. Christ as Priest *(Daniel 8:1–27)* 173

9. Christ as King *(Daniel 9:1–27; 7:1–28)* 196

10. Summary of Daniel 7–9 221

11. The Final Message—Part 1 *(Daniel 10:1–12:13)* 230

12. The Final Message—Part 2 *(Daniel 10:1–12:13)* 250

13. Daniel's Walk With God 279

Preface

My interest in a serious, in-depth study of the book of Daniel began a number of years ago in a class titled, "Introduction to the Old Testament," taught by the well-known Adventist archeologist, Dr. Siegfried H. Horn. This was not my first introduction to Daniel, but it was my introduction to the serious, critical questions concerning the book.

One of those questions has to do with the identity of Darius the Mede brought to view in chapter 6. After dealing with that issue in class, Dr. Horn admitted the answer remained incomplete and suggested that someone should examine the Darius tablets in the different museum collections in an attempt to better identify the king mentioned in Daniel 6 from historical sources. Some years later, I took up that challenge. Since then, I have written several articles on the subject, but the identity of Darius the Mede still remains debatable. All that I can say is that I have narrowed the field of historical sources in which the answer to this question must be found. My interest in the historical backgrounds of Daniel 6 led me into the other historical chapters of the book.

The history brought to view in Daniel is a special kind of history—a theological history in which selected events are given while others are ignored. Of course, his own personal participation was one major factor in Daniel's selection of which events to record. There is something autobiographical about the historical chapters of Daniel's book. But they are more than just the story of what happened to Daniel in Babylon. They also reveal the hand of God in history and in Daniel's life. Thus, we can study Daniel 6 to see if there really was a historical figure such as Darius the Mede. But more importantly, we can also see how God acted on Daniel's behalf at this time in Babylon's history. Above and behind the historical accounts given in Daniel is the overarching perspective of the interaction of God in human history to work out His own eternal purposes.

In this way, history and theology come together. In Daniel, we have a selective religious history that reveals not only the political history of nations at that time, but also God's interaction with them and with His people who lived in these nations.

Beyond that, the history of the book gives us the context and starting point for the prophecies that appear in it. In Daniel, history and prophecy are not to be set apart in separate realms; they are interwoven. The two blend as the prophecies begin in the historical time of the prophet himself and then extend into the future beyond the prophet's day. Daniel actually lived under the first two of the nations found in the "outline" prophecies of the book—Babylon, Media-Persia, Greece, and Rome. And the fulfillment of those prophecies beyond his time have given testimony to the inspired nature of the prophecies given to him.

In terms of subject matter, Daniel's book is divided almost equally, with the first half being mostly history and the second half being mostly prophecy. Of course, we find elements of prophecy in the historical chapters, and there are, likewise, some historical elements in the prophetic chapters. But the general division of the book into roughly equal sections of history and prophecy is an accurate and helpful distinction.

I began my research into Daniel's prophecies by looking at the close connection between chapters 8 and 9. In the early 1980s, about the time I had completed my initial study, controversy broke out in the Seventh-day Adventist Church regarding these particular prophetic chapters. As a result, my work with the Biblical Research Institute of the General Conference required me to give more detailed attention to the prophetic portions of Daniel. This study resulted in an unpublished manuscript, "Daniel and the Judgment." Eventually BRI published certain chapters from this manuscript as volume one of the Daniel and

Revelation Committee Series, under the title, *Selected Studies in Prophetic Interpretation.* As the title suggests, this work was not a chapter-by-chapter commentary on Daniel's prophecies, but dealt rather with certain topics only.

In contrast, this study of Daniel does deal with the entire sweep of the prophetic chapters and presents them more or less in consecutive order. This enables the reader to study the text in a more orderly fashion. However, I have chosen to deal with the text of Daniel in a way that does not strictly follow the original order as given in the book itself. For example, in examining chapters 7, 8, and 9, I have reversed the order—taking up chapter 9 first, then chapter 8, followed by chapter 7. I have done so because I believe the text becomes more meaningful if viewed in this order. I have also followed this "reverse" order based on insights that have come from studying the literary structure of various Old Testament texts—especially the Psalms. In the various chapters that cover these prophecies, I have provided further justification for altering the order of the chapters for the purpose of studying them.

The history presented in the earlier portions of Daniel's book flows quite naturally into the prophetic sections. There is a sense in which prophecy is merely history written from the divine viewpoint before it happens. Some elements of history provide a basis for reviewing the fulfillment of prophecies after the events have happened. Thus, we will not find a sharp separation in Daniel's book between history and prophecy. The great outline prophecies in Daniel begin quite naturally with Babylon and Media-Persia—the kingdoms that existed in the prophet's own time. They go on to point to kingdoms yet to come—Greece and Rome. Finally, they come down to our own time and beyond—until God's kingdom makes its appearance. God's eternal kingdom is the great goal of history. It is also the great goal of prophecy, and it should be the great goal of our own personal, spiritual journey as well.

The final reason we need to carefully study the historical chapters of Daniel is for the spiritual lessons we can learn from them. In the reaction of Daniel and his friends to the pagan culture of Babylon we can find an example of how to live in the pagan culture of our own century.

Their lives can provide a model for the way we should live today—honest, dedicated to God, and courageous in His faith.

Therefore, as we see the unfolding of history and prophecy in Daniel, we see God's hand guiding that history by His mighty acts on behalf of His people—national Israel in the Old Testament, and the church in the New Testament. As surely as He has guided that history in the past, just so surely will He eventually bring about its culmination in His glorious kingdom. That was Daniel's inspired focus, and it should be ours as well. Our own spiritual experience with God should have as its goal living with Him forever in the kingdom He has promised to set up at the end of time.

It is my hope that this study will contribute in some measure toward that end.

William H. Shea
Silver Spring, Maryland

INTRODUCTION TO THE BOOK OF DANIEL

This survey of the book begins with a brief review of the author's personal biography. We should become acquainted with Daniel the man before we come to the subject of Daniel the prophet.

Daniel was born in the late seventh century B.C. and lived his early years in Jerusalem or its vicinity. By the time he had grown to manhood, political and military struggles in the great nations of his time altered the fate of little Judah in which he lived. From the time of Daniel's birth until 605 B.C., Judah was nominally under the control of Egypt. In that year, however, a major battle took place; Egypt was defeated, and Babylon came to exercise control over Judah and Jerusalem. Nebuchadnezzar II, commander of the Babylonian army, led his troops to the gates of Jerusalem and demanded the payment of tribute and a selection of choice hostages. Daniel was among those chosen. He was selected, along with the others, because of his future potential as a civil servant in Babylon—a task he fulfilled, after the requisite training period, for more than sixty years.

But God had something more in mind for Daniel than mere service at the court of Babylon. God called him to the office of prophet and gave him dreams and visions. Some of these dreams, visions, and prophetic statements were addressed to the people of his time. On three different occasions, Daniel was given prophecies which dealt with, or were delivered to, kings at the royal court in Babylon. This type of prophecy—dealing with contemporary persons and issues—is sometimes called *classical* prophecy. Daniel spoke with prophetic voice to the kings of Babylon just as Jeremiah spoke to the kings in Jerusalem.

On other occasions, he was given prophecies which involved a longer range of vision, looking into the future history of the nations. This second type of prophecy is commonly called *apocalyptic* prophecy because it deals more specifically with revealing the future. It is also called outline prophecy because it outlines the history of nations in advance.

Thus in Daniel's book we find these two different types of prophecies—classical and apocalyptic. We also find another distinct type of narrative—history. Different sections of the book clearly contain these different types of literature. In general, the book of Daniel divides in half; the first half is history, and the second half is prophecy. It is in the first half of the book—in the context of history—that we find the classical prophecies that deal with contemporary persons and events. The prophecies of the second half of the book are more apocalyptic in character.

The languages used in Daniel's book also emphasize the distinction between the two main sections. Most of the historical chapters were written in Aramaic, while most of the prophetic chapters were written in Hebrew. Hebrew was Daniel's native tongue, and Aramaic was a related language that was used for part of the official correspondence of the Neo-Babylonian and Persian Empires. More than any other book in the Bible, Daniel is bilingual. Ezra was also written in both Hebrew and Aramaic, but only a small part of Ezra—the royal decrees—is in Aramaic.

This twofold nature of Daniel provides a convenient outline with which to study the book. Some commentaries on Daniel hold that this book was not written by a single individual, Daniel, who lived in sixth-century B.C. Babylon, but rather by an unknown, anonymous author who lived in Judea in the second century B.C. The nature of the materials found in the historical chapters bear upon this question.

The prophecies of Daniel also have been interpreted in very different ways. Three main schools of thought exist on the interpretation of Daniel's prophecies. *(1) Preterist.* This method of interpretation places all the emphasis on the past and sees the fulfillment of portions of the prophecies as past. *(2) Futurist.* This school of thought places the fulfillment of Daniel in the future. *(3) Historicist.* This view of the prophecies emphasizes a flow and continuity from the past through the present and into the as-yet-unfulfilled future. It is sometimes called the continuous historical view because it sees the prophecies as part of a continuum from the past to the future. The introduction to the prophetic section of Daniel's book explores the strengths and weaknesses of each of these schools of interpretation. The approach taken in this book falls in the category of the historicist view.

Daniel's experience included more than just being a historical figure. There was even more to Daniel than his experience as a prophet. There was also the matter of his own personal spiritual experience with God. This side of his experience and his book should not be neglected or overwhelmed by the other elements. The last chapter of this book considers the important matter of Daniel's own spiritual experience as a chosen instrument of God.

So that will be the order of march in this look at the book of Daniel: history, prophecy, and spiritual experience.

A NOTE ON THE ORDER OF TREATMENT

The reader will notice that the order in which this study takes up the different aspects of Daniel's book varies somewhat from the standard and canonical order of the chapters in the book itself. However, if one looks carefully at the datelines of the biblical chapters—when they are given—it is apparent that Daniel does not present his material in strict chronological order either. For example, the prophecies of Daniel in chapters 7 and 8 were actually given *before* the historical events of chapters 5 and 6. Although all of the events recorded in Daniel are historical in the sense that they actually happened, they have been arranged in a certain way for a certain purpose. *To a degree, this study on Daniel has endeavored to follow the thought order rather than the written order. For that reason, the reader will find some irregularity in the order in which the chapters are presented.*

In the first part of this book—the historical section—the chapters studied follow something of an inverted order. Chapters 2 and 7 have been grouped together because they are concerned with prophecies about the nations. Chapters 3 and 6 have been grouped together because they deal with persecution of the Jews in exile, Daniel and his three friends in particular. Chapters 4 and 5 have been grouped together because they deal with Nebuchadnezzar and Belshazzar, the kings of Babylon. This type of inverted order is sometimes known as a *chiasm* (from the Greek letter *chi* which looks like an X). That something like this was intended by the original author is evident from the fact that it is precisely these six historical chapters that were written in the Aramaic language.

When we come to the prophetic chapters, the order is not inverted; rather, it is reversed. Thus we have chosen to study the three main prophetic chapters in the heart of the book of Daniel in reverse order; beginning with chapter 9, then going on to chapter 8, followed by chapter 7, and finally concluding that section with a summary of these three chapters. The reason for this order of study has to do with thought order, not chronological or historical order. In terms of the events to which these prophecies refer, chapter 9 comes first because it focuses especially upon the Messiah. The contents of chapter 8 go on well beyond that point into the Christian Era. But it is Daniel 7 which carries the prophecy on into the final kingdom of God and pictures the saints of the Most High as entering and possessing it.

There is a reason for following this thought order; it is not the arbitrary selection of a modern commentator who simply wants to do something different. In modern western-European thought, we reason from cause to effect. We collect all the data and then synthesize it into a hypothesis. Finally, we refine that hypothesis to a theory. That is the procedure of the modern scientific method.

But the ancients were not moderns nor were they scientists, so they worked out things in their own way. While they were quite capable of working through things in chronological order as we do, they also utilized an approach that involved reasoning from effect back to cause. The prophets could depict a scene in such a way that their listeners were led to inquire, "Why did this happen?" This question led them back to the cause. An inspired prophet could say, "This land will be destroyed and left desolate," leading back to the natural question, "Why will this land be destroyed?" The answer to that question commonly lay in the fact that the people to whom the prophet was sent were a wicked and rebellious people who had broken their covenant with God. For an example of this approach see Jeremiah chapters 4 through 7 and Micah chapter 1. Wickedness was the cause, and desolation was the result—but the prophet gave the result first in order to lead his readers to a discussion of the cause.

That is the kind of thought order followed in these three prophecies at the heart of Daniel. If Daniel were presenting these prophecies to a modern audience today, he would naturally give chapter 9 first, because that chapter deals with the first events to happen. He would follow with chapter 8 because that prophecy presents the next events to happen. Finally, he would give chapter 7 because that prophecy presents the grand climax to the series. Only when these prophecies are put in this thought order does the modern reader appreciate fully their great sweep and connection with each other—something that would have come more naturally to an ancient listener or reader because of the way in which his or her thought processes had been conditioned. By reversing Daniel's original order of presentation, we have attempted to unveil the full beauty of the way in which these prophecies were first presented.

The final major line of prophecy in Daniel's book is found in chapters 10–12. Chapter 10 presents the introduction, or prologue, to this prophecy, and chapter 12 contains its epilogue, or conclusion. The body of the prophecy in chapter 11 is very detailed and follows a historical and chronological order.

There are four major apocalyptic, or outline, prophecies in the book of Daniel. They are found in chapters 2, 7, 8, and 11. Outline prophecies cover the rise and fall of nations from the prophet's day to the end of time.

The other major prophecy in Daniel's book is found at the end of chapter 9. While the four major outline prophecies deal with the rise and fall of nations, chapter 9 deals more exclusively with the people of Daniel's city and country—Jerusalem and Judah. Although the events of this prophecy run parallel to those of the other major outline prophecies, they focus upon a particular part of that world not covered in the other prophecies—the history of the Jewish people in Judea down to the time of the Messiah. The fact that the four major lines of prophecy in this book go over the same outline of nations is called *recapitulation,* or *parallelism.* Just as the four Gospels go over the same events from different perspectives, so these four lines of complementary prophecies go over the same territory, filling in more details each time. The presentation starts out on the most broad scale in chapter 2, with the nations represented by different metals in an image. By the time we reach chapter 11, we are down to the individual kings of each nation and their personal actions. Chapter 2 starts out with the use of the telescope, while chapter 11 ends up with the use of the microscope.

The final chapter of our examination of Daniel ends on the theme of spiritual relationship. This element is found not so much in the prophecy itself as in the experience of the prophet. That is where I feel it should also end up for the reader.

CHAPTER ONE

INTERPRETING HISTORY

The first half of Daniel, chapters 1 to 6, is essentially historical in nature. These historical narratives include some prophecy, but clearly they contain more history than prophecy. The historical nature of this portion of the book raises several significant questions:

- What is the biblical view of history?
- What is Daniel's view of history?
- Does the book address Neo-Babylonian history or some later period?
- What is God's activity in history? What is His relationship to it?

These questions all boil down to two main ones:

1. Does God interact with human history, or has He gone off to some other portion of His universe leaving earth to go along on its own?
2. With what period of history does Daniel's book deal?

The second question involves historicity more than history, and the text of the book itself gives a direct and readily available answer: Daniel's book presents itself as a record of the experiences of some persons who lived during the period of the Neo-Babylonian kingdom, during the late seventh and much of the sixth century B.C. But beyond this simple answer lies another issue: Is the book of Daniel really a true record of events which happened in the sixth century B.C.? Or is it something that was written down later by someone other than the prophet Daniel to make it sound as if it occurred in the sixth century B.C.?

Many current commentaries on Daniel often answer these questions by taking the position that God does *not* intervene in human affairs and that the book was actually written in the second century B.C., not the sixth, by someone other than Daniel. Therefore, these commentators don't expect the book of Daniel to be historically accurate or true to the sixth century B.C. setting it describes. In down-to-earth language this is what is known as "Daniel in the critics' den."

THE BIBLICAL VIEW OF HISTORY

Does God interact with human history? This is a philosophical question. It involves the biblical view of history and goes back to the question of the essential nature of Scripture at its very core. What is the Bible? More specifically to our discussion of Daniel's book, what is the Old Testament? It is a revelation of the nature, character, and purposes of God. But it is more than that. It provides a history that begins with Creation in Genesis and ends with Ezra and Nehemiah in the Persian period. That history extends through the books of Moses and Joshua, the book of Judges, 1 and 2 Samuel, and the books of Kings, paralleled by Chronicles. Finally, that history comes to an end with the records of Ezra and Nehemiah. In all, it extends over more than two millennia. But there is more to this history than mere raw records of what happened. There is a particular view of history, and that view is intimately involved with God as the central actor on the stage of that history. It is, as one historian-theologian has described it, a record of "the mighty acts of God." God has been active throughout all of that history, interacting with human beings, guiding and directing them, not only in terms of their earthly affairs but also in terms of how to obtain His salvation.

This same view of history is also evident in the book of Daniel. Here, the story starts with the first conquest of Jerusalem by Nebuchadnezzar. This turn of events must have looked disastrous to many of the Jews living in Jerusalem at that time. Yet behind it all, God was working out His purposes. He permitted the conquest of Judah and Jerusalem because the nation was led by Jehoiakim, a wicked and rebellious king, and because its society was morally corrupt. Even in the tragedy of conquest, however, God brought good out of evil. His servants—Daniel and his friends—were brought into circumstances where they were able to witness in a way that extended far beyond their little family circle in Judah. They became witnesses for the true God among all the courtiers of Babylon and before the most powerful monarch of the time. God gave Jehoiakim into Nebuchadnezzar's hand, but He also gave favor to Daniel and his friends before that very same king. Thus, in the personal and national events of the time, we can see God's hand at work. And since we have the inspired word of the prophet Daniel who viewed those workings and was given information from heaven about them, we can see the intervention of God in these human circumstances all the more clearly.

We see God's intervention in human history in other aspects of Daniel as well. God not only intervenes in the course of history between nations, such as Babylon and Judah, but He also involves Himself in the history, the personal story, of individuals. For Daniel's friends, we see God's miraculous intervention especially in chapter 3 with the story of their deliverance from the fiery furnace. In the case of Daniel, God's involvement is operative all the way through the book, but it comes especially to the forefront in chapter 6 with the miraculous deliverance of Daniel from the hungry lions in their lair. So God operates on the level of nations and historical events of epic proportions, but He also interacts with people on an individual level.

The third way in which the book of Daniel demonstrates God's attention to, and involvement in, the history of nations and individuals is through the prophecies given there. The four major outline prophecies of the book, those in chapters 2, 7, 8, and 11, provide a preview from the time of the prophet down through the ages of history to follow. God not only has an interest in the course of the history of the nations; He not only intervenes on occasion to affect it; but He also knows the course that it will take. Readers of the book of Daniel may rest assured that there is indeed a caring God behind the scenes of action in history.

This view of the world that is presented in Daniel and throughout the Bible is not very compatible with modern philosophical thought.

DANIEL

The modern worldview has its origin not so much in the Bible as in the philosophy of the ancient Greeks. In particular, this modern worldview was shaped by revolutions in thought that occurred in the eighteenth century A.D., known as the Age of Reason. Working from the physical model constructed from the mathematics of Sir Isaac Newton and others, the view was developed that the human mind was all-sufficient and there was no need for an external source of knowledge or inspiration such as God. This humanistic view came to prevail in intellectual circles, leaving little room for God. For a time He was tolerated on the periphery of human experience. Deism was a movement that saw God as a watchmaker. He created the world, the solar system, and the universe—then wound it up so that it would run on its own, according to its own laws that scientists were discovering.

Soon, however, the theory of evolution came along in the mid-nineteenth century and removed God from even that small role. Now there was no longer any need for a watchmaker to make the watch in the first place. The watch had evolved on its own. All of this led to a direct confrontation between the biblical school of thought and rationalistic humanism. The Bible says there is a God and that He has revealed Himself. Rationalistic humanism says there is no God and there is no revelation from Him. The Bible thus becomes central to this debate.

One aspect of the Bible that demonstrates that there is a God and that He has revealed Himself is the matter of predictive prophecy. It might be that an especially well-informed person could accurately guess the course of events in the immediate or near future. But to propose that someone, utilizing only natural human resources, could correctly predict what was going to happen five, six, or seven centuries in advance, as is the case in the book of Daniel, goes far beyond any natural human knowledge. Such insight could come only from the realm of the supernatural. As a consequence, the issue of predictive prophecy has played a significant part in discussions between those who accept the biblical view and those who do not.

Those who deny the biblical view of God and history must find a humanistic explanation for the predictive aspect of the prophecies given in the Bible. One way to nullify the predictive content of a prophetic book such as Daniel is to say that its prophecies were not fulfilled, that the events predicted did not come to pass. Later chapters of this book will take up the evidences for the fulfillment of the prophecies of Daniel.

But there is another way to cancel the predictive element of a prophetic book, and that is to demonstrate that the book's local historical content is inaccurate. For example, Daniel's prophecies purport to have been given in the setting of sixth-century B.C. Babylon. If Daniel, supposedly writing from the vantage point of sixth-century B.C. Babylon, does not have his Babylonian history straight, then one need not give credence to any of the prophetic details he gives either. In other words, one way to undermine the prophetic section of Daniel is to first undermine the accuracy of its historical section. If the historical accuracy of the book can be impugned, its prophecies need not be taken seriously.

But if this argument has validity, then the reverse must also be valid. If we can demonstrate that Daniel's historical sections *are* accurate and dependable, then we must take seriously what he says in the prophetic sections as well. We turn, then, to that issue—the historical accuracy of Daniel.

THE HISTORICAL ACCURACY OF DANIEL

Those who do not accept the view that God is intimately involved in human history and who have no place in their thinking for predictive prophecy, have pointed to a number of supposed historical inaccuracies in Daniel's book as a means of denying the predictive element of the prophetic portions. So the problem for those who see Daniel's prophetic portions as predicting events far in the future is to meet these objections and demonstrate the historical accuracy of the book. We will do this by taking up five of the major objections that have been raised against the historical accuracy of Daniel. There is evidence in each of these cases to indicate that rather than being historical inaccuracies in the biblical record, they are actually misunderstandings by modern historians of what the record really says.

However, before we take up these five individual objections to the historical accuracy of Daniel, let's examine the basic presuppositions that underlie them as a whole.

DANIEL

Scholars who study Daniel from the viewpoint of rationalistic humanism cannot accommodate supernatural revelation into their understanding of the book. Such a view, of course, excludes the possibility that Daniel's prophecies were actually given in the sixth century B.C. and predicted subsequent events centuries in the future. The usual explanation has been that the book of Daniel was actually written much later—most probably in the second century B.C. The writer is supposed to have been an anonymous individual who lived in Jerusalem in 165 B.C., during the time of Antiochus IV Epiphanes, a Greek king from Syria. Antiochus IV persecuted the Jews and disrupted their religious services in the temple, so much of the prophecy in Daniel is thought to focus upon him and his persecuting activities. Thus, these scholars argue, the so-called prophecies of Daniel are really history written in the form of prophecy. That is, a second-century B.C. writer based his material on contemporary events taking place around him, but presented them in the form of prophecies that purported to have been written in the sixth century B.C. predicting these events.

And if the writer of Daniel actually lived in the second century B.C., naturally he would not be able to present the history of sixth-century B.C. Babylon without making mistakes. Thus, according to this argument, inaccuracies in the history of Babylon and the sixth century B.C. are proof of a late authorship for the book and the lack of a true predictive element in the prophecies.

Let's turn, then, to the five major examples that have been cited as historical inaccuracies in the book of Daniel. What is the evidence? Are these indeed historical mistakes—or misunderstandings on the part of the critics?

THE DATE IN DANIEL 1:1

Daniel 1:1 gives the date of Nebuchadnezzar's first siege of Jerusalem as "in the third year of the reign of Jehoiakim king of Judah." Critical scholars argue that the correct date is actually the *fourth* year of Jehoiakim, or 605 B.C., when correlated with the events described in Nebuchadnezzar's own chronicles.

The sequence of events runs like this: Josiah, King of Judah, died when he went out to fight Pharaoh Neco at Megiddo in the summer of

609 B.C., as the Egyptian ruler was on his way north to fight with the Babylonians (see 2 Kings 23:29). An accurate date for this campaign of Neco can be obtained from the Babylonian Chronicle, the official record of the first eleven years of Nebuchadnezzar's reign. Upon his return from northern Syria in the fall of that same year, Neco deposed Jehoahaz of Judah and carried him off to Egypt (see 2 Kings 23:33–35). In his place he installed Jehoiakim as king (verse 34).

The important chronological point here is that this final transition, the installation of Jehoiakim as Judah's king, took place after Rosh Hashana, the fall New Year. Thus the first official year of Jehoiakim's reign began in the fall of 608 B.C. The period of time before that fall New Year was known as the "accession year" or Year 0. Thus Jehoiakim's third year, mentioned in Daniel 1:1, began in the fall of 606 B.C. and extended to the fall of 605 B.C. Within that year, Nebuchadnezzar fought the battle of Carchemish in Syria in the spring (Jeremiah 46:2). He came up to Jerusalem in the summer of that year before Jehoiakim's fourth year began in the fall.

Thus if one interprets this date according to the principle of accession year reckoning and the Jewish (fall-to-fall) calendar, the date works out correctly as the Jewish fall-to-fall year of 606/605 B.C. which is historically accurate.

BELSHAZZAR AS KING OF BABYLON

Another criticism of the historical episodes in the book of Daniel has centered around the figure of Belshazzar in chapter 5. It is clear from various historical sources that the last king of the Neo-Babylonian Empire was Nabonidus, not Belshazzar. Yet Daniel 5 portrays Belshazzar as the king in the palace of Babylon the night the city fell to the Persians.

Knowledge about the existence of Belshazzar was lost from the time of the ancient world down to the year A.D. 1861. During those years, he was unknown from primary historical sources, and various theories were advanced about his identity, especially during the eighteenth and nineteenth centuries A.D. In 1861 the first cuneiform tablet was published mentioning Belshazzar by name. Twenty years later, Nabonidus' *Chronicle* was published; it told about a series of years during which

Belshazzar managed governmental affairs in Babylon while his father Nabonidus was in Arabia. Finally, in 1924, another cuneiform text was published, now called the Verse Account of Nabonidus. It tells, among other things, that when Nabonidus left Babylon he "entrusted the kingship" to his son Belshazzar. Thus a whole interconnected series of tablets have been discovered in recent years which reveal the role that Belshazzar played in political and military events of Babylon in the sixth century B.C.

On this point, the critics of Daniel's history have had to retreat. One wrote candidly, "presumably we shall never know how the author of Daniel knew of these events." Actually, it is easy to understand when one takes the evidence of the book itself into account. The answer is that Daniel was on the scene of action at the time as an eyewitness.

Still trying to rescue some credibility from this turn of events, critics have exploited another aspect of this problem. They have noted that there is no specific Babylonian tablet which directly refers to Belshazzar as "king." This observation is accurate as far as it goes. But what does it mean when the Verse Account of Nabonidus says he "entrusted the kingship" to Belshazzar?

A Hebrew who came out of the political environment Daniel did would be well aware of the practice of co-regency. David put Solomon on the throne with him so that there were two co-kings ruling Israel for a time. This also happened again at various times in Israel's history. Daniel, therefore, simply referred to Belshazzar as "king" because he occupied the position of king and functioned as a king. Daniel was historically correct because he knew who was ruling in Babylon while Nabonidus was away from the capital for ten years.

There is a small, but important detail, in Daniel 5 that shows just how accurate Daniel's knowledge of Belshazzar and his fate really was. Daniel tells us who was in the palace in the city that night—and who was not. Belshazzar was there, but Nabonidus, the chief king, was not. This detail is something that could have been known only by a witness to those events in the sixth century B.C. A writer in the second century B.C. might well have made the mistake of putting Nabonidus, the last chief king, in the palace that night. But Daniel did not make that mistake, and the Nabonidus Chronicle tells us where Nabonidus was. He had taken one division of the Babylonian army out to the Tigris River to fight Cyrus and his troops as they approached from the east. Belshazzar was left in the city with the other division to protect it. The writer of Daniel knew that Belshazzar was in the city the night it fell, and he makes no mention of Nabonidus for the obvious reason that he was elsewhere. This small, seemingly insignificant, detail reveals just how historically accurate Daniel was in the case of Belshazzar.

THE SEPARATE MEDIAN KINGDOM

For centuries, orthodox interpreters of the book of Daniel have seen its fourfold sequence of kingdoms in chapters 2 and 7 as representing Babylon, Media-Persia, Greece, and Rome. Since the book of Daniel mentions a king named Darius *the Mede,* critical scholars have argued that the writer of Daniel thought there was a separate Median kingdom *after* the Babylonian kingdom. Therefore, they feel that on the evidence of the book itself, the sequence should be shortened to Babylon, Media, Persia, and Greece. In this way the series ends not with Rome, but with Antiochus Epiphanes who came out of the Greek kingdom. This, they say, is consistent with what a second-century B.C. author would write, but that it is a historical mistake to speak of a separate Median kingdom after the time of Babylon.

There *was* a separate Median kingdom back in the ninth, eighth, and seventh centuries B.C. That is well known and is not at issue. But the critics are correct that it would be a historical error to insert a separate Median kingdom in this sequence *after* 539 B.C. when the Babylonian kingdom fell. The Medes had been conquered by the Persians earlier in the sixth century B.C. and for the next two centuries were an integral component of the Persian Empire.

Did the writer of Daniel make such a mistake and identify a separate kingdom of Media? Not on the basis of the evidence in the text. The ram in the prophecy of chapter 8 is identified in verse 20: "the two-horned ram that you saw represents the kings of Media and Persia." The single symbolic ram represented the single kingdom of Media-Persia.

The same point is made in the narrative of chapter 6 where the law given by Darius was said to be "in accordance with the laws of the

Medes and Persians, which cannot be repealed" (verse 12). If Media and Persia were separate kingdoms at this time the reference would have been to "the laws of the Medes and the laws of the Persians" rather than to "the laws of the Medes and the Persians." One codex of laws governed the dual kingdom.

The writing on the wall in chapter 5:28 teaches the same thing for Belshazzar's kingdom was "divided and given to the Medes and Persians." There are no grounds in the book of Daniel for separating an individual Median kingdom. The sequence should stand as it has been interpreted—Babylon, Media-Persia, Greece, and Rome.

DARIUS THE MEDE

The identity of Darius the Mede is still a matter of some dispute even among conservative scholars who accept his historical existence. This case is not yet as clear as the one that deals with Belshazzar. Several candidates have been mentioned as possibilities, including two Persian kings, two Median kings, and two Persian governors. These will be discussed in more detail in the chapter that deals with Daniel 6. Here only two points need to be mentioned.

First, we know there was a co-regent in Babylon during the first year of Persian control. The everyday, business tablets of Babylon at this time carry the names of the kings and their titles along with a date expressed in terms of the king's regnal year. From these documents, it is clear that Cyrus did not carry the title "King of Babylon" for the first year after the Persian conquest; none of the tablets written then assign that title to him.

Second, there is the matter of throne names. In ancient times, kings commonly had personal names before they took the throne; after taking the kingship, they assumed another official name. This was very common in Egypt, and was practiced occasionally in Israel. Azariah who was also named Uzziah is an example. This custom was used rarely in Mesopotamia, but perhaps somewhat more commonly in Persia, according to some modern historians. Thus Darius, as mentioned in Daniel, could well be a throne name, but we still need to be more accurate in identifying the personal name of the individual who may have taken that throne name.

THE DATE OF DANIEL'S ARAMAIC LANGUAGE

Earlier studies argued that the Aramaic language used in chapters 2–7 of Daniel more closely matched the Aramaic of the second century B.C., than that of the sixth century B.C. However, when those studies were carried out, only one set of ancient Aramaic texts was well known—the Elephantine Papyri from fifth-century B.C. Egypt. Since Daniel's Aramaic differed somewhat from the language used in the Elephantine Papyri, it was argued that Daniel's Aramaic was from a later period.

A steady stream of discoveries of Aramaic inscriptions has since given us a much more complete picture of that language and its development—and a better basis of comparison with the Aramaic appearing in Daniel. The differences between the Aramaic of Daniel and that found in the Elephantine Papyri were thought at one time to represent a chronological development in this language, but are now known to be a regional dialect development instead. The Elephantine Papyri that formed the original basis for comparison all came from Egypt and reflected an Egyptian dialect of Aramaic. This dialect differed from the way the language was written and spoken in Judah, Syria, Babylonia, and Iran. Each of these regions had its own regional dialect. A number of the Aramaic features in the book of Daniel that were thought to be late characteristics—such as the position of the verb, for example—are now known to be early characteristics peculiar to eastern regions, in other words, like the Aramaic of Babylonia where Daniel lived!

Another major development in this area has come from the discovery of the Dead Sea Scrolls. The Essenes who worked at the monastery at Qumran by the Dead Sea from the second century B.C. to the late first century A.D., wrote and copied a number of Aramaic documents as well as Hebrew texts. As these documents have been published, it has become clear that Daniel's Aramaic is considerably older than these Dead Sea documents. Since modern critical scholars believe Daniel was written at about the same time as the Dead Sea Scrolls, it is awkward for their view that there is not a closer correspondence in terms of language. The Aramaic Dead Sea scrolls have also revealed that Daniel's Aramaic is not Palestinian by geographic distribution. Rather it is an eastern type of Aramaic, as one would expect of a resident of Babylonia.

Thus the major developments in the study of the Aramaic language appearing in Daniel have all tended to move the date for that writing earlier than the critics believed. At present, Daniel's Aramaic is simply classified as "Imperial Aramaic" meaning that it fits well within the dates of the Persian Empire from the seventh through the fourth centuries B.C. The linguistic argument is no longer a serviceable argument against the earlier date of Daniel's Aramaic.

Thus after examining the major objections to the historical accuracy of Daniel, we can say with assurance that its language and historical content corroborate the testimony of the book itself that it was written in the sixth century B.C. Thus the argument of the critics that we cannot trust its prophetic statements because of its historical inaccuracies is shattered.

THE LITERARY STRUCTURE OF THE HISTORICAL CHAPTERS

In concluding this chapter, we need to look at one other feature of the first half of the book. This feature does not have to do with dating or determining historicity; rather it deals with why the chapters of Daniel are arranged in the order in which they are.

The careful reader will realize that the historical narratives of the book are not arranged in a strictly chronological order. For example, chapters 5 and 6, which are dated in the Persian period, precede chapters 7 and 8, which belong to the earlier Babylonian period. A chronological order would require that chapters 7 and 8 should precede chapters 5 and 6. So some other organizing principle must have been used. As noted earlier, Daniel does divide—with some overlap—into roughly equal sections of historical and prophetic chapters.

More than that, however, the chapters that were written in Aramaic—chapters 2 through 7—exhibit a specific literary order. These six chapters stand apart from the rest of the book on the basis of the language used. They also stand apart in terms of literary structure—the way they are ordered within their own section. These chapters are clearly related to each other in pairs based on content. Chapters 2 and 7 form one pair; both chapters are outline prophecies that deal with the rise and fall of kingdoms over great portions of human history.

Likewise, chapters 3 and 6 are also similar in content. Chapter 3 describes the persecution of Daniel's three friends in the fiery furnace; chapter 6 describes Daniel's own persecution in the lions' den. In both cases God's servants suffer trials of their faith, and in both cases they are supernaturally delivered from those trials.

This leaves chapters 4 and 5 standing together as a pair within the Aramaic and historical portion of the book. These chapters also deal with the same subject—an individual Babylonian king. In chapter 4, it is Nebuchadnezzar who is in view. In chapter 5, it is Belshazzar. Both of these narratives begin with a local setting—Nebuchadnezzar in his palace, and Belshazzar in that same palace. Both of these kings had become cases of vaunted ego, and both were judged by the true God. In both instances, their judgments came in the form of prophecies which were subsequently fulfilled. Daniel was present to interpret both of these prophecies. The two stories have slightly different endings, but even here, they still bear a relationship to each other. In chapter 4, Nebuchadnezzar fell into a period of insanity, but then was able to rise again and return to his throne. In chapter 5, however, there is no subsequent redemption for Belshazzar. He and his city fell that night to the Persian conquerors.

Thus the narratives of the Aramaic and historical section of the book of Daniel line up according to thematic pairs along the following kind of outline:

A. Daniel 2—prophecy about the rise and fall of kingdoms
B. Daniel 3—narrative about the persecution of Daniel's friends
C. Daniel 4—prophecy about fall and rise of King Nebuchadnezzar
C. Daniel 5—prophecy about the fall of King Belshazzar
B. Daniel 6—narrative about the persecution of Daniel
A. Daniel 7—prophecy about the rise and fall of kingdoms

Such an outline is like a step ladder with steps on both sides in which one ascends in the same order that one descends the steps on the other side, A : B : C : C : B : A. The technical name for this order of writing is a *chiasm*. This word comes from the name of the Greek letter *chi* which looks something like an X. The idea is that the outline proceeds up one leg of this kind of X and then follows in reverse order down the other. It is organization based on inversion or a mirror image. What we have here in Daniel is a relatively simple *chiasm* based upon thematic links between two stories of a similar nature. A glance at the chiastic outline above shows that chapters 2 and 7 are thematically linked, as are chapters 3 and 6, and chapters 4 and 5. This kind of arrangement is fairly common in the Old Testament, especially in the psalms, so it is evident that the people of Daniel's time were well aware of this type of writing.

What purpose did it serve for them, and what value does it have for us today? It served several functions. First, it was an easy memory device. If you had to memorize the contents of these six chapters of Daniel, that might be a difficult assignment. However, it would be much easier to remember what each chapter is about once you recognize this inverse order.

Second, this kind of organization makes it possible to see explanatory links between the paired narratives. For example, many commentators have recognized that the prophecy of chapter 7 is a further and more detailed explanation of the prophecy given in chapter 2. The two prophecies are related; they are not referring to different and distinct periods of history. The literary structure, then, becomes simply another way to reinforce that link.

Third, there is the matter of aesthetics. It is good to recognize that the Bible speaks to us in many different ways and cultures. But it is also good to realize that there is literary beauty in these expressions as well. We recognize the literary beauty of some of the psalms. Why not recognize the literary beauty of some biblical prose, such as these chapters in Daniel? Daniel is not the small, insignificant work of an unimportant editor; this is the work, under God, of a literary artist, and we need to recognize his skill.

Finally, this literary structure emphasizes the unity of this section of Daniel and the whole book. These narratives have been very precisely fitted together in a specific order, like the bricks used to build a fireplace. One cannot be removed without having the whole structure crumble. Each is vital to the order and relationship. Literary critics of Daniel have missed this point. They have tried to separate chapter 7 from the rest of the historical chapters. For them, the prophecy of chapter 7 was written about 165 B.C. in the time of Antiochus Epiphanes, but the preceding historical chapters were written earlier, they say, perhaps in the fourth or third centuries B.C. But these narratives, embedded as they are in this literary architecture, cannot be so easily dismembered. Chapter 7 belongs with chapter 2; the two are a pair. And that pair forms a frame around the other four chapters that have been paired together. Thus the historical chapters are all a unit, a package, and the fact that they were also all written in the same Aramaic language emphasizes that point. For a century and a half, source critics have been breaking up Daniel into smaller and smaller pieces. Finally, an appreciation of the literary artistry and structure of the book has demonstrated how wrong such an approach has been. The book of Daniel is one literary unit, and an aesthetically attractive one at that.

Because of this unique literary structure of the historical section of Daniel, we will study these chapters in the pairs to which they belong.

CHAPTER TWO

EXILED

With the exception of a small part of the first chapter, the entire book of Daniel is set in Babylon. That is because Daniel lived there most of his adult life, and he lived a long time. The first date in the book, at the beginning of chapter 1, is equivalent to 605 B.C. in our calendar. The last date, the date that accompanies the last prophecy of the book (Daniel 10:1), is equivalent to 536 B.C. That gives us a span of almost seventy years that Daniel spent in Babylon. During most of this time he lived under Neo-Babylonian kings, but he spent the very last years of his life under the Persian kings who conquered Babylon. Daniel probably died soon after receiving the last prophecy recorded in his book. In fact, when the angel Gabriel gave him that prophecy, he appears to have indicated to Daniel that that would soon be the case.

Daniel was probably in early adulthood when he was taken to Babylon. Some have suggested that he was perhaps around eighteen years of age, an age that would fit well with Babylonian policy for captives. Thus of the almost ninety years that Daniel lived, he spent approximately the first twenty in Judah and the last seventy in Babylon. Living so long in Babylon meant that Daniel was well acquainted with the city and the nation, its rulers and its procedures at court. He came to Nebuchadnezzar's court soon after his exile and probably served there a long time since Nebuchadnezzar enjoyed a lengthy rulership of forty-three years and Daniel seems to have held an important position in public service at least during Nebuchadnezzar's lifetime. After the death of Nebuchadnezzar, however, Daniel appears to have fallen from favor of the later rulers of Babylon. It was not until the very last of these, Belshazzar, that Daniel was rehabilitated to his former position of prominence, and then only briefly. But his popularity continued into the Persian period when he also achieved some prominence though at the cost of considerable difficulty to himself.

In good times or in bad, Daniel was a model of faithfulness and perseverance. He was also a model in his constant and dedicated devotional life, though this too came at a considerable cost to himself. Daniel is, therefore, a bright example to us of one who had courage, loyalty to his God, perseverance, and a living communion with that God. Since several of his prophecies close with the time of the end in which we now live, Daniel's example in these areas is an excellent reminder for us that we, too, should live for God in spite of the circumstances, good or bad, we may encounter.

As a person who lived in Babylon for many years and who also worked at its power center, Daniel obviously knew Babylon very well. Prophets of God may speak to the distant future on occasion, as Daniel did. But they also spoke to their own times and people. For Daniel, that was Babylon in the sixth century B.C. and the people of God who lived in exile there. It is only natural, therefore, that Babylon and its history would play a prominent part in the prophecies that God gave to him. Babylon appears in no less than four of the prophecies God gave to Daniel—appearing in chapters 2, 4, 5, and 7 of the book. A knowledge of Babylon and its history in the seventh and sixth centuries B.C. should be of use to us, then, in terms of understanding the prophet in the context of the time and place in which he lived. Such an understanding serves as a jumping off point for the successive steps in the prophecies which God has revealed to us through Daniel.

DANIEL'S TIMES

One way of looking at Daniel is to suggest that he was merely a small pawn who got caught up in the international power politics of his time. Such an evaluation has to do with the shifting politics and loyalties in the late seventh century B.C.

It was a time of transition. Judah existed on a narrow strip of land between the Mediterranean Sea and the eastern desert. That narrow corridor of land stood squarely in the path of conquest for both the Egyptians to the south and the Mesopotamian powers of Assyria and Babylon to the north. Repeatedly, powerful military forces from the north and the south pushed through Palestine. In rapid succession, the little kingdom of Judah came under the control of three different nations in the late seventh century B.C.

First, there was Assyria. Ashurbanipal, the last great king of the Assyrian Empire, died in 626 B.C. just two or three years before Daniel was born. With his death, major changes took place in the Near East. The Assyrian Empire broke up into many pieces, and for a time the people of Judah enjoyed a respite as Assyrian control was weakened. King Josiah took the opportunity of that interval to begin a religious reformation in the country (see 2 Kings 22:8–23:25). As the prophet Jeremiah indicated, however, Josiah's reform did not go deep enough or last long enough.

In this power vacuum, the aggressive pharaohs of the twenty-sixth dynasty in Egypt soon moved into position to take control of Western Asia as far as the Euphrates River where they held sway for approximately a decade. Meanwhile, a new power was rising in the east. The Babylonians, joining with the Medes from the mountains of northern Iran, successfully attacked the major population centers of Assyria—Nimrud and Nineveh. They conquered these cities and then destroyed them. As they moved up the eastern branch of the Euphrates, their activities brought them into confrontation with the Egyptians in the area of the upper river.

After an initial skirmish in 611 B.C., the Babylonians and Egyptians fought a major battle in 605 B.C. Jeremiah mentions this battle in Jeremiah 46:1–12 where he provides a view of the disastrous defeat of the Egyptians. We also have the words of Nebuchadnezzar's own royal annals for these events. There his scribe recorded:

> Nebuchadnezzar his [Nabopolassar's] eldest son, the crown prince, mustered [the Babylonian army] and took command of his troops; he marched to Carchemish which is on the bank of the Euphrates, and crossed the river [to go] against the Egyptian army which lay in Carchemish, . . . [they] fought with each

> other and the Egyptian army withdrew before him. He accomplished their defeat and beat them to non-existence.

These decisive events turned the whole political landscape of the ancient Near East upside down. What had formerly been under the control of Egypt now came under the control of Babylon, including all the territory south to the border of Egypt. Quite naturally, that included the kingdom of Judah. Royal records from Babylon—the Babylonian Chronicle texts—illuminate this situation. These texts, written in cuneiform, or wedge-shaped writing on clay tablets, were year-by-year accounts of the major events during the reign of the king. They do not give details for this particular conquest but state in general terms: "At that time Nebuchadnezzar conquered the whole area of Hatti-country." The designation "Hatti-country" was a holdover from the days when the Hittites ruled Syria and Palestine. The Hittites were long since gone, but the designation still remained. It included all the kingdoms from Syria in the north to Judah in the south.

One may ask why Nebuchadnezzar's records did not specifically mention Jerusalem as one of the cities he conquered. The probable reason was because Jehoiakim, the king of Judah at the time, could see that resistance to Nebuchadnezzar was futile, and he surrendered. Thus it wasn't necessary for the Babylonians to mount a full-scale war against the city. The Babylonian Chronicle texts mention only those cities which held out until Babylonian troops overran them. Cities which surrendered before that point, like Jerusalem, were not mentioned by name.

An observer of the historical scene in the Near East in 605 B.C. might have thought that all of this was merely the result of shifting human loyalties and power. But there was more to it than that. Daniel indicates this additional dimension at the very beginning of his book. Jehoiakim surrendered and fell into the hands of Nebuchadnezzar not just because he was a bad king, which he was, but because God permitted and directed events in this way. There was an unseen factor involved in the course of these events, and that factor was a divine one. Daniel 1:2 says, "And the Lord delivered Jehoiakim king of Judah into his hand." While this was not God's original intent for His people, their apostasy—led by King Jehoiakim—brought about this sad course of events.

Since God's people had relinquished their faith in Him and had given up participating in His covenant, they had also forfeited His protection from enemies such as Babylon (see Deuteronomy 28:1–30:20).

DANIEL'S PERSONAL EXPERIENCE

Even though a vigorous faith in the true God was largely lacking in Judah at this time, there still were those who were faithful to God. Daniel and his friends were among those who held on to their faith in spite of the generally prevailing apostasy. This did not prevent them from being taken into exile, but it did give them the opportunity to witness for their faith during that exile. In fact, the faithfulness of these servants of God in even the most trying of times is one of the bright spots in the book of Daniel. The question comes to us then: Do we meet similar, or even lesser, trials in our lives with a corresponding measure of faith? With such a strong example of courage and faith left for us by Daniel and his friends, should we not exercise the same devotion and trust in God to meet the trials that come to us?

Imagine yourself in Daniel's situation. You are young, just on the verge of beginning your adult life. Every opportunity seems to stretch before you. But then a sudden curve in the pathway of experience appears before you. Instead of being able to take advantage of the opportunities in your own home city and country, you are dragged off to a foreign land quite remote from your own. Further, you are given no privileges in your journey and have to walk four hundred miles across the desert to get to your destination. You have no assurance that you will ever see your home or family again. In fact, it looks very much as though you will not. What would your attitude have been? Discouragement? Depression? Would you have questioned how God could have done all this to you? Now that no one from your homeland could see you, would you have decided that you might as well live any way you could to get along in the land of your captors?

Some of these ideas may well have passed through the minds of Daniel and his friends, but they gave them no permanent heed in reacting to their difficult circumstances.

Taking hostages from captive countries was standard policy exercised by both the Babylonians and the Egyptians. Young men of considerable potential were taken back to the heartland of the empire to be trained in Babylonian or Egyptian ways and culture. This was done for a purpose. The point was to train these young men for future service to the empire. When the current king or administrators of the captive countries passed off the scene of action, their places could be taken by natives of those countries who had now been trained in Babylonian or Egyptian thinking. In that way Babylon, for example, could obtain administrators who had an intimate knowledge of the local customs of the people whom they governed, but who would have their ultimate loyalties cultivated toward Babylon through their education.

When Daniel and his friends arrived in Babylon, they began an extensive course of study. The different disciplines which they mastered were to enable them to become better Babylonian bureaucrats, better government servants. They undoubtedly studied the Babylonian cuneiform writing. This involved learning an elaborate system of signs to be incised upon soft clay with a pointed stylus. Cuneiform writing has provided us with some of the oldest samples of writing produced by the human race. Many examples have survived the centuries and with good reason—when the clay hardened, it provided a relatively permanent record. If the records were very important, such as state documents of a king, the cuneiform tablets involved were fired in a kiln. This hardened them even more than drying in the sun and made them very durable, much more durable than the paper we use today. If the records were not so important, they were left to dry naturally and harden more gradually. These less durable tablets were more easily broken, which is why excavators digging in ancient Near Eastern ruins often find many more fragments than whole tablets. It takes careful work in a museum to piece together those fragments of tablets that belong together.

Even though the Babylonian writing system was cumbersome to learn, the language itself probably was not very difficult for Daniel and his friends. Babylonian belongs to what is known as the East Semitic language family, while Hebrew belongs to the West Semitic group. Both are in the same general language family, and it would not have been very difficult for Daniel and his friends to pick up the Babylonian language. In addition, some of the work at the Babylonian court was done in Aramaic, a language even closer to Hebrew.

Nebuchadnezzar himself was not a native-born Babylonian in the ethnic and cultural sense. He, and his father Nabopolassar before him, belonged to one of the tribes of the Chaldean people who lived in southern Babylonia. These tribes spoke Aramaic, thus Nebuchadnezzar's own native tongue would have been Aramaic. It was quite natural, therefore, for Daniel to converse with Nebuchadnezzar in this language and for several of the dialogues between these two individuals to be recorded in Aramaic. This provides a partial explanation why the book of Daniel was written in two languages—chapters 1, 8–12 in Hebrew and chapters 2–7 in Aramaic.

We know a lot about the sciences as they were studied and practiced in Babylon. Those durable clay tablets have provided us with many of the Babylonians' astronomical calculations and their system of mathematics. Our modern system of mathematics is based upon units of ten, the decimal system. But the Babylonian system was based on units of six, known as sexagesimal mathematics. Some of this system has come down to us today; it explains why there are sixty seconds in a minute, sixty minutes in an hour, and 360 degrees in a circle. The Babylonian system shows up in Daniel 3 where the measurements of the image that Nebuchadnezzar set up—sixty cubits high and six cubits wide—are given in typical Babylonian sexagesimal measurements.

One of the more unpleasant problems the Hebrews faced in their Babylonian curriculum was the subject of astrology. The scientific side of that subject is astronomy, and that was not a problem. The interpretive, subjective side of this subject, however, is astrology. Babylonian culture was steeped in this sort of thing, and the Hebrew captives were probably introduced to it in their classes.

Here we find a sharp, distinct difference between the Bible and the ancient world. The ancient world was much devoted to the subject of astrology, observations based on the motions of the heavenly bodies used to predict human events and their outcomes. The Bible, however, is diametrically opposed to this sort of thing. This opposition is clearly stated in both Mosaic legislation (see Deuteronomy 18:9–14) and by the prophets (see Isaiah 8:19, 20). In this respect, therefore, the Bible stands diametrically opposed to some of the practices that went on in the environment surrounding the Israelites. Daniel and his friends would undoubtedly have opposed the use of these astrological methods in their work for the government of Babylon. They had a source upon which to rely for a knowledge of the future that was much more sure than the divination practices of Babylon. That source was the true God.

It is a paradox, therefore, that Daniel was eventually placed in charge of the wise men of Babylon (Daniel 2:48) who were active practitioners of astrology. Some of the episodes described later in his book demonstrate the superiority of the knowledge received from the true God as opposed to the false methods of the wise men (see Daniel 2–4).

Although we agree with Daniel's opposition to the thoughts and practices of Babylonian religion, we should also be fair to the Babylonians in terms of what they did and did not try to do with these captives. This issue comes up in terms of the names that were assigned to the Hebrews. Once he arrived in the capital, Daniel was given the new name of Belteshazzar (Daniel 1:7). This is a sentence which breaks down into three components: *Belit,* the title of a goddess; *shar,* the word for "king"; and the verb *uzur,* which means "to protect." Literally, therefore, Daniel's Babylonian name means, "May [the goddess] Belit protect the king." The Babylonian ruler, Belshazzar, carried a very similar name, the only difference being that the title of Bel, "lord," referred to a masculine rather than a feminine deity.

Daniel's three friends were given similar names that conveyed meaning, and that meaning was, in some cases, connected with Babylonian gods. This does not mean, however, that the Babylonians were trying to forcibly convert Daniel and his friends to the Babylonian religion simply by giving them names which contained a divine element. The goal was much more pragmatic than that. The Babylonians simply wanted to give these captives names which would be easy to recognize by the Babylonians with whom they would be working.

THE TEST

Soon after enrolling in the scribal school in Babylon, Daniel and his three friends ran into trouble. The trouble was not over astrology, or their Babylonian names, or worshiping idols. It was over food. Students complaining about the food they are served at school is not a modern phenomenon; it goes back a long way, 2,500 years in this case! But in this instance there were excellent grounds for lodging the complaint: "Daniel resolved not to defile himself with the royal food and wine, and he asked the chief official for permission not to defile himself this way" (1:8).

The question arises, Why did Daniel refuse to eat the food that was provided from the royal quartermaster depot or kitchen? The text gives us a very clear and direct answer: "Daniel resolved not to defile himself."

It would have been an interesting conversation to listen to as Daniel was trying to explain to the Babylonian official this defilement based upon the dietary laws set out in Leviticus 11 and Deuteronomy 14! Among the cuneiform texts which have been cataloged and translated are some which list the foodstuffs that were provided to the Babylonian army. Supplies included pork. For an Israelite, pork was unclean and considered unfit to eat. If pork was supplied to the army in the field, it probably was supplied to the bureaucrats in the palace and to students in the scribal school. Thus Daniel and his friends would have had to face the issue of unclean meat being served to them. This they declined to eat because it would "defile" them.

Other reasons were probably involved as well. As in the New Testament case at Corinth, some of the meat provided in Babylon may have been offered to idols (see 1 Corinthians 8). Then, too, there was the matter of the preparation of the food. Babylonian butchers would not have prepared any of their meats in a way that would have been considered kosher for a Jew (see Leviticus 17:10–14). The preparation could also have involved highly spiced foods.

The easiest and most direct way to avoid all of these problems was to eat a vegetarian diet and drink only water. That is what Daniel requested of the official. Literally, he asked for "seed-food," that which grows from seeds, or plant food (1:12). Daniel could see the problems involved in the Babylonian diet, and he could also see that the most direct way to avoid them was to avoid the problem altogether rather than to try to eat his way around it. He asked for a vegetarian diet and the principal non-alcoholic beverage available—water.

The official, however, was reluctant to put Daniel on that kind of regimen (1:10). He was afraid that it would have adverse effects upon the Hebrews. But Daniel persisted and was eventually given permission to eat his preferred diet for a period of ten days (1:14). Ten days out of his three-year course was not too much to risk, but even so, the official only reluctantly gave Daniel and his friends permission to do so. The official was responsible for the captives' welfare, and if they suffered from this new diet, he would suffer from Nebuchadnezzar's wrath (1:10). Kings of the ancient world were noted for their tendency to punish the messengers who brought bad news.

Could a period of only ten days really make a difference? In modern society's approach to health there are a number of examples which demonstrate that ten days can indeed make a difference. One special diet plan advertised on American television promises, "Give us a week, and we'll take off the weight!" More intensive was the regimen of Dr. Pritikin, a nutritionist whose severe low-fat diet was aimed at rapid cholesterol and weight reduction as part of a rehabilitation and conditioning program for seriously ill heart patients. To participate in such a program one had to spend a week at Pritikin's center. It should also be noted that a patient can recover from major surgery and be discharged from a hospital in well under ten days. In fact, the length of hospital stays are getting shorter and shorter. Thus Daniel's request for ten days as a period of test was reasonable, even though he probably would have liked to have had more time.

Once again, it was not just the ordinary force of human circumstances that opened up this possibility to Daniel and his friends. They were not just better nutritionists or exercise physiologists or intellectually superior to the other students enrolled. They were able to obtain the favor of the official and carry out this program because "God had caused the official to show favor and sympathy to Daniel" (vs. 9). Intelligent as he was, Daniel had still another factor operating in his favor, and that factor was the most important—divine favor. In this situation, God was able to use and bless Daniel and his friends because of their faith in Him and His promises.

Likewise, God can use us today in similar situations. This part of the narrative places emphasis upon the fact that God not only wants us to have spiritually alert minds, but He wants us to have healthy bodies as well. The two are directly related. "At the end of the ten days they looked healthier and better nourished than any of the young men who ate the royal food" (Daniel 1:15). Having passed this ten-day test, Daniel and his friends were able to eat the diet that they wanted for the rest of their three years in school. Continuing on this diet for that length of time also contributed to their excellent outcome at the end of the course.

THE FINAL RESULT

At the end of their three-year course, the final graduation examination was an oral one (1:19, 20). Indeed, their oral examiner was the most important person of all, more important than any of the professors they had had during their studies. The final oral examiner was none other than the king himself. He wanted to see what they had accomplished during their period of training and to see if they were satisfactorily qualified to take up posts in the Babylonian government. Once again, Daniel and his friends came through with flying colors: "The king talked with them and he found none to equal Daniel, Hananiah, Mishael and Azariah; so they entered the king's service" (vs. 19). Using hyperbole, the text describes them as being ten times better than the other wise men in Nebuchadnezzar's kingdom. This does not mean that Daniel got 100 percent on his exam and that the other wise men of Babylon got only 10 percent. It simply means that the Hebrews were clearly more outstanding than the other students in the course and that they were superior even to the professional wise men who had already taken up their posts. A similar sort of literary phenomenon is found in the story of the burning fiery furnace in Daniel 3. Nebuchadnezzar's workmen were told to heat it "seven times hotter" (vs. 19). This does not mean that the furnace went from 500 degrees, for example, to 3,500 degrees. Rather it means that it was stoked to a much more intensely hot state, regardless of the absolute temperature involved.

What was the real reason Daniel and his friends did so well on their oral examination before the king? Was it because they had higher IQs? Was it because they were on a healthier program? These things may have helped, but more than these things, it was the direct blessing of God. "To these four young men God gave knowledge and understanding . . ." (1:17). Without the blessing of God, these young men would not have done as well as they did. God had a plan and a purpose for them, and He wanted to demonstrate that fact before all of the wise men of Babylon, before their fellow students, and before the king. God has a plan and a blessing for your life, too, although it may not work out just exactly the way it did for these captive students in Babylon.

DATES

We conclude our examination of chapter 1 with a technical note about three minor chronological details related to this chapter. The first has to do with the date in the first verse of the chapter. It says that Nebuchadnezzar came up and besieged Jerusalem in the *third* year of Jehoiakim, king of Judah. Some have criticized this date as inaccurate, claiming that the siege actually took place in Jehoiakim's *fourth* year. This objection is dealt with more fully in chapter 1 of this volume (see pages 22, 23). It is sufficient here to point out that if one interprets this date according to the principle of accession year reckoning and the Jewish (fall-to-fall) calendar, the date works out correctly as historically accurate.

The second chronological problem involved here focuses upon the length of time Daniel and his friends studied—three years according to Daniel 1:5—and the date upon which the events of Daniel 2 took place "in the second year of [Nebuchadnezzar's] reign" (2:1). These statements can be harmonized readily when it is realized that Daniel 1:5 does not necessarily mean three full years of twelve months each. The first and last years of this study sequence probably were only partial years, just as the academic school year in North America today is more like nine months than twelve.

This explanation involves what is known as "inclusive reckoning" which deals with the way the ancient Hebrews reckoned fractions. For modern readers, 50 percent is the dividing line; anything above that is rounded to the next whole number, and anything below it is deleted. That was not the way the ancient Hebrews did it. For them, any fraction became "inclusive" to the next number. Thus Jesus could be in the tomb for three days even though those three days included only a portion of Friday afternoon, all day Saturday, and a portion of early Sunday morning. According to "inclusive reckoning," that is still three days. Another biblical example of this can be found in 2 Kings 18:9–11 where the siege of Samaria began in the fourth year of Hezekiah and ended in his sixth year, which was "at the end of three years" (2 Kings 18:10). Thus Daniel's three years of schooling may not have been three full years of twelve months each.

The final minor chronological problem in chapter 1 is found in its last verse which says, "Daniel remained there until the first year of King Cyrus" (verse 21). Since this is the King Cyrus of Persia with whom the book ends (10:1), this is a reference to the entire ministry and lifetime of Daniel in Babylon. But it is put at the end of the very first story of the book which deals with Daniel's arrival in Babylon and his first experiences there.

Obviously, this mention of Cyrus comes from a time seventy years later in approximately 536 B.C. It was put here in chapter 1 editorially to anticipate what follows in the book. It is not intended to be a dateline as is the time statement in verse 1. Rather, it sets the perspective for all of what follows. Some of Daniel's narratives may have been written earlier and some of them may have been written later, but the last of them and any editorial comments such as this clearly came from the Persian period when the book was finished.

CHAPTER THREE

FALLEN KINGS

Chapters 4 and 5 of Daniel deal with the fate of two kings of the Neo-Babylonian Empire—Nebuchadnezzar, the founder and first great king of that empire (chapter 4), and Belshazzar, the last king of that empire who was not nearly so great (chapter 5). The fact that Daniel's life could encompass the entire history of the Neo-Babylonian Empire shows how short its existence really was. Daniel came to Babylon as a teenager early in Nebuchadnezzar's reign, and he was still there as an old man when Belshazzar died in the palace the night the Persians conquered the city.

Daniel not only lived in Babylon during this long time period, he also interacted on a professional level with both these kings. God used Daniel to bring prophecies to them—prophecies about their kingdom and prophecies about themselves. Thus these two chapters deal not only with these Babylonian kings, but also with Daniel and how he served them. Daniel's role for both kings was similar; he served as an inspired wise man who brought them messages from the true God about their life and times.

Nebuchadnezzar received a message from God through a dream; God spoke to Belshazzar through the writing of a disembodied hand upon the wall of the audience hall of the palace. In both cases the kings needed somebody to interpret God's message, and in both cases the wise men of Babylon were inadequate for the task. Daniel had to be called because the mysterious messages came from the true God whom he served. Both messages were messages of judgments that would fall upon the kings. They were both to be judged according to the contents of the prophecies which Daniel interpreted for them. And in both cases all happened just as Daniel predicted.

However, there is a significant difference between the fate of these two kings. Nebuchadnezzar received a prolonged sentence of insanity, but he eventually came back from it, repented, and turned in faith toward the true God. Belshazzar, on the other hand, received his judgment in the very night the prophecy came to him. With his death that night, the Neo-Babylonian Empire passed into Media-Persian hands.

The themes of these two chapters are similar, then, even though they are developed in different ways. This thematic link binds these two chapters together at the center of the chiastic literary structure of the Aramaic section of the book (chapters 2; 7). In this structure chapter 2 is linked thematically with chapter 7; chapter 3 is linked thematically with chapter 6. And at the center of this ladder, chapter 4 is linked with chapter 5. Thus, chapters 4 and 5 stand as a linked pair at the center of this chiastic structure. They are linked together by the nature of their contents, and they have been placed side by side to further emphasize that connection. (For a further discussion of the chiastic literary structure of the historical section of Daniel, see chapter 1, pages 28–31.)

THE DREAM OF THE GREAT TREE

The story in chapter 4 is cast mainly as a first person report from Nebuchadnezzar himself. He begins the account in this way:

> King Nebuchadnezzar, To the peoples, nations and men of every language, who live in all the world: May you prosper greatly! It is my pleasure to tell you about the miraculous signs and wonders that the Most High God has performed for me (4:1, 2).

After a brief poetic passage in which the king praises this great God for His majesty and dominion, he goes on to relate his experience. Nebuchadnezzar's expressions of praise are a good lesson for us. We, too, should praise God for the great things He has done for us. This is one of the lessons of chapter 4. Just as God worked on Nebuchadnezzar's behalf in ancient times, so He can work for us today. Perhaps the way

He works for us will not take the same form as His actions in Nebuchadnezzar's behalf, but the narrative in this chapter assures us that God is powerful and that He intervenes in the affairs of life for the benefit of His children. When He does, and we see His hand at work, we should praise Him as Nebuchadnezzar did.

Nebuchadnezzar did not date this account of God's dealings with him, but we have some indication of the time frame in which these events occurred. The king reports that he was in his palace, contented and prosperous. Such a description would apply most naturally to a period sometime during the middle of his forty-three-year reign. During the first third of his reign, Nebuchadnezzar took the army out in almost constant campaigns. During the last third, he went back on the road with the army again. Thus, it was especially during the middle third of his long reign that he was at peace and prosperous because his major military conquests had been accomplished by that time.

One night during this prosperous and peaceful period the king was asleep in the palace when there came to him a most impressive dream. This was no ordinary dream, and Nebuchadnezzar felt that it was of vital importance to him to find out what it meant. In the case of his earlier dream described in Daniel 2, Nebuchadnezzar could not remember the content when he awoke; this time, he remembered his dream clearly. So he called his wise men and diviners, recounted the dream to them, and demanded an interpretation. No one could explain it to him (vss. 7, 8).

Finally Daniel was called. The junior wise men could not accomplish the task, so their chief was called. Note that at first Nebuchadnezzar refers to Daniel by his Babylonian name of Belteshazzar. The king told Daniel that in his dream he had seen a great tree. The tree was enormous and strong and visible to the ends of the earth. It also provided shade for the animals that lived under it and fruit for the birds who lived in its branches (vss. 10–12).

The second scene of the king's dream, however, was not so pleasant. A holy messenger angel came down from heaven with a decree that the tree be cut down, including branches, leaves, and fruit; the birds and animals that had previously lived in its protection were to be scattered. But all was not lost, for the stump of the tree was to be bound after the tree was cut down, and it would remain in the ground (vss. 13–15).

At this point in the dream, the angel made a transition in his instruction and explanation, moving from the symbol of the tree to the actuality of what the tree represented. The tree clearly represented a man and his fate. The angel indicated that the man so represented would live among the animals and plants of the field, just like the stump of this tree. This man's mind would be changed into the mind of an animal, just like those he was to live among. All of this would last until seven "times," or years, would pass over him (vss. 16, 17). Presumably, the judgment would then be lifted, although the angel did not directly prophesy the man's actual restoration at the end of the seven years.

If you had been one of the wise men summoned by the king to explain this dream, what would it have meant to you? Remember, you would not have the clear hindsight we have today in reading the entire story.

It would have been clear that the dream applied to a man, for the words of the angel made that plain. But what man? It seems obvious to us, as we read the story today, that Nebuchadnezzar was the man involved. But would this have been the natural explanation to occur to the wise men facing the task of interpreting the dream? Probably not. More likely, they would have immediately thought in terms of an enemy of Nebuchadnezzar. Because of the fate of the man in the dream, their first inclination would probably have been to pick out the king or opponent who was giving Nebuchadnezzar the most trouble and apply the dream to him.

If you had been one of the wise men commanded to interpret the dream, the one thing you would *not* want to do would be to apply the dream to Nebuchadnezzar! After all, messengers who brought bad news to the king could easily suffer his wrath. However, the wise men probably would not have thought of this interpretation anyway. It simply would not have occurred to them that a king so rich and powerful and famous could suffer such an affliction. At the time, mental illness was thought to be the work of demons, and how could demons afflict a man so obviously blessed by the gods?

Thus Daniel's interpretation ran contrary not only to what the wise men thought about Nebuchadnezzar, but to the very theology of their belief system. A man so blessed by the gods could not be cursed by them at the same time too! If things had been going badly for

Nebuchadnezzar, it could indicate that the gods were angry with him. If so, such an application of the dream might be true. But not now in a time of prosperity and peace.

DANIEL'S INTERPRETATION

When Daniel received the interpretation of this dream from the true God, he too was shocked (vs. 19). Like the other wise men, Daniel was astounded that such a fate could happen to so prominent and powerful a figure. In chapter 1 Daniel had written that God had given Jehoiakim of Judah into Nebuchadnezzar's hand (1:2). And if God had given Nebuchadnezzar control of the king of His own covenant people, how much more true must that be of those kings and kingdoms elsewhere in the world that Nebuchadnezzar had conquered? In his prayer of thanksgiving for the gift of the dream and its interpretation in chapter 2, Daniel had praised God because He "sets up kings and deposes them" (2:21). Given the prominence to which Nebuchadnezzar had come, it certainly looked as though God was the One who had placed him in his lofty position. Clearly, God had exalted Nebuchadnezzar and given him great power. But now He was going to demonstrate the other side of the coin. Whom He had set up, He could also depose, and Nebuchadnezzar was about to be deposed. That was what shocked and surprised Daniel about the interpretation of the dream in chapter 4. But in spite of his surprise, he went ahead and told the king what the dream meant.

Like Nathan before David, Daniel reluctantly carried out his assignment. With tact he pointed out that the dream applied to Nebuchadnezzar. But he couched the prophetic word with concern for the king, "My lord, if only the dream applied to your enemies and its meaning to your adversaries!" (vs. 19). Before God gave him the interpretation, Daniel probably thought the dream *did* apply to Nebuchadnezzar's enemies. Certainly, that is what the other wise men would have thought. Once God spoke to him, however, Daniel could do nothing but clarify and present God's message for the king.

After describing the great tree, Daniel said, "You, O king, are that tree!" (vs. 22). This part of the message was not so difficult for he could go on to praise the strength and greatness of the tree-king. Then came the harder part found in the second act of the dream:

> You will be driven away from people and will live with the wild animals; you will eat grass like cattle and be drenched with the dew of heaven. Seven times will pass by for you until you acknowledge that the Most High is sovereign over the kingdoms of men and gives them to anyone he wishes (vs. 25).

Daniel did not end his prophetic sermon without offering hope. The prophecy included restoration as its final element. Daniel concluded with an appeal to the king, calling him to repentance:

> Therefore, O king, be pleased to accept my advice: Renounce your sins by doing what is right, and your wickedness by being kind to the oppressed. It may be that then your prosperity will continue (vs. 27).

Daniel did not appeal for the king to repent merely with words; he called for actions that were commensurate with the depth and sincerity of his repentance. He called for right deeds and restoration. In the name of the oppressed, Daniel challenged this fearful conqueror who had wrought so much destruction across the Near East. Nebuchadnezzar had oppressed others to the limit; now he had the opportunity to redress those wrongs and make them right. He had the power to do so. The question was, Would he do so?

The dream and the prophet's appeal pointed the king to repentance, confession, and restoration. Nebuchadnezzar's military exploits were noteworthy; could he also leave behind him a record of restoration after those conquests? It would take a great man and a humble man to do so. But if Nebuchadnezzar were not humble enough to do so himself, God would do the humbling for him.

THE RESULTS

The kings of Judah would not repent of their folly, which led to the downfall of their kingdom and the exile of their people. Could we really expect a pagan king such as Nebuchadnezzar to repent in response to the prophet's appeal? Think about what would be involved in such a repentance.

The king would be admitting that he should not have made the conquests he had carried out. That the oppression he had imposed upon the various countries of the ancient Near East should not have been imposed. That he should not have imprisoned the war captives. That exiles, such as the very prophet who stood before him, should not have been brought to Babylon and that they should be returned to their own lands. In essence, the king would be saying that a large part of what he had done as king—some of his greatest exploits—were wrong. It would have taken a great and humble man to admit this, and Nebuchadnezzar was not up to—or down to—the task. He would not bow in repentance.

Although the king refused to submit to God when He appealed to him through Daniel and the interpretation of the dream, God gave Nebuchadnezzar more time to think it over. He gave him plenty of time. He gave him a whole year. Still Nebuchadnezzar would not yield and repent. One year later, he was walking on the roof of his palace. Perhaps he was thinking about the impressive dream he had had a year earlier (vs. 29). His response—a stubborn rejection of the prophet's appeal—was unchanged.

The form in which he expressed his refusal is interesting. It was couched in a statement of boastful pride: "Is not this the great Babylon I have built as the royal residence, by my mighty power and for the glory of my majesty?" (vs. 30).

Was there any basis in fact for this boasting? Yes, quite a bit. Nebuchadnezzar had enlarged and beautified Babylon on a grand scale. Prior to his time, the city had consisted mainly of a smaller area—"the inner city" or central portion. Nebuchadnezzar added a new line of outer walls. This had the effect of strengthening the city's defenses and enlarging its area at the same time. Inside these outer walls, he built a new palace. He also built the western section of the city across the Euphrates River. We know he was responsible for much of this construction because thousands upon thousands of the broken clay bricks which survive in the ruins of ancient Babylon have Nebuchadnezzar's name stamped upon them.

In addition to physically building up the city of Babylon, Nebuchadnezzar also built the nation into an empire by his political and military conquests. His father, Nabopolassar, threw off the Assyrian yoke, freeing Babylonian forces to undertake more wide ranging campaigns. But it was his son, Nebuchadnezzar, who welded the conquests made in those campaigns into an empire.

Then, too, there is the matter of the length of Nebuchadnezzar's reign. The foundation of the Neo-Babylonian Empire can be dated to 605 B.C., the year Nebuchadnezzar came to the throne. The demise of this empire can be fixed in 539 B.C., the year the Media-Persian army conquered Babylon. Since Nebuchadnezzar reigned for forty three years, his rulership spanned some two-thirds of the entire time the Neo-Babylonian Empire existed.

So Nebuchadnezzar had solid reasons for glorying in his achievements in terms of building the city of Babylon, building an empire, and ruling over it for much of the time it existed. There is, however, another side to his accomplishments, a darker side. If Assyrian practices are any example, much of the construction of the city of Babylon was carried out by slave laborers captured in various military campaigns. The extension of Nebuchadnezzar's empire exacted a high cost in human lives—both of the defeated and of his own soldiers who died in battle.

It used to be thought that Nebuchadnezzar's reign was one long, uninterrupted rule. But now that we possess his annals for the first eleven years of his reign, we know that in his tenth year there was a revolt against him in Babylon. This revolt was so serious that even in the palace there was hand-to-hand fighting in which the king himself was involved! Nebuchadnezzar's achievements may have been impressive, but they came with a high price tag for many of his subjects—some of whom were not entirely peaceful and accepting of his rule.

In spite of the suffering his projects had cost, Nebuchadnezzar could still boast about his own greatness and the greatness of his accomplishments. But the heavenly watchers recorded his boasting and pride. The whole picture of what these accomplishments had cost in terms of human suffering was open before God, and He did not approve. Nebuchadnezzar was raising himself up to an almost quasi divine status, like the figure of the king of Babylon who represents the devil in Isaiah 14:12–15.

Now Nebuchadnezzar was to receive his deserved punishment predicted in the prophetic dream of a year earlier. Now he would be cast down to the ground and take his position with the lowliest of the low, with the animals themselves. He had had a full year of probation in which to repent of what he had done and his pride in it, but he made no such move toward the true God. Now it was time for his sentence to be carried out.

The type of insanity to which Nebuchadnezzar was subjected is uncommon, but not unknown in modern psychiatric practice. The technical name for animal-like, or more specifically "wolf-like," behavior by human beings is *lycanthropy*.

In view of the general situation that would exist in the case of a king who was incapacitated in this way for such a long period of time, the question arises: How did Nebuchadnezzar manage to hold on to his throne in spite of his madness? This would have been an ideal time for a usurper to assassinate the insane king and take the throne in his place.

The probable reason this did not happen has to do with the ancients' view of mental illness. They believed it was caused by demons, minor gods who were malevolent toward human beings. They also believed that if a person was deliberately killed while suffering from insanity, the demon god who had caused the mental illness would cause it to come upon the murderer. Thus no one would risk acquiring mental illness by killing a person so afflicted. Babylonian theology, or psychology, probably protected Nebuchadnezzar during the time of his incapacitation.

Several times the text gives the length of time the madness was to last as "seven times" (vss. 16, 23, 25). By a process of elimination, it can be seen that "years" is the only time unit with which the word "times" fits in this chapter. So it has been understood since pre-Christian times. The Greek Old Testament of Daniel chapter 4 translates this word as "years." Thus in Nebuchadnezzar's dream, "times" means "years." The king was to be incapacitated and insane for seven years.

We may consider the judgment severe, but it had the desired effect. At the end of the time, when Nebuchadnezzar came back to his normal senses, he also came back to a recognition and knowledge of the true God (compare 2:47; 3:28, 29). He acknowledged God in his psalm of praise at the beginning of the chapter (vss. 2, 3) and also in his song of praise at the end of the chapter (vss. 34, 35). Notice that he glorified and praised the God of heaven *first* before he told about the return of his kingdom and his restoration to his position and power (vs. 34). He now saw divine and human affairs in their correct priority. In this entire recital, Nebuchadnezzar's closing statement was: "Those [like me] who walk in pride he [the Most High God] is able to humble" (vs. 37).

One of the questions we asked at the beginning of this chapter was this: Was God fair to judge Nebuchadnezzar in this way? And now we can see that the ultimate answer to that questions is Yes. It *was* fair of God. Even Nebuchadnezzar himself acknowledged that fact at the end of the story. While he was out with the animals, he probably was not able to see the great central fact of God in his experience. But when he was restored to his right mind and looked back over the entire affair, he could see God's hand in it all. At this juncture in his life he became a believer in the true God, in contrast with the false gods of polytheism he had worshiped previously.

Daniel, the prophet of God, was on the scene of action to explain to the king what all of this meant. And God continued to speak to Nebuchadnezzar. As severe as God's judgment on Nebuchadnezzar may appear, ultimately this experience brought about his conversion to the true God. So it is not surprising that after chapter 4 we hear nothing more about Nebuchadnezzar in the book of Daniel. There is a spiritual pilgrimage in the book that tells of Daniel's own experience, and there is also the story of Nebuchadnezzar's spiritual pilgrimage. He traveled the road from being the most powerful king of his time—a proud, egotistical ruler—to the point where he became a humble, trusting, and praising believer in the true God. At the close of chapter 4, we leave Nebuchadnezzar rejoicing in the salvation that had come to his royal house that day.

NEBUCHADNEZZAR'S LESSON IS FOR US

Although we don't have the personal power and authority Nebuchadnezzar wielded as ruler of Babylon, we still can learn from his experience. Like him, we probably tend to think better of ourselves than we should. Like him, we praise our own achievements, large or small. "Is this not great Babylon which I have built," still echoes in our experience today. This kind of pride and self-congratulation did not die with the death of the Neo-Babylonian Empire. It lives on today in human nature and continues to manifest itself in various ways. It is the foundation of the modern religion of humanism, which holds that human beings are so competent mentally and physically that we do not need help from any outside source such as God. But just when we get to this point in our experience, something comes along to disturb that self-confidence and to throw us back into the arms of our heavenly Father who alone can meet our ultimate needs. The problem can be individual—a health crisis. Or it can be family related—the death of a loved one. It can be something local—a flood or fire. Or national and international—war or famine. Whatever form the crisis may take, we learn that our own devices are not adequate to cope. Our dependence cannot be on self; it must lie in something greater than our own abilities. Like Nebuchadnezzar, we must ultimately find our reason for living in something greater than, and outside of, ourselves. The philosophy of humanism and our human pride are ultimately bankrupt when it comes to the deepest needs of our beings. We find our highest position in life when we kneel humbly at the foot of the cross. Nebuchadnezzar found that out, and our experience leads us to the same conclusion.

We sometimes complain about these testing situations. "Why me?" is a constant cry when trouble comes. The reverses we experience in life may not be as direct or as severe as those which Nebuchadnezzar faced, but they should have the same end result. We should be able to see the hand of God leading us through those trying experiences; we should ultimately be able to see how He has used them to refine our characters and teach us to rely upon Him in trying times. At the end of his experience, Nebuchadnezzar voiced no complaint against God for the insanity which had fallen upon him. It was not too severe. It did not last too long. There was no argument with God; Nebuchadnezzar simply stood back and praised Him for the part that He had taken in his life.

We, too, should be able to look back upon our past experiences and see the way God has led us. Properly understood, we would not change anything the leadership of God allows to come into our lives, even though some episodes may have been hard and painful at the time. When we come to the final point that Nebuchadnezzar did, the hardness of those experiences fades away and is swallowed up in praise to the God who has led us, even through the valley of the shadow.

DANIEL

THE BANQUET

Daniel 5 opens with Belshazzar appointing a banquet. This may seem strange when one remembers that at the very time Belshazzar was calling for a banquet, a division of the Persian army was posted outside the walls besieging the city! Was not this a foolish time to be involved in such a celebration?

It might look so at first, but in light of all the defenses behind which this banquet took place we can better appreciate Belshazzar's self-confidence. Babylon was defended by *two* sets of walls, the outer walls and the inner walls. Both were actually double walls. The two inner walls were twelve and twenty-two feet thick respectively. The two walls making up the outer defenses were twenty-four and twenty-six feet thick. Thus any enemy who wanted to get into the inner city, where the palace and main temple were located, had almost eighty-five feet of walls to get through or over, and these came in four different sections, all of them defended. No wonder Belshazzar felt secure enough to hold a banquet in spite of the besieging army outside the city!

The invitees to this banquet included the upper class of official Babylonian society—a thousand of the lords or nobles of the realm. The king also invited his wife, his secondary wives, the concubines from the royal harem (5:1, 3), and possibly his mother—the "queen" of verse 10, although this could be a reference to Belshazzar's main wife.

The banquet involved a lot of drinking, both wine and probably beer (vs. 2). The Babylonians were famous for their beer making, and some of the tablets describing their procedure for making beer have been found. Beer is probably what the Bible calls "strong drink" and which it condemns more strongly than it condemns fermented wine. Modern statistics for crimes and auto accidents demonstrate that alcohol is involved in a large percentage of such situations—with disastrous results. Alcohol is a drug that affects the faculties of judgment in the human mind and its higher, moral thought patterns. Belshazzar was no exception to this effect.

The king went beyond merely having a banquet at which quite a bit of drinking was done. He brought out the vessels that had been taken from the temple of Yahweh, or Jehovah, in Jerusalem and used them as receptacles from which to drink alcohol (5:3; see also 2 Kings 24:12,

13). Belshazzar may have also used vessels from the temples of other Near Eastern gods. Clearly, the use to which he put these vessels indicated his contempt for God from whose temple they had come.

Belshazzar's drinking from the temple vessels also involved certain theological beliefs. According to Babylonian theology, many gods existed in heaven. These gods acted on earth through their representatives so that when a particular event took place on earth it meant that the same action had also taken place in the realm of the gods. For example, when Babylon scored a victory over one of its enemies this indicated that in the heavens, Marduk, the god of Babylon, had defeated the god of that country. Thus earthly events reflected what had happened as well among the gods. So for Belshazzar to drink from the vessels that had come from Yahweh's temple was an expression, for him, of the superiority of his god over that of the Jews. Unfortunately for Belshazzar, his theology was false; he was actually engaged in an act of blasphemy against the true God.

THE HANDWRITING ON THE WALL

God's response to this act of blasphemy by Belshazzar and his nobles was sent in the form of a prophecy written upon the wall of the throne room or audience chamber in which the banquet was held (vss. 5, 6). Thanks to the spade of the archaeologist, we have a pretty good idea where this occurred. The palace area of Babylon was located just inside the great Ishtar gate on the north side of the inner city. Coming south through the processional way, a traveler would pass through that gate and turn right toward the Euphrates to enter the palace area. The buildings of the palace were arranged around a central courtyard; the building on the south side was the one in which the king held audiences, and so it probably was the building in which Belshazzar held his banquet.

The outside of this building was covered with ornate and elaborate figures framed in colored enameled bricks. Among the figures portrayed were lions reminiscent of the first "beast" of Daniel 7:4 which symbolized Babylon. The walls inside the building, however, were plain white, so in whatever medium the disembodied hand wrote, the letters would have stood out distinctly against that background.

Belshazzar, and no doubt his nobles as well, were shocked when the writing appeared on the wall. In his fright, his "legs gave way," and he "turned pale" (vs. 6). Everyone in the room was astounded. Naturally, everyone wondered what the strange writing meant. An immediate search began for someone who could read the mysterious writing. The wise men of Babylon came, but they could not offer an answer (vss. 7–9).

Then the queen (vs. 10), probably the queen mother of Belshazzar, remembered the old days half a century earlier when Daniel had served at the court as a wise man superior to all of the other wise men of Babylon. On at least two occasions, Daniel had been able to unlock the mysteries of Nebuchadnezzar's dreams, and this stuck in the memory of the queen mother. At her urging, Daniel was summoned (vss. 10–13).

The interview that ensued between Daniel and Belshazzar covered three main points. One, of course, was the interpretation of the writing on the wall. As a preface, however, Belshazzar made an offer to anyone who could interpret the writing. He proposed to make that person the third ruler in the kingdom and to give him the emblems and tokens of that office (vs. 16).

Why would Belshazzar offer to make the successful person the "third" ruler in the kingdom? It would be much more natural to offer to make him the "second" ruler. Or failing that, to simply give him great honor. But an offer of the "third" position in the kingdom seems oddly specific. Why the "third" position?

It all becomes clear when we understand the political situation in Babylon at the time. The kingship of Babylon was involved in an unusual arrangement just then. The official king was Nabonidus, Belshazzar's father. But because of his extended absence from the kingdom he had made Belshazzar co-regent. In his own words, he "entrusted the kingship to him [Belshazzar]." For ten years while Nabonidus was away in Tema of Arabia, Belshazzar had remained in Babylon and administered the kingdom.

Now, however, Nabonidus had returned. But the situation had become even more threatening than it had been when he was off in Arabia. With the Medes and Persians assaulting the eastern frontier of the empire, Babylon was in danger of crumbling. Two rulers were vitally necessary at this time—one in the field to meet the onslaught of the enemy, and the other in the capital to hold the kingdom securely in his control. Nabonidus took the role of field commander and led one division of the Babylonian army out to the Tigris River to meet Cyrus and his troops. Belshazzar stayed in the city with another division of the army to protect the capital. Nabonidus was defeated on the fourteenth day of Tishri, and the city of Babylon fell to the Persian army two days later. Through the use of tables compiled by modern astronomers and Assyriologists, the day that Babylon fell can be identified as October 12, 539 B.C. in terms of our calendar.

This explains Belshazzar's offer of the "third" position in the kingdom to anyone who could interpret the writing on the wall. Nabonidus occupied the first position as senior king. As co-king, Belshazzar was the second in the kingdom, and the successful interpreter would be elevated to the third highest position, that of prime minister, serving under these two kings.

Later historians lost the knowledge of this situation in Babylon and even of Belshazzar's existence. Only an inhabitant of Babylon in the sixth century B.C. could have known of such an unusual arrangement and used such a specific, yet irregular, designation as "*third* highest ruler in the kingdom" (vs. 16, emphasis supplied). Daniel received that honor because he interpreted the writing (vs. 29), but he occupied the post only a few hours. Then the Persian army conquered the city, and Belshazzar was killed (vs. 30).

The last part of the interview between Daniel and Belshazzar involved Belshazzar's knowledge of recent Babylonian history. Daniel referred Belshazzar to the case of Nebuchadnezzar and the results of his pride as outlined in chapter 4. Not only did Daniel recall this experience to Belshazzar, he fearlessly declared that he ought to have paid attention to it. It should have been an instructive example to Belshazzar, but he did not humble himself (vss. 18–21).

If Belshazzar had taken Nebuchadnezzar's experience into account, he would never have committed the sacrilege of drinking from the vessels from Yahweh's temple. Nebuchadnezzar's experience should have taught him to respect the true God whose might and power could humble the greatest ruler of the kingdom. But he chose to ignore this warning. "You . . . have not humbled yourself, though you knew all this," Daniel accused the king (vs. 22). Belshazzar was sinning against light and knowledge; he was not in darkness and ignorance concerning the true God (vss. 22–24).

As a matter of fact, Belshazzar and his father Nabonidus had deliberately chosen other gods to worship. They worshiped not only Marduk, the regular and prominent god of Babylon, but Sin, the moon god as well. Nabonidus was a special devotee of this god. He selected temples of the moon god to rebuild and refurbish, in Syria as well as in Babylonia. He even built a temple to Sin in Arabia.

It is interesting to see this connection with the moon god in the light of events as they occurred in Babylon that October night the city was taken. The final Persian assault on Babylon began on the night of the fifteenth of Tishri and was completed by the morning of the sixteenth (the Babylonian day extended from sundown to sundown). On the night of the fifteenth of a lunar month such as Tishri, a full moon would be shining. Thus Babylon fell when Sin, the moon god, was at his fullest and most powerful. Although elevated by Nabonidus to a position of prominence in the Babylonian pantheon, the moon god had no power against the decree of Yahweh, the true God, who had predicted the overthrow of Babylon by the Medes and Persians. God's power was shown to be sovereign over all of the elements of nature and man. Nothing could turn Him aside from the accomplishment of His purposes—certainly not the power (weakness!) of the false god of the moon.

These events display another interesting detail in terms of the calendar. The month of Tishri was the seventh month of both the Jewish and the Babylonian calendar. The Hebrew festival of Yom Kippur, the Day of Atonement, occurred on the tenth day of Tishri. In other words, the Jewish Day of Atonement occurred just five days before the city of Babylon fell. When Daniel read the writing on the wall he interpreted the meaning of the third word written there, *tekel,* as signifying, "You have been weighed on the scales and found wanting" (vs. 27). The verb here is in the past tense—"you have been weighed." When might God have made such a judgment concerning Babylon? Of all the days in the Jewish calendar, the Day of Atonement was the day of judgment *par excellence.* It was a day of judgment in the camp of ancient Israel, and it is still considered to be a day of judgment in modern rituals of the synagogue. There would have been no more appropriate time for God to have passed sentence upon Babylon and Belshazzar than the Day of Atonement, which preceded the overthrow of the kingdom by just five days.

There actually were four words written on the wall (vs. 25). The first two were the same word repeated—*mene.* This word meant, according to Daniel, "God has numbered the days of your reign and brought it to an end" (vs. 26). It is interesting that this word was repeated. This can be meaningful in terms of the two rulers—Nabonidus and Belshazzar—who ruled together on the same throne at the time. One would not outlive the other and reign on; the reign of both was to come to an end at the same time—Belshazzar through death, and Nabonidus through defeat and exile.

We have already looked at the third word written on the wall, *tekel,* and its meaning. *Parsin,* the fourth and final word, told of the power that would receive the kingdom when the Chaldean dynasty fell. *Parsin* referred to the Persians; the Media-Persian Empire was to expand and incorporate into it what had formerly belonged to Babylon. Or as Daniel interpreted it, "Your kingdom is divided and given to the Medes and Persians" (vs. 28).

The story of how the Media-Persian army conquered Babylon is told by the Greek historian Herodotus, who visited the region a century after these events took place. The inhabitants told him that the Persians diverted the Euphrates River and then marched into the city through the riverbed, thereby bypassing the intricate system of fortress walls (*The Histories,* I:189–192). All this occurred in Tishri, the month we call October. That is the month in which the Euphrates River is at its lowest ebb. Thus it is not entirely clear just how much water the Persians would have had to divert from the river. At any rate, they gained entrance to the city through the riverbed.

There was still the obstacle of the city gates on the piers beside the river. These were probably only lightly defended, but the Persians would still have had to force them open. The question is, how?

The most prevalent theory is that a traitorous fifth column in the city, made up of Babylonians who were disgusted with the rule of Nabonidus, were willing to open the gates for their conquering deliverers. Nabonidus was an unpopular king, and texts exist, written after the fall of Babylon, which even suggest that he was mad. Of course this could be Persian propaganda written to ensure a ready acceptance among the populace. But one answer to how the Persians were able to breach the city walls along the river is that traitors inside the city willingly opened them.

Another possibility can be suggested from Isaiah 45:1–3 where God promises to go before Cyrus's troops and give Babylon into his hand:

> This is what the Lord says to his anointed, to Cyrus, whose right hand I take hold of to subdue nations before him and to strip kings of their armor, to open doors before him so that gates will not be shut: I will go before you and will level the mountains; I will break down the gates of bronze and cut through bars of iron. I will give you the treasures of darkness, riches stored in secret places, so that you may know that I am the Lord, the God of Israel, who summons you by name.

This remarkable prophecy has been a stumbling block to critical interpreters of the Bible. They cannot see how Isaiah who lived in the eighth century B.C. could prophesy so specifically of these events which did not occur until the sixth century B.C. The prophecy even points out Cyrus by name almost two centuries before he accomplished these deeds. To fit these facts with their understanding of how Scripture was written, some interpreters have hypothesized a "second Isaiah" who lived in the sixth century B.C. and who would have known of these events and Cyrus's name.

To those who believe that Scripture is inspired by God, however, this prophecy is simply an evidence of His remarkable foreknowledge and of how He has chosen to give this knowledge to His servants the prophets. With such evidences of God speaking through His prophets, what faith we should have in God's word through them!

When God prophesies events to take place in human history, He can use a variety of means to bring them about. He can simply foresee what human actors will do on the stage of history. In other instances, He intervenes more directly. We see that intervention clearly in certain places in the book of Daniel, especially in chapters 3 and 6 which we will study in the next chapter of this book.

In chapter 5, the mysterious handwriting that appeared on Belshazzar's wall was a clear example of God's direct, miraculous intervention in human affairs. Everyone present at the feast knew that this writing was supernatural in origin. No Babylonian artist painted those words on the wall; it was either an angel or God Himself. And if God intervened so directly in Belshazzar's palace, then the distinct possibility exists that He, or His angel, acted in a similar way with the latches on the river gates of the city.

Certainly, God sent an angel to miraculously open prison gates to free Peter (Acts 12:10). So perhaps it was not Babylonian traitors who opened the river gates after all; maybe it was the same angel who had written on the palace wall a short time earlier. If one supernatural action occurred in the palace, then surely it isn't difficult to conceive of another supernatural action following soon thereafter a short distance away. Perhaps God did not rely upon a human hand to fulfill His word to Isaiah regarding Cyrus; perhaps He Himself acted to fulfill His own word, just as He said He would.

THE RESULTS

The events of this historic night ended with several significant results. Belshazzar was deposed and killed (Daniel 5:30). Although the prophecy of the writing hand had broad, political implications, it was, first of all, a personal prophecy to Belshazzar. To him, the prophecy specifically meant his own individual downfall. "That very night Belshazzar, king of the Babylonians, was slain" (vs. 30) as the Persian troops broke into the undefended palace. The Greek historian Xenophon (*Cyropaedia* VII, V, 24–32) confirms the Bible statement. He doesn't refer to Belshazzar by name, but he relates how there was a banquet taking place in the Babylonian palace that night and how a king of Babylon was killed. He also tells us why that king was killed. On a hunting trip, Nabonidus, chief king of Babylon, had earlier killed the son of Gobryas, the Persian general who was to lead his troops into the city the night Babylon was overthrown. In revenge for the death of his son, Gobryas killed the son of Nabonidus.

But more important than Belshazzar's fate was the fate of nations that occurred that night. The shifting fortunes of history turned away from Babylon to crown Persia as the next great world empire. Media-Persia was to extend its borders even further than Babylon had. The city of Babylon was incorporated into the Persian Empire and for a time served as one of the winter capitals of the Persian kings. When Babylon finally rebelled against Xerxes (the Ahasuerus of the book of Esther) in 482 B.C., he put down the revolt with such violence that from that time forward, the city began to fade in importance. The first turn of the screw in Babylon's fall from power, however, occurred at the time of the Medo Persian conquest in 539 B.C.

The book of Daniel integrates history and prophecy. The great lines of prophetic history Daniel outlined are rooted in the history of his time. The first world power of which the prophecies in Daniel chapters 2 and 7 spoke was Babylon—represented by the head of gold in chapter 2 (vss. 32, 37) and by the lion in chapter 7 (vs. 4). Daniel himself lived under this world power of Babylon (chapters. 1–5, 7, 8), and he lived on to serve under Persian overlords as well (chapters. 6, 9–12). So Daniel himself saw the fulfillment of the first part of these great prophecies that God gave him.

Daniel acknowledged this transition of world empires in an interesting and subtle way in his words to Belshazzar that final night before Babylon's fall. He pointed out to Belshazzar that the king had "praised the gods of silver and gold, of bronze, iron, wood, and stone" (vs. 23). This sequence has a familiar sound to the reader of the prophecy given in Daniel 2. There the great image was made up of gold, silver, bronze, iron, and clay, followed by a great stone (2:31–35). Aside from the fact that Daniel has substituted "wood" for "clay," the sequence is the same in his words to Belshazzar on the night of the transition from the golden kingdom of Babylon to the silver empire of Media-Persia. Daniel made an interesting variation here in chapter 5, however, for when he started to enumerate these metals, he put silver first, before the gold. Why the minor, but significant, alteration? Because the fulfillment of the prophecy given in chapter 2 was actually taking place that night; the silver was superseding the gold, and Daniel signifies this in his speech to the king.

LESSONS OF A PERSONAL NATURE

Deep spiritual truths of a personal nature can be found in this narrative apart from the historical and prophetic lessons present. We look back at Belshazzar with 20/20 hindsight and say, "What a foolish man! How could he have gone against the word of the prophet and the example of his grandfather Nebuchadnezzar's experience?

Perhaps we should look at Belshazzar with a little more charity—not to excuse his blasphemy, but to take it to heart as an example for ourselves. Do we, too, fly in the face of the words of the prophets and the clear-cut examples of God's action in past history to cling stubbornly to our own ways? In our lives, have those words and actions fallen upon deaf ears and blind eyes? We may not be guilty of gross blasphemy and idolatry as was Belshazzar, but our own perverse ways can equally frustrate the grace of God.

Belshazzar spurned God's mercy and grace, extended to the royal house of Babylon since the time of Nebuchadnezzar. God's grace has also been extended to our forefathers, but that is not the issue. The issue is whether we have accepted God's grace for ourselves and have fashioned our lives according to it, rather than turning to our own ways. May God grant that the foolish example of Belshazzar will prevent our falling into similar ways today.

There are lessons of judgment in this chapter. God keeps accounts with nations and individuals. Babylon and Belshazzar were weighed in the balance of judgment and were found wanting (vs. 27). In one pan of the balances were placed God's mercy and righteousness; in the other, the rapacity, violence, and pride of Babylon and Belshazzar. The mercy of God far outweighed the pride of Belshazzar, but he chose not to accept that mercy. Judgment is not a popular topic in the modern world. At least not God's judgments. We want our fair share of justice in the courtroom, but when it comes to dealing with God we would prefer a God who does not call us to account. We would rather evade our moral responsibility if at all possible. The topic of divine judgment was no more popular in the time of Daniel, Jeremiah, or Ezekiel than it is in our day. If the Old Testament prophets teach us anything, it is that in all ages a significant portion of God's people have tried to evade their moral responsibility and yet escape God's judgment.

Jesus illustrated the same thing in His parable of the rich man who tore down his barns to build bigger ones. This man lived his life according to the principle of greed. He wanted to merge more and more corporations. Then came the fateful night: "You fool! This very night your life will be demanded from you" (Luke 12:20). That was Belshazzar's condition as well. It could also be ours, but it need not be.

At the other extreme, we see the spiritual example of Daniel. He stood before the king confident in the God whom he served. He had received the word of the living God, therefore he did not need to fear the word of any king regardless how powerful he was. Whether he was honored with position (as he was by Nebuchadnezzar and Belshazzar) or cast into the den of lions (as he was by Darius) Daniel's faith and confidence in God remained strong. It mattered little to Daniel whether the Babylonians or the Persians controlled the world. Such details did not change his prayer habits or his personal integrity in the least. Regardless of how the political winds of the world blew, Daniel remained like the needle to the pole faithful to his duty and to his God. Our example in chapter 5 is not Belshazzar, but Daniel. Belshazzar provides a warning of a path not to follow; Daniel stakes out the path of faith and trust that leads to the kingdom of God.

By faith, Daniel recognized that regardless of which armies were successful or which kingdoms were established at any particular moment, history was still under God's control. Ultimately it was moving toward His goal. And his faith was realized when he saw the fulfillment of the very first step of the great prophecies as the Persians conquered Babylon.

We stand now at the other end of the line. In terms of Daniel 2 we stand at the very bottom of the image, among the feet and toes in the time of the iron and clay. We are waiting for the next and final step, the setting up of the stone kingdom, God's kingdom. We can look back over history and see that the beast kingdoms of Daniel 7 have risen and fallen as God predicted. How much more then should we have faith and confidence in our God today, that He knows the future and has revealed it to His servants the prophets.

LESSONS OF A HISTORICAL NATURE

Not only can we have confidence in the prophetic future as revealed to us through Daniel, but we can have confidence in the historical word that is conveyed to us in Daniel's book as well. Critics of the Bible have attempted to undermine the historical accuracy of Daniel and thus undermine his prophetic accuracy. The attempt has failed, and nowhere has it failed more than in chapter 5.

First the critics denied that there even was such a person as Belshazzar. Then the tablets coming out of the mounds of Mesopotamia demonstrated his existence and his position and why the book of Daniel evaluated him the way it does.

A close examination of the historical setting of this chapter reveals just how precise and exact was the writer's knowledge of Babylon in the sixth century B.C. We can ask a very specific question of Daniel: "Who was the king in the palace the night that the city fell to the Persians?" This would be a good place to catch a writer of a later time in details of inaccurate knowledge. Based on the information preserved through classical historians, the answer would have been "Nabonidus." As the last known official king of Babylon, he should have been the monarch for whom Daniel interpreted the writing.

But the writer of Daniel did not erroneously put the well-known Nabonidus in the palace that night. Instead, he put the virtually unknown Belshazzar there. Daniel makes no mention of Nabonidus. If a banquet was held in the palace and Nabonidus was in the city, he certainly would have attended. Yet Daniel makes no mention of his presence. Why not? Where was Nabonidus? We did not know the answer to these questions until archaeologists dug up the tablet that we now know as the *Nabonidus Chronicle.* That tablet tells us clearly where Nabonidus was and why he was not in the city. He had taken another division of the Babylonian army out to the Tigris river where he fought Cyrus and his army in a nearby city named Opis. Two days before the city of Babylon fell, Nabonidus's army was defeated in the field by Cyrus's Persian troops. Nabonidus fled and did not return to the city of Babylon until well after the city was in Persian hands. So Daniel 5 is correct to ignore Nabonidus. He was not in Babylon the night it fell.

When Daniel came into the throne room of the palace that night, he saw a king. But that king was Belshazzar, not Nabonidus. How could Daniel have known that Belshazzar was in the palace that night, to protect the city, but that Nabonidus his father was absent? How could he have known these intimate details about the personnel present in the palace on that very night?

Only one answer to this question is possible. Daniel was an eyewitness to these events just as he tells us in his record. We may have confidence in the accuracy of the historical events described in the book of Daniel, and we may have confidence that the future events which it predicts will come to pass.

LESSONS OF A STRUCTURAL NATURE

The portion of Daniel written in Aramaic covers chapters 2 through 7. At the very center of this section, chapters 4 and 5 deal with similar subjects—the king. In chapter 4, the king is Nebuchadnezzar; in chapter 5, the king is Belshazzar. Even though the events of these two chapters probably took place more than forty years apart, Daniel has chosen to tell these two stories side by side. He has deliberately arranged them in this way.

Although these two chapters both deal with the same type of subject—the king—they deal with that subject in different ways. Those two treatments give us a picture of comparison and contrast which can influence the direction of our spiritual lives. In the end, Nebuchadnezzar provides us with a good example; Belshazzar never does. The first king came to a reluctant conversion; the second king refused to be converted at all.

To emphasize the similarities and the contrasts in these two historical narratives, Daniel located them at the center of the literary framework of this part of the book. As the center of the chiastic structure in Daniel chapters 2 through 7, this arrangement focuses on individual responsibility. One king finally made a good choice, while the other king did not. The emphasis is on individual responsibility. Just as the monarchs of Babylon had an individual responsibility to God, so do each of us. We have a choice to make for or against God's grace and His kingdom. Although Belshazzar's example might urge us to delay and finally say no to God, Nebuchadnezzar's experience gives us motivation to meet and accept this true, personal God and to enter His kingdom.

There may seem to be some distance between literary structure and personal spiritual lessons, but the form in which Daniel wrote and arranged his book emphasizes the fact that a close relationship actually exists between the two.

CHAPTER FOUR

Kingly Persecution

The particular experiences of the Hebrew exiles in Babylon singled out in these two chapters begin on a very negative note, but they end with a glorious and miraculous deliverance in both cases. In the first, the trial involves Daniel's three friends (chapter 3). The second involves Daniel himself (chapter 6).

People often wonder where Daniel was while his friends were undergoing their test on the plain of Dura. We don't know the answer to this question because the text simply doesn't tell us. Common speculation is that Daniel was absent on an errand for the king. That is a reasonable suggestion, but we do not know for sure why Daniel wasn't present when the king set up his image. What we do know is that Daniel himself later faced the same kind of test. He did not have to suffer with his friends on the plain of Dura, but he did not escape persecution. In chapter 3, Daniel's companions face the fiery furnace, but in chapter 6, Daniel faces the den of lions.

These two stories contain a number of common features. Both start with an experience of persecution by the king who was reigning at the time—Nebuchadnezzar in the first instance, and Darius the Mede in the second. Both stories tell of the faithful courage of the Hebrews and their trust in God in spite of the circumstances. Both tell how the Hebrew exiles were plunged into trials that were intended to take their lives. Both stories tell of a miraculous deliverance. And in both cases the king involved recognized the Hebrews' faithfulness to the true God as illustrated by their deliverance.

Not only do these two chapters deal with similar themes, they are also placed at complementary locations in the literary structure of

Daniel's book. As we have seen earlier, the literary structure of the historical section of Daniel is carefully constructed to bring out the similarities between the chapters that are paired together due to common themes. In the case of chapters 3 and 6, the common themes are persecution and ultimate victory through faithfulness to God.

As has been noted before, the historical section of Daniel (chapters 2–7) was written in Aramaic, thus setting it off from the rest of the book. Likewise, the narratives in that section were arranged in a chiastic order in which paired narratives were located at similar junctures in that structure. In the preceding chapter we saw that chapters 4 and 5, dealing with the theme of fallen kings, comprise the two central narratives of this historical section. We come now to chapters 3 and 6—the intermediate narratives in this chiastic arrangement. The final part of this chiastic outline is treated in the next chapter of this book which examines chapters 2 and 7 in terms of their description of fallen kingdoms.

THE TEST

Nebuchadnezzar ordered that a great image be set up on the plain of Dura (3:1). Considerable confusion has existed about exactly what and where Dura was.

Scholars used to think Dura was the name of a city somewhere in the kingdom of Babylon. Identifying such a city, however, has been difficult. Another suggestion has been that Dura was the name of an irrigation canal and that the plain of Dura was located close by. This suggestion has not worked out well either, so search has been made in another direction.

Some refinements have been made recently in identifying the location of the plain of Dura. The name *Dura* is also the simple Babylonian word for a "wall." *Dur* is the word for "wall," and the letter *a* at the end of the word is the article "the" in Aramaic. So translating this phrase directly, instead of leaving it as an unknown place name, indicates that Nebuchadnezzar set up his image on "the plain of the wall."

But the question remains: "What plain and what wall?" There were two major walls surrounding the city of Babylon. The inner wall, about a mile long on each side, surrounded the central part of the city. The territory inside this inner wall was urban, containing many buildings and streets along with the palace and the largest temple in the city.

Later, Nebuchadnezzar added an outer wall several miles long that extended to the east bank of the Euphrates River and around the city. In Nebuchadnezzar's time, Babylonian engineers and builders had not yet filled this area between the inner and outer walls with buildings, although construction was taking place. The open area served as a parade ground for the army and a place within the city walls where the troops could bivouac. This large open space between the two walls could properly be called the "plain of the wall," or "the plain of Dura." In all likelihood this was where the events of chapter 3 took place.

Such a location would have facilitated attendance at this great assembly by officials from Babylon (vs. 3). It would also have put the image close to the palace of the king. There is no reason to suppose that the assembly gathered at some site in the kingdom remote from the capital.

Another consideration is the great size of the image. Its measurements are interesting from several points of view. Daniel says the image was sixty cubits high and six cubits wide (vs. 1). The Babylonians employed a sexagesimal mathematical system based on the number six, unlike our decimal system based on the number ten. So the measurements Daniel gives are typically Babylonian. But some have objected that an image sixty cubits high and only six cubits wide would be too tall for its width. A 1:10 ratio would look very skinny.

It's true that such measurements would result in a very tall, thin statue. Yet the ancients depicted their gods exactly this way. The figurines of Baal that come mainly from Syria and Palestine are good examples. The arms, legs, and bodies of these figurines are long and spindly, what we would call a matchstick kind of image. So for Nebuchadnezzar to make a statue with these proportions would not have been unusual.

What *was* unusual was the image's height. Some have objected that Nebuchadnezzar would not have made a figure so tall and that the sixty-cubit height (approximately ninety feet) is an exaggeration belonging to legend rather than historical fact. However, some examples of similarly tall statues can be cited in the ancient world. Probably the most famous of these was the colossus that stood on the island of Rhodes. At seventy cubits, it actually stood ten cubits higher than Nebuchadnezzar's image. The colossi of Memnon at Thebes in southern Egypt consist of two representations of the king Amenhotep III, one of which still stands to a height of sixty-five feet. So although Nebuchadnezzar's image would have been exceptionally tall, such statues were by no means unknown in the ancient world. As a modern comparison, it is interesting to note that the figure of the Statue of Liberty, excluding the pedestal, stands twenty feet higher than did Nebuchadnezzar's image.

Another factor to consider in terms of the height of this image is the height of another structure that may have been in the area. If Nebuchadnezzar set up his image in the plain between the city walls, and if it faced west, it would have been looking at the old central city of Babylon. In the center of the city was the temple area of Marduk which contained the great temple tower, or ziggurat, of Babylon. At some 300 feet high, it dominated the landscape. Its base was approximately 300 feet square and extended upward in a solid pyramid shape through seven levels, each covered with enamel bricks of a different color from the previous level. The top level consisted of a temple to the god Marduk in addition to the main temple located at the foot of the ziggurat. With such a monumental structure nearby, Nebuchadnezzar's image, standing a "mere" ninety feet high, would not appear so exceptional.

WHO OR WHAT DID NEBUCHANEZZAR'S IMAGE REPRESENT?

Basically, there are two possibilities. Either it represented a god or it represented a man. If the image was designed to represent a man, no doubt that man was Nebuchadnezzar himself. If it represented a god, it most likely represented Marduk, the city and national god of Babylon and the personal god of Nebuchadnezzar.

Which of these two possibilities is more likely? Daniel 3 does not tell us precisely what the image represented, but it does tell us that the assembled crowd was to bow down and "worship" the image (vss. 7, 12, 14, 15). Although the citizens of the kingdom were expected to perform obeisance to the kings of Babylon, they did not worship them. In Egypt, the kings were considered to be gods, but in Mesopotamia, kings were only the special servants of the gods. Only a very few Mesopotamian kings claimed to be divine, and Nebuchadnezzar was not among them. In fact, Babylonian theology held that it was a sin for the king to claim divinity and that those who did so would be punished by the gods. So it is considerably more likely that the image was intended to represent Marduk, the god of Babylon, than Nebuchadnezzar.

Why did Nebuchadnezzar have this image erected? Again, Daniel 3 does not tell us. But it is easy to see a connection between chapters 2 and 3. In chapter 2 the king dreamed of a great image made of different metals which represented the successive kingdoms that would rule over the earth. The immediate meaning of this dream to Nebuchadnezzar was that another kingdom would follow Babylon (2:39). This was not good news to Babylon's king! Hitler thought that the Third Reich would stand for a thousand years, and Nebuchadnezzar probably had a similar future in mind for his kingdom. In Daniel 2:32, 36–39, Babylon is represented as the golden part of the image. Thus by making an image similar to the one he had seen in his dream, but by making it all of gold (probably gold foil sheathing a wooden form underneath), the king denied the dream's meaning—the succession of kingdoms that was to follow Babylon on the world stage. In Nebuchadnezzar's thinking, Babylon was to stand forever. Constructing an image all of gold represented that fact.

However, there probably was more to the erection of the image than just a response by the king to the message of his dream. The Babylonian Chronicle proves helpful at this point. Prior to the discovery of these tablets containing the official record of Nebuchadnezzar's kingship, scholars thought that his lengthy forty-three-year rule was a monolithic, unchallenged reign. But the Chronicle tells a different story. In fact, there was such serious opposition to Nebuchadnezzar that on one occasion a revolt arose from within the city that resulted in hand-to-hand combat in the very palace itself with the king fighting for his life! The Chronicle entry reads:

> In the tenth year [595/594 B.C.] the king of Akkad [Babylon] was in his own land; from the month of Kislev [December] to the month of Tebet [January] there was rebellion in Akkad. . . .

> With arms he [the king] slew many of his own army. His own hand captured his enemy (quoted in Wiseman, *Chronicles of Chaldean Kings,* 73).

Daniel does not give a date for the events of chapter 3. But it is tempting to link them to the rebellion described in the Babylonian Chronicle and to see in the king's demand that all the officials of the kingdom bow down to the image, a loyalty oath required in response to the problem of disloyalty in their ranks. If this speculation is correct, then the Babylonian Chronicle provides a possible date for the events described in chapter 3. If the rebellion took place in 594 B.C., then the episode with the image could have taken place later that year or early the next year as a response to the rebellion.

Continuing that hypothesis, it is important to note who was present at the dedication of the great image. Not all the citizens of Babylon were called to assemble. It was a select group, identified as "the satraps, prefects, governors, advisers, treasurers, judges, magistrates and all other provincial officials" (vss. 2, 3). These Babylonian government officials were "summoned" (vs. 2) by the king to attend the dedication ceremony. If the summons was a response to the rebellion that had taken place, it is easy to see why the king would have selected this group. Government officials and those working in the palace were the most likely to formulate plots against the king. They were the ones potentially most dangerous to him, and they were also the ones whose support was most crucial to the king. Any disloyalty in this group would plunge the monarch and his kingdom into serious trouble again.

To prevent such a development, the king assembled these officials and had them swear an oath of allegiance. It took a religious form. If one bows down and worships the god of Babylon, then one is also pledging allegiance to faithfully serve that god and his earthly representative, the king. Thus the events of chapter 3 can be seen as preventive politics practiced in religious garb on the plain of Dura.

The demand to worship the image was not specifically targeted at Daniel's three Hebrew friends. They were simply caught up in the situation because they were civil servants of the government of Babylon—positions for which they had been brought as exiles to Babylon from

Judah and to which they had been appointed by the end of chapter 2 (see vs. 49).

Like them, we, too, may be carried along by the force of circumstances over which we have no direct control. There comes a time, however, when those who follow God have to take a stand for the right and be counted. We cannot always flow with the crowd, no matter how tempting it may be to do so. One lesson from chapter 3 is that faith in the true God will bring us through such trials just as it did the three Hebrews facing the king's anger on the plain of Dura.

THE RESPONSE

Heralds instructed the assembled officials to bow down and worship the great image when the players in the orchestra struck up their music. And with the exception of the three Hebrews, that is exactly what they did (vss. 4–7).

We do not know how many persons gathered before the image, but the list of officials given in verse 2 seems to be all-inclusive. Perhaps 2,000 officials would have been involved. Imagine that large crowd of 2,000 people all bowing down at one time. Then imagine the three Hebrews standing all alone as everybody else was prostrate on the ground. These three men must have felt very much alone as they stood out distinctly from the bowing multitude. They felt keenly the pressure of 2,000 other officials all conforming, all obeying the king's decree. Some of these officials probably worked with Shadrach, Meshach, and Abednego. They may even have been friends. Can't you imagine an official who is bowing near these three Hebrews whispering, "Get down! Get down, for your own good! You don't have to mean it; just get down!"

But the Hebrews did not flinch or bow. They were not swayed by the crowd, all of whom were bowing before the image. There are times when Christians, like these men, have to take an unpopular stand. Early Christians refused to burn incense to the emperor, and in some instances it cost them their lives. Burning incense to the emperor was an act of worship; bowing down on the plain of Dura was also an act of worship. Worshipers of the true God could not participate in either ceremony.

No doubt, the pressure the three Hebrews felt from the conforming crowd intensified when they were brought before the king (vs. 13). Nebuchadnezzar was the world's most powerful monarch. Whatever he wanted to do with them, would be done; they were completely in his control. There was one thing, however, he could not do. He could not violate their will and choice. He could attempt to persuade them. He could try to coerce them. He could punish them. But he could not force them to act against their will.

One or more furnaces probably stood nearby, adding to the monarch's threat. We must not think these were constructed specially for the Hebrews when it was discovered that they would not obey the king and worship the image. Rather, the furnaces had been constructed in advance and were standing ready for anyone foolish enough to resist the king's loyalty oath. As the music played and the Hebrews remained standing, they could look out over the huge crowd bowing to the ground and see clearly the instruments of punishment for those who refused.

Most likely, these furnaces were brick kilns. Bricks were made in two ways in ancient times—by drying them in the sun and by firing them in kilns. Kiln-fired bricks were harder and were used especially for the outer surfaces of buildings. The great plain between the two sets of city walls was a place of ongoing construction projects, and the main construction material used was not wood or cement, but clay. The city of Babylon was made of thousands, if not millions, of clay bricks. The kilns used to fire these bricks were shaped like a beehive with a hole at the top of the cone through which flammable material was dropped; there was another tunnel-like opening on one side. Pallets of bricks were put in the side opening, and the material with which the kiln was fired was dropped into the kiln from above. Steps went up the side of the kiln to the upper opening. The Hebrews were probably dropped into the kiln through the hole at the top.

The kilns were probably already fired up by the time the ceremony took place. Thus the Hebrews not only knew they would be thrown into one of these kilns for their refusal to worship the image, they could actually see it burning and smoking in the distance. But in spite of looking right into the terrifying face of their fate, they stood firm in their refusal to bow down (vss. 16–18). Fear of a horrible death could not induce them to be unfaithful to God!

It's also interesting that they didn't break ranks over this issue. Two didn't stand firm with one bowing. Two didn't give in and leave the third alone in his faithfulness to God. All three were united in the common bond of faith and courage so that when one spoke to the king, he spoke for all three. This is the kind of unity in the faith that is needed as the church approaches its final crisis. When Christians break ranks and divide in their response over test and trial, they only make it harder for themselves and for their fellow Christians.

The king was already angry, and he was getting progressively more so. Upon hearing that the three Hebrews had disobeyed his order, he was "furious with rage" (vs. 13). When they rejected a second opportunity to bow down to the image, "his attitude toward them changed" and he became even more "furious with Shadrach, Meshach and Abednego" (vs. 19). It's not a good thing to have the world's most powerful ruler angry at you, with his instruments of torture and annihilation standing by at the ready.

Why was the king so enraged? As a matter of policy, Assyrians and Babylonians did not force captive peoples to convert to the worship of their conqueror's gods. Why didn't Nebuchadnezzar have more tolerance for these Hebrews who didn't choose to worship his god?

Something more is involved here. If the scenario suggested earlier is correct and the events of chapter 3 are seen in terms of a recent revolt in Babylon, then we can understand why the king would have been so upset with these officials who would not take his loyalty oath. In Nebuchadnezzar's mind, here were the seeds of another revolt in the making. No wonder this was such a sensitive issue with him and that he took the Hebrews' refusal so seriously.

Yet, in spite of all this, the king was still willing to give them another opportunity to bow to the image. He was willing to have the orchestra strike up again and see if the Hebrews would obey (vs. 15). But their mind was set so firmly upon remaining faithful to God that they told the king not even to bother with another stanza of music. Their decision was set in a cement stronger than that which held the city's walls together. They put it this way:

> O Nebuchadnezzar, we do not need to defend ourselves before you in this matter. If we are thrown into the blazing furnace, the God we serve is able to save us from it, and he will rescue us from your hand, O king. But even if he does not, we want you to know, O king, that we will not serve your gods or worship the image of gold you have set up (vss. 16–18).

This was a death-before-dishonor response, but it was more. They clearly enunciated the reason they could not obey. It sprang from "the God we serve." They served Yahweh (Jehovah), not Marduk. Their refusal to bow to Nebuchadnezzar's image involved more than just the refusal of these three men to obey the order of one king. Two gods were involved—Marduk and Yahweh. Nebuchadnezzar served Marduk; the three Hebrews served Yahweh. The scene on the plain thus became a contest between the true God and the false god, played out through their human representatives.

From all appearances, it looked as though the Hebrews were the certain losers in this contest; in actuality, they were in a win-win situation. If they died as a consequence of their steadfast trust in God, they could be seen as martyrs courageous enough to die for their faith. If, on the other hand, their God did deliver them—as they stated in their second option—then His glory and honor would be made even more manifest. But this does not subtract in the least from the courage and faithfulness they demonstrated. As far as they knew, they were about to die when they told the king they did not need a second chance to bow to the image. Their reply is a remarkable testimony to their faith and trust and courage.

Their example raises a question for us: Is our faith and trust in God strong enough that we would be able to stand up to such a test and exhibit the spiritual courage they showed? Are we sufficiently grounded in His Word and in our experiences with Him that we, too, could stand before a king and declare that under no circumstance would we dishonor the God who has loved us?

Sometime in the future we may indeed have to face such a test. For the present, however, our lives are confronted with lesser challenges. How we respond to these prepares us for greater tests. They indicate how we will respond when larger issues arise. The Bible has a principle of spiritual life that applies here: "Whoever can be trusted with very little can also be trusted with much" (Luke 16:10). The wear and tear of ordinary, everyday life are directly related to the great challenges of life. God prepares us to meet the great trials of life in the everyday school of hard knocks. Moses spent forty years in the wilderness tending sheep, but it was that preparation that enabled him to meet with Pharaoh on equal terms. We, too, can develop a spiritual preparation for whatever life may hold for us.

THE RESULT

Nebuchadnezzar was not happy with the response of the three Hebrews. The punishment previously designed was not sufficient in the face of such insolence. He ordered that the furnace be heated seven times hotter (vs. 19). How would he have accomplished this? Remember, this took place in Babylon. Today we call this area, Iraq. Iraq is a country rich in oil. Most of that oil is underground and has to be pumped out by modern oil companies. But there are places where oil seeps to the surface. These open asphalt wells have been used in modern times, and they were known and used in ancient times as well. The best way to have a brick kiln heated to a much higher temperature would be to throw some petroleum into it.

The king's order to increase the temperature was obeyed, and it succeeded so well that the men who carried the three bound Hebrews up the steps on the side of the furnace and threw them in, were themselves killed by the blast of the furnace (vs 22). If the overheated furnace did that to the men who threw the Hebrews in, you can imagine what it would do to the Hebrews themselves who were directly in the furnace itself. But it didn't. The king came over to see how the punishment was progressing. He probably bent down to look in the tunnel at the side of the kiln. He expected to see the charred and burning bodies of his three unfaithful officials; instead he saw them perfectly unharmed and unburned! The three men had been firmly tied when they were thrown into the furnace (vs. 23). Now as the king looked in, they were unbound and walking around in the fire! When they finally came out of the kiln, the report was, "the fire had not harmed their bodies, nor was a hair of their heads singed; their robes were not scorched, and there was no smell of fire on them" (vs. 27).

This was a very selective fire! It had burned the ropes right off the Hebrews' wrists. It had even burned the men who had thrown them into the fire. But it did not touch the bodies of these three men, nor their garments, nor even a single hair of their heads! There was no smell of smoke about them! It was as if they had never been in the fire at all. It was as if there was a kind of protective nonflammable envelope surrounding them. Thus God honored the faith and trust of His faithful servants.

From that dramatic answer to prayer we can see that we serve a prayer-answering God. He may not answer our prayers in such a dramatic way, but the fact that He did so for Shadrach, Meshach, and Abednego assures us that He will hear and answer our prayers in the way that He sees is best.

Our prayers should express the same confidence and faith that the prayers of these three Hebrews did. They did not demand a single, specific answer from God; they recognized the possibilities and left the decision to God. He can deliver us and will do so if He sees best; but He may also answer, No. In such cases, we should be willing to accept that answer and live with it—or die with it, as Shadrach, Meshach, and Abednego were ready to do. Their example is an example of faith and courage to us, but it is also an example of accepting God's will.

As recorded in the Gospels, the miracles Jesus performed had an additional purpose beyond benefitting specific individuals.They were also teaching vehicles designed to convey a spiritual lesson. For example, Jesus performed seven miracles on Sabbath. These not only blessed those who were involved, they also taught something about the Sabbath. They taught that Jesus was Lord of the Sabbath and that the Sabbath could be used for His purposes in the healing and salvation of mankind (see Matthew 12:8). They also taught that He was the Creator and re-Creator (see John 5; 7). Likewise, the miracle God performed for the three Hebrews in the fiery furnace had a purpose beyond their deliverance. Through this miracle, Nebuchadnezzar and the hundreds or thousands of Babylonian officials on the plain of Dura were brought face to face with the true God of heaven.

Nebuchadnezzar understood the lesson and said so. As he looked into the fire and saw Shadrach, Meshach, and Abednego unharmed, he addressed them as "servants of the Most High God" (vs. 26). The king even decreed that all those in the nations he ruled should honor the God who had so dramatically demonstrated His power to deliver His servants—thus ensuring that the miraculous event would be known throughout his empire (vss. 28, 29).

But God did not leave it to chance that Nebuchadnezzar would understand clearly who had performed this miracle. As the king looked into the fire, he saw the three Hebrews walking about unharmed in the flames, but he also saw a fourth being in the fire with them. He immediately recognized this figure as divine—a "son of the gods" (vs. 25). Later, he identified this divine being as an angel (vs. 28). We must not suppose that Nebuchadnezzar identified this fourth person with God's Son in the sense that we Christians think of Jesus Christ today. Remember that the king was still in his pagan, unconverted state at this time. This is clear from the way he commands all his officials at the beginning of this narrative to bow down to the image of his god. It is also clear in his response to Shadrach, Meshach, and Abednego when they refused to bow to the image because they served another God. Clearly, this miraculous deliverance made a deep impression upon Nebuchadnezzar and caused him to recognize the superiority of the Hebrews' God. But he was not converted to serve their God at this time. This experience surely helped prepare him for such a conversion, but that experience was not complete until the end of his seven years of insanity described in Daniel 4. Not until then did Nebuchadnezzar come to accept the true God whom he called the Most High God (4:34–37).

Nebuchadnezzar did not see a clear picture of the Messiah in the fourth figure walking about in the fire. He recognized this being as a "son of the gods" (vs. 25), as his description can be most literally and accurately translated. This is not at all the same as "the Son of God." A "son of the gods" simply means a being from the realm of the gods, that is a supernatural being. His identification of this being as an angel brings up the references to other angels in the book of Daniel. Two of them are named Gabriel and Michael. Gabriel was the one who brought some of the prophecies to Daniel (9:21, 23). Michael, the archangel (or prince of the heavenly princes, Daniel 8:11, 25; 10:13; 12:1) was the one who stood up for and defended the people of God, both in Babylonian and Persian times and at the end of time (Daniel 10:13; 12:1). Given the defensive posture in which we find Michael, he would have been the ideal angel to have protected and defended the three Hebrews in the fire. From a New Testament perspective we know that Michael is Christ (Revelation 12:7), but that would not necessarily have been evident to Nebuchadnezzar on this occasion. He simply knew that the God of the Hebrews had sent a divinelike being to rescue them. That very vivid impression would have been adequate for the time being in the course of Nebuchadnezzar's spiritual pilgrimage.

An interesting contrast is involved here when one compares the concluding scene of the vision of Daniel 7. There Daniel looked into the heavenly courts and saw the Ancient of Days, God the Father, conducting the heavenly tribunal. At the conclusion of that scene, one like a "son of man . . . approached the Ancient of Days" (7:13) to receive the kingdom. The language here is similar to Nebuchadnezzar's pronouncement in chapter 3:25, but there is a contrast as well. In chapter 3 we see one like "a son of the gods" here on earth, a divinelike being come down from heaven to earth. In chapter 7 we see one like "a son of man" in heaven, a humanlike incarnate being who has entered heaven where He will receive the kingdom for ever and ever. Michael is the Protector of His people here on earth, and He will be their great Ruler here for all eternity. He is none other than Jesus Christ who will come again at last as King of kings and Lord of lords to fulfill the prediction of Daniel 7:14 and Revelation 19:16.

THE SETTING FOR DANIEL 6

The events recorded in Daniel 5 and 6 took place within a relatively short period of time spanning the fall of Babylon and the short-term aftermath of that conquest by the Persians. Chapter 5 describes the kingdom's collapse from the Babylonian viewpoint of what was going on within the city and the palace. Chapter 6 recounts what took place soon after, as the Persians set up their administration of the newly conquered territories. Daniel played a part both in the final events under the last Babylonian king, Belshazzar, and in the setting up of the new

Persian administration. In fact, he played a prominent part in that transition. Unfortunately, it was his prominence that got him into difficulty.

In the ancient world, the Persians were fairly benevolent conquerors. For example, they commonly, though not always, left in place the indigenous rulers and officials of conquered territories. Instead of removing them, they adapted them to their use. Sometimes, this applied even to conquered kings who were left to rule their previous holdings under the authority of the Persian Empire. Another evidence of Persian benevolence was their return of captive peoples to their homelands. As the books of Ezra and Nehemiah make plain, it was under Persian kings that the people of Judah were allowed to return home.

The Persians did not extend preferential treatment to the kings of Babylon, however. Belshazzar was killed the night the city was taken; the Persians captured his father Nabonidus and exiled him to far-away Carmania. Actually, exile was probably an act of kindness, for Nabonidus could easily have been executed.

With Belshazzar and Nabonidus both out of the picture and the kingdom taken over by the Persians, it was necessary to appoint a new person to head up the Persian government of Babylon. Cyrus, the ruler of the empire, appointed Darius the Mede to this job. Darius was to rule in Babylon as a vassal king subject to Cyrus who continued to rule the Persian Empire of which Babylon was now a part.

At this juncture we encounter a historical question: Who was this person called Darius the Mede in Daniel 6? No one by that name is known from secular sources of the time.

A number of suggestions have been made regarding the identity of this biblical Darius, but no consensus has yet been reached. Those who accept the historicity of Daniel 6, all accept the premise that "Darius" is the throne name of someone who was known by a different, personal name before being appointed to the rulership of Babylon. Such a solution would not be unusual. The practice of assuming a throne name at the time of accession was well known throughout the ancient Near East. In Egypt, kings took on a whole set of five different names when they succeeded to the throne. In Mesopotamia, two Assyrian kings who conquered the city of Babylon and placed themselves upon its throne, assumed throne names when they did so. Tiglath-pileser III assumed the throne name of Pulu (both names are used in 2 Kings 15:19, 29), and Shalmaneser V was known by the throne name of Ululaia.

In Judah we have the clear case of the leper-king Uzziah who was also known by the name of Azariah (2 Kings 15:1; 2 Chronicles 26:1). Azariah was probably his original name and Uzziah his throne name. It is also possible that Jedidiah was Solomon's personal name (2 Samuel 12:25), and the latter his throne name—or the reverse. Some historians of Persia have suggested that the names by which the famous Persian kings are known—Cyrus, Darius, Xerxes—may have been throne names and that they had other personal names before they became king. Therefore, the suggestion that "Darius the Mede" is a throne name used in the book of Daniel reflects a well-known practice in the ancient world.

What is more difficult is the task of identifying the individual who bore this throne name. Darius the Mede should not be confused with Darius I Hystaspes, also known as "Darius the Great," who ruled Persia from 522 to 486 B.C. This individual came from a Persian, not Median, line and ruled later than the Darius of Daniel 6. The readings suggested at the end of this chapter discuss in detail the different suggestions that have been made for identifying the historical person Daniel 6 refers to as "Darius the Mede."

THE PLOT

From the point of view of Daniel's book, what Darius *does* is more important than who Darius *is*. It's important to note that Daniel was not originally singled out for punishment or persecution. Instead, the Persians intimately involved him in their reorganization of the government of the province of Babylon. Darius had appointments to make on two different levels of officialdom. One hundred twenty lower-level officials needed to be appointed or confirmed in office, and three officials were to be installed on the highest level. Daniel was one of these three uppermost administrators, and Darius was soon to consider making him the most pre-eminent of the three (6:1–3). This would have been equivalent to making Daniel the chief governor of all Babylon.

Naturally, his civil-service colleagues reacted negatively to Daniel's impending elevation. They were jealous and set out to make sure that he didn't receive this highest post. The plot they hatched centered on Daniel's religious practices because they knew that this was the only "flaw" they could exploit. He was so conscientious in all the affairs he carried out for the king that these jealous colleagues knew they would never catch him in rank dishonesty or inefficiency (vss. 4, 5). So they set a religious trap for Daniel. They approached the king with a proposal. "The king should issue an edict," they urged, "and enforce the decree that anyone who prays to any god or man during the next thirty days, except to you, O king, shall be thrown into the lions' den" (vss. 6, 7).

Now this is a very strange-sounding request. One might well ask, "What about the other gods of Babylon?"

In order to understand the appeal of such a decree, one needs to understand the disturbed religious conditions in Babylon immediately after the Persian conquest. Nabonidus, the last Babylonian king, set out to protect the city of Babylon as the final bastion of defense against the Persians. He attempted to do so not only with troops and arms, but also with the help of the gods. His representatives went to the major cities of Babylonia and took the images of their gods out of the temples and brought them to Babylon. The rationale was that by gathering the images of the gods in Babylon, the gods themselves would be obliged to defend the city. Nabonidus wanted the gods on his side.

The Persians were successful in spite of this ploy, of course. But when they took over, they faced not only political problems; they faced a religious problem as well. With the images of the gods gathered in the capital city, people throughout the kingdom were having difficulty praying in empty temples. The Persians set about to rectify this situation by sending the gods back to their respective cities and temples, but the logistics and the ritual that had to take place made it certain that the transfer would take some time to accomplish. Not until the end of the Babylonian calendar year, some four months later, did all the gods find their way back to their locations, says the *Nabonidus Chronicle.*

Under such confused conditions, a request to divert prayers away from any god except the king himself becomes easier to understand. During more normal times, such a request would have bordered on the absurd, but these were not normal times either religiously or politically.

The Babylonian officials who proposed this regulation were not actually concerned whether someone prayed to these other gods. They were interested in only one God—Yahweh, or Jehovah, the God to whom Daniel prayed. They took advantage of the times in order to devise a plot to bring Daniel down. They knew how regular he was in his prayer habits. Three times a day, Daniel prayed to his God, facing west toward Jerusalem where the temple had once stood (vs. 10). Daniel probably prayed at the times when the morning and evening sacrifices would have been offered in that temple had it still been standing (Daniel 9:21).

Daniel didn't flaunt his prayers in a display of superficial religiosity, but neither did he try to hide these personal spiritual exercises. His fellow officials knew his habits well. They knew how regular and faithful he was in this practice. They also knew that he was a man of such integrity and faithfulness to his God that he would not interrupt his prayer life simply because of a mere human prohibition. Daniel had faith in his God, but his colleagues had faith in Daniel!

Their confidence in Daniel's steadfastness is a remarkable example to us of faithful devotion. If we were to find ourselves in a situation similar to that in which Daniel found himself, would others feel sure that our steadfastness would not change? Daniel's vibrant, active faith found its source in his regular time for prayer and devotions. He didn't start praying only when some crisis came along. Nor was he engaging in some spiritual showmanship by continuing his prayers in spite of the decree. Although his prayers may have become more fervent as a result of the king's decree, Daniel's basic relationship with God had already been established in the habits of life. Long before this plot was formed against him, he had found prayer to be the vital ingredient in his busy life in Babylon as a high-ranking official. The decree simply brought to the forefront the habits of a lifetime on the part of this faithful servant of God.

HOW LONG HAD DANIEL BEEN PRAYING LIKE THIS?

He was deported to Babylon in 605 B.C. when he was approximately eighteen years of age. The present episode took place during the brief reign of Darius the Mede, therefore it must have taken place either in 539 B.C. or 538 B.C. If we add Daniel's sixty-seven years in Babylon to his age of eighteen when taken captive, we come to an age of about eighty-five years for Daniel at the time this episode occurred. Daniel was an old man when the Persians took over, but he was still intellectually capable, and his life of faith still burned bright. This was the result of a lifetime of faith and prayer, a beautiful example of faithfulness.

Daniel's faithfulness did not go unnoticed by God. On two different occasions an angel was sent to him and addressed him in these words: "O Daniel, man greatly beloved" (Daniel 9:23; 10:11, KJV; "highly" or "greatly" esteemed, NIV). God had not forgotten His servant simply because he was an old man. On the contrary, His regard for Daniel grew even greater as the man grew older in the faith and came to know God better. This should come as an encouragement to those who have grown older. Companions and relatives on earth may forget, but God never forgets. Daniel's case demonstrates the divine concern.

The decree was to cover a span of thirty days during which no one was to pray to anyone other than Darius (6:7). Daniel's enemies didn't have to wait this whole time to see whether Daniel would violate the new command. They undoubtedly caught him praying on the first or second day. So they rushed off to the king and told him of Daniel's disregard of his decree.

Now the laws of the Persians were irrevocable (vs. 15). Having once been enacted, the decree could not be changed to fit the new circumstances. Daniel, a favorite of the king, had been caught in the king's own ordinance. And the king had been caught in the scheme of the officials plotting against Daniel. He tried all day to work out some sort of arrangement whereby Daniel could be released and escape punishment, but he was unable to do so (vs. 14). By sundown, it became clear that the king could not deliver Daniel. God's prophet would have to be given to the lions.

THE RESULT

We can get some idea of where the lions' den would have been located in ancient Babylon. The famous royal hanging gardens of Babylon were considered to be one of the seven wonders of the ancient world. The story behind their origin is that Nebuchadnezzar married a wife from the mountainous country of Media. Coming down to the flat, dry, hot plain of Mesopotamia, she longed for the pleasant features of her mountain homeland. To lessen her homesickness, Nebuchadnezzar built the renowned hanging gardens of Babylon. Recent studies have suggested that these gardens were located in the northwestern corner of the palace, adjacent to the Euphrates River.

In all likelihood the royal zoo was located beside the royal gardens. Thus the same water that was used to irrigate the gardens could be used to water the animals, and the gardens would provide a proper habitat for some of the animals in the zoo. Thus the lions' den into which Daniel was thrown probably was located in the northwestern corner of the palace area.

Reports arose prior to World War I that the lions' den from which Daniel was miraculously delivered had been located and excavated by archaeologists. Excavations were going forward at Babylon, and Christian pilgrims came back from these diggings with the report that the lions' den had been found. The source of these erroneous rumors was Robert Koldewey, the excavator of Babylon. Koldewey was an unbeliever and an irreverent man. He was also a practical joker. Pilgrims would arrive asking questions about things such as the lions' den. Without hesitation, Koldewey would take them to some part of his excavations and say, "This is exactly the spot where it happened."

The pilgrims went home rejoicing to have seen where Daniel suffered and was delivered. When one of Koldewey's associates argued with him about what he was doing to these gullible people, Koldewey replied, "Why should I take from them one of the great experiences of their trip?"

Although we haven't located the scene of Daniel's deliverance from the lions, the clay tablets upon which the Babylonians kept their records do shed light on his experience. From the city of Ur, farther south, have come records which tell about the supplies for the feeding of the lions. Just as bureaucrats recorded the foodstuffs distributed to different officials, they also recorded the food that was distributed to animals in the royal zoo—including the lions. These texts come from the time of the Ur III Dynasty or approximately 2000 B.C., the time of Abraham. Not only did Babylon have lions in the royal zoo in the time of Daniel in the middle of the first millennium B.C., the records show they already had them there as early as the beginning of the second millennium B.C.

Darius was upset. Although he had no choice but to throw Daniel into the lions' den, he didn't like it. He didn't like it because he had been tricked into it by his own officials. More than that, he was genuinely concerned for Daniel; he had a great affection and respect for him. The king could not sleep all that night (vs. 18). Darius already knew of Daniel's God, and he had some inkling that He could act on Daniel's behalf (vs. 16), but he was not yet a believer. He might have gotten a full night's sleep if he had had a little stronger faith in Daniel's God!

God did not desert Daniel in the lions' den any more than He had deserted Daniel's three friends in the furnace. As on the earlier occasion, He sent His angel to be with Daniel and to protect him. Daniel told the king on the following morning when he came to inquire about the prophet's welfare, "O king, live forever! My God sent his angel, and he shut the mouths of the lions. They have not hurt me, because I was found innocent in his sight. Nor have I ever done any wrong before you, O king" (vss. 21, 22). Daniel did not claim credit for his own deliverance. He acknowledged God's mighty angel who had done this for him. In answer to his prayers, God had granted Daniel divine protection. God may not always answer prayers in such a dramatic way, but we can be certain He hears us when we pray today as surely as He heard Daniel's prayers in the lions' den.

Does God still perform such miracles today? Or is Daniel's experience just a story from long ago and far away that has little to do with modern life as we live it? From Recife, Brazil comes a story illustrating that God is still active and can do for modern believers what He did for Daniel so many centuries ago. A man, working in the Recife city zoo, came in contact with Seventh-day Adventists, began studying the Bible, and was eventually baptized. Following his baptism, he came to work the next Monday morning with his new-found faith shining on his face. "A wonderful thing happened to me this Saturday," he told his fellow workers. "I was baptized into the Seventh-day Adventist Church!"

One of those listening to his testimony was particularly cynical toward Christianity. He replied, "Well, if you are such a great Christian, why don't you jump down into this cage with the lions? Why don't you see if God will protect you?"

Immediately, without hesitation, this new Christian jumped down into the lions' cage! Now, I would not recommend doing that; there is such a thing as presumption rather than faith. But I also think the Holy Spirit honored this man's action as a testimony of his new-found faith.

As the man jumped into the cage, the movement attracted the attention of a large, male lion who came over to see what was happening. The lions in this cage, it should be noted, had not been fed for twenty-four hours. The large male lion came over to the man in his cage and sniffed his trousers. Then he turned around, went back to his place, lay down, and went to sleep! Perhaps God has sent His angel to deliver not only Daniel in times past, but this zookeeper in Recife, Brazil.

The purpose? Some time later seven of his fellow zookeepers were baptized.

Daniel was delivered from the lions. But the effect was quite different when his enemies, who had plotted against him, were placed in the same den where Daniel had spent the night. The lions attacked them immediately (vs. 24), demonstrating how hungry they really were. Daniel says that one of the reasons God delivered him was because he was innocent (vs. 22). In plotting against Daniel, his enemies were also plotting against his God. As a result, they were judged guilty and punished accordingly. The *lex talonis,* the law of an eye for an eye and a tooth for a tooth, was operating here—not from any desire for revenge on Daniel's part, but by the will of Darius the Mede.

Although at this time the king was still probably a Zoroastrian by religious conviction, he could see the greatness and power of Daniel's God in this miraculous deliverance.

> Then King Darius wrote to all the peoples, nations and men of every language throughout the land: "May you prosper greatly! I issue a decree that in every part of my kingdom people must fear and reverence the God of Daniel. For he is the living God and he endures forever; his kingdom will not be destroyed, his

> dominion will never end. He rescues and saves; he performs signs and wonders in the heavens and on the earth. He has rescued Daniel from the power of the lions" (vss. 25–27).

Because of Daniel's faithful witness, God's character became known throughout the kingdom of Babylon to a degree it had never been known before. When he knelt to pray in spite of the prohibition, Daniel probably never dreamed of the far-reaching effect such an apparently insignificant act would cause. He probably saw it merely as a part of his normal round of daily activities, unimportant in and of itself except that, through it, he came into contact with his God. Yet, through that act of prayer, in defiance of the law, the name and character of the true and living God became known throughout the kingdom.

In the same way, our little acts of kindness, faith, and love may also have an effect that reaches as far as eternity. Through the faithful witness of Daniel, God calls us to a similar life of faith.

DANIEL 3 AND 6 IN SUMMARY

These two chapters present similar pictures; in both Hebrews are being persecuted by a foreign king. In the first case, the king was Nebuchadnezzar of Babylon, and in the second, it was Darius the Mede, a vassal king of Babylon under the Persian emperor Cyrus. Both kings utilized Hebrews in their civil service. In both cases, these Hebrews were faithful in their service to the king, and also to their God. It was this latter quality—their faithfulness to God—that got them in trouble. Because of their dedication to God, Daniel's three friends were thrown into the fiery furnace. Because of his dedication to God, Daniel himself was cast into the den of lions. In both cases miraculous deliverances took place—from the furnace and from the lions' den. And in both instances the foreign king was convinced that divine intervention had taken place on behalf of these servants of the true God. Both kings proclaimed throughout the kingdom the power and majesty of the God of heaven.

In terms of themes, then, these two chapters relate events that share many similarities. Of course, these similarities were worked out in different ways. The two events probably took place more than fifty years apart. The nature and location of the trial were different, the king on the throne was different, the deliverances took place in different ways, and the words chosen by the monarchs with which to praise the God of heaven were different.

Nevertheless, the overarching concerns of both episodes were the same. In both, the saints of God were put on trial and were delivered from that trial through divine intervention. So, we can say that the similarities between these two events are major in scope, while their differences are matters of detail.

The chiastic literary structure to be found in Daniel's book, in which form complements function, also underlines the similarities between chapters 3 and 6. In this volume, we have already noted the chiastic structure of Daniel and the fact that in the Aramaic section of the book, the chapters are arranged in pairs (see page 29). Chapters 3 and 6 form one such pair describing persecutions suffered by the Hebrews in exile. Daniel intentionally arranged his writings in this way to show the interrelated nature of the chapters and the unity of his writing. Literary critics who attempt to divide these units and distribute them to different sources written at different times have missed the point of the writer who expresses the unity of his book in a very bold and aesthetic way.

CHAPTER FIVE

Fallen Kingdoms

Chapters 2 and 7 of Daniel deal with the same general subject—prophecies regarding the rise and fall of four major Mediterranean world powers. The first of these prophecies was given to a pagan king, Nebuchadnezzar, in a dream as he slept at night (Daniel 2:1). The second was given to the prophet Daniel himself as he slept in his bed at night (Daniel 7:1, 2). So although the mode of revelation was virtually the same in both instances, the recipient was quite different. This contrast clearly accounts for some of the differences in content between the two prophecies.

Even a cursory look makes it apparent that the dream given to Nebuchadnezzar was much more simple than the one given to Daniel. Nebuchadnezzar saw only a great image composed of four metals from top to bottom with its feet a mixture of clay and metal. Then a great stone struck the image on the feet, smashed it, and disposed of it. This stone then grew until it filled the whole world.

The interpretation is that the four metals represent four kingdoms, so the meaning is quite straightforward and direct. Four great Mediterranean world powers were to occupy the stage of history, one after the other. Then the fourth power would become mixed up with other elements. Finally, the kingdom of God would replace all earthly kingdoms, and in contrast to them, it would stand forever.

In Daniel 7, the message is given directly to God's prophet and thus to God's people. The outline of kingdoms remains the same, but includes more details. In this prophecy, four beasts, or animals, represent the four world kingdoms. The four beasts that appear in chapter 7 correspond to the four metals found in the image of Daniel 2. But there is a much greater opportunity to express details in the second prophecy because animals are animate, whereas metals are not. Thus the kingdoms that were outlined with mere generalizations in Daniel 2 have their features fleshed out in Daniel 7. As the text progresses from revelation to a pagan king to the revelation given to a prophet of God, it also progresses from a more general prophetic outline to one that contains more details. This is a pattern that continues throughout Daniel's book. Even more details are added in chapters 8 and 11.

This feature of Daniel's book brings up the subject of hermeneutics or rules of interpretation. There are two different schools of thought about how the prophecies of Daniel should be approached.

In one case, critical scholars advance the theory that the proper method is to start with chapter 11 and work backward through chapters 8, 7, and 2. Thus Daniel 11 becomes the yardstick by which to approach the other prophecies of Daniel's book. These scholars feel that most of Daniel 11 deals with the Greek king Antiochus Epiphanes who ruled the Seleucid kingdom from Antioch to Syria from approximately 175 B.C to 164 B.C.. Having determined that he is the main subject of the prophecies in Daniel 11, these critical scholars then read him back into the other prophecies of Daniel's book. Thus, Antiochus Epiphanes comes to be the all-encompassing figure of Daniel's prophecies.

The other approach starts with Daniel 2 and works progressively through the successive outline prophecies of the book—chapters 7, 8, and 11. This approach results in a very different view of Daniel's prophecies. In this approach, the succession of world kingdoms is clearly Babylon, Media-Persia, Greece, and Rome. Under the first scheme, Antiochus Epiphanes becomes the major figure of Daniel's prophecies throughout the book. Under the second, Antiochus Epiphanes is scaled down to a very modest subheading under the Greek kingdom.

Which of these two approaches is correct?

The development we have already noted between Daniel 2 and 7 points the way to the method inherent in the biblical text itself. Since Daniel 2 is the more simple prophecy and Daniel 7 adds detail and is the more complex, it seems natural and logical to begin with the more simple prophecy and work on through the book to the more complex, adding the details presented by each successive prophecy.

In either system it is clear that the book contains four main outline prophecies, chapters 2 and 7 in the Aramaic portion of the book and chapters 8 and 11 in the portions written in Hebrew. (The prophecy of chapter 9 is of a somewhat different nature since it concentrates on the future of the Jewish people and their Messiah, instead of viewing the nations of the world around them.) These four major outline prophecies are connected like a series of parallel electrical circuits. All four go over the same ground, but they progressively fill in more and more details. This parallelism is evident from the language used in the prophecies, the symbols found in them, and the interpretation given to them in the book itself.

Chapter 2, the first of these four outline prophecies, has the longest introduction. It recounts the circumstances under which this prophecy was given and how it was interpreted. In contrast, the prophecy in chapter 7 has a very short introduction consisting of a dateline and Daniel's statement that the prophecy came to him directly in a dream. The longer historical introduction to the prophecy of chapter 2 serves as a transition to connect the history of Daniel's book with the prophecies to be found in it. In chapter 2, in what is still commonly known as the historical section of Daniel, we find a significant transition from history to prophecy.

THE SETTING

Daniel had not been in Babylon long before his life was threatened! The threat grew out of an event that occurred by the second year of King Nebuchadnezzar's reign (2:1) which was either Daniel's second or third year in Babylon (the Babylonians did not number the year that the new king came to the throne as one of his regnal years). This threat was aimed not just at Daniel, but also at his friends, Shadrach, Meshach, and Abednego—and indeed, at the whole class of wise men in Babylon. By belonging to that class, Daniel and his friends found their lives endangered.

The danger arose from a dream the king had. Nebuchadnezzar did not understand the dream. In fact, when he woke up, he couldn't even remember what he had dreamed. However, he was impressed that it was very important. So he requested that his wise men help him. He summoned them and commanded them to tell him the dream and its interpretation. The wise men were quite willing to work on the interpretation, but told the king he must first tell them the contents of the dream. The king tried every class of wise man available. "So the king summoned the magicians, enchanters, sorcerers and astrologers to tell him what he had dreamed" (vs. 2).

But each of these classes of wise men needed something to work with. The astrologers used the stars; the diviners used sheep livers; others used different signs in nature that signaled something to them—such as the birth of an animal with a congenital deformity. Nebuchadnezzar supplied none of these things. He had had a dream—an impressive dream—that now he could not remember. His wise men must supply the dream and its interpretation.

The king and his wise men were at loggerheads. The wise men said, "Tell your servants the dream, and we will interpret it" (vs. 4). The king responded, "So tell me the dream and interpret it for me" (vs. 6). Of course, the king was the only one with the power and authority to solve the impasse. The wise men merely served in an advisory capacity. The king was not pleased. He could see that his wise men's pretended ability to tell the future was dubious at best and they were stalling for time.

Again he demanded, "Tell me the dream, and I will know that you can interpret it for me" (vs. 9). The heat of the dialogue escalated—along with the king's anger. He had the last word. He pronounced a death decree upon all of the wise men of the kingdom. If they were so worthless that they could not do what he asked of them, something supposedly well within their powers, he would do away with them all (vss. 12, 13).

Daniel and his three friends were not involved in this dialogue, but they did belong to the class of government workers that had been condemned. When news of the king's decree reached them through Arioch, commander of the king's guard, Daniel went in to the king to ask for more time so that he could attempt to present the dream and its interpretation to the king (vss. 14–16). Nebuchadnezzar had just accused the other wise men of trying to buy time (vs. 8), so one could imagine

Daniel's request did not fall upon very welcoming ears. Nevertheless, since Daniel had not been party to the initial discussions, Nebuchadnezzar permitted him more time. Daniel came back with the answer the next day.

To achieve that goal Daniel went into a prayer meeting with his friends (vss. 17, 18). Have you ever entered into prayer when your life counted on it? If Daniel did not come up with the contents of the king's dream, he would be killed—along with his friends and all the wise men of Babylon. A lot of people were counting upon Daniel as he knelt to pray with his friends! One can only imagine the earnestness of the prayer.

And God answered! He had not forsaken or abandoned Daniel and his friends. They were still precious in His sight; He was looking out for them and protecting them. "During the night the mystery was revealed to Daniel in a vision" (vs. 19). At this point in the story, the text does not reveal the content of the dream to the reader. That comes later when Daniel reports to Nebuchadnezzar.

The story does recount, at this point, the song of joy that the Hebrews sang when they received the answer from God that would deliver them and the other wise men of Babylon. Their praise to God comes in the form of a brief psalm, or song—a piece of poetry (vss. 20–23). Not only is it a beautiful piece of poetry, it also expresses some of the key theological concepts of the history and prophecy that follow in the book of Daniel:

> Praise be to the name of God for ever and ever;
>   wisdom and power are his.
> He changes times and seasons;
>   he sets up kings and deposes them.
> He gives wisdom to the wise
>   and knowledge to the discerning.
> He reveals deep and hidden things;
>   he knows what lies in darkness,
>   and light dwells with him.
> I thank and praise you, O God of my fathers:
>   You have given me wisdom and power,
> you have made known to me what we asked of you,
>   you have made known to us the dream of the king.

According to this brief poem, God is not an absentee landlord. He is present and active in the world and takes an active role in the nations. He can set up kings or he can depose them (vs. 21). To the unaided human eye, human history may appear to be a chaotic interplay of forces and counterforces. But Daniel assures us that behind all of this stands God, looking down upon it and moving within it to achieve what He sees best. At present, we may not understand all of these movements, but we can rest in the assurance of Daniel's words that God is truly active in the affairs of men and that He is working them out to His own best ends.

In addition, God makes known at times what will occur ahead in all this seemingly random play of world events. He gives this knowledge to His servants—not the wise men of Babylon, but prophets such as Daniel. God heard the prayer of Daniel and his friends for knowledge, and He gave "wisdom to the wise" (vs. 21).

God may not speak to us in visions and dreams today, but those who are sufficiently wise to seek Him will receive additional wisdom about the course they are to pursue and the course that history will follow. The light that dwells with God is sufficiently powerful to illuminate even the dark corners of history and the future of nations (vs. 22). The poem opens with a statement that wisdom and power belong to God (vs. 20); it ends with God providing wisdom and power to Daniel and his friends, revealing the king's dream to them (vs. 23).

When Daniel appeared before the king, Nebuchadnezzar asked him what he had asked the other wise men earlier: "Are you able to tell me what I saw in my dream and interpret it?" (vs. 26). The wise men had protested that the king's demand was not reasonable, that no man could perform what he asked of them (vs. 20). Daniel agreed that no human could tell the king what he had dreamed. In fact, he made it even more emphatic and specific. "No wise man, enchanter, magician or diviner can explain to the king the mystery he has asked about," declared Daniel (vs. 27). But what the wise men of Babylon and their gods were unable to accomplish, Daniel's God could do easily. "There is a God in heaven who reveals mysteries. He has shown King Nebuchadnezzar what will happen in days to come. Your dream and the visions that passed through your mind as you lay on your bed are these" (vs. 28). There is only one true God in heaven in contrast to the various gods of Babylon. This God reveals mysteries; He does not keep them hidden. He revealed the dream to Daniel to give to the king (vs. 28).

THE DREAM

If Daniel got the dream wrong, it could have cost him his life. But he did not get the dream wrong because he received it from God, and God was the One who had given it to Nebuchadnezzar in the first place. God had spoken to the king in a dream, and now He was using His servant Daniel to make His message even more plain and clear to Nebuchadnezzar.

As explained by Daniel to the king, the dream consisted primarily of one great object—an image. The word used for *image* is the word commonly used in the Old Testament for an image, or idol. It is the word also used in Daniel 3 for the great image the king later erected on the plain of Dura. So the concept of an image would not have been unfamiliar to Nebuchadnezzar. Normally, however, the images of the gods with which he was acquainted were covered with a single type of metal—either gold or silver foil—or possibly cast in bronze. What was distinctive about the image Nebuchadnezzar saw in his dream was that it consisted of a series of metals, not just one. Nebuchadnezzar's response to this can be seen in Daniel 3. He built his own image to correspond to the one that he had seen in his dream, with one difference—his image was all of gold. This expressed his reaction against the image he had seen in his dream.

The metals in the image of Nebuchadnezzar's dream decreased in value but increased in strength. Moving from the golden head, through the silver and bronze, to the iron at the bottom, there was an ascending scale of strength and a descending scale of value. The feet of the image were its most curious part; the iron continued, but mixed with clay (2:33), obviously a poor choice of material for attempting to hold the iron pieces in place.

One final scene in the vision introduced another element—the rock (vss. 34, 35). It was an unusual rock in that it was cut out, or quarried, but not by human hands. No chisel marks of the stone masons defaced it. It was not part of the image. Instead, it struck the image like a ballistic missile hurled from the outside, causing the image to shatter and crumble into pieces. The stone was stronger than all the metals that had been used in the image—even the strongest of them, the iron in the legs. Nothing could withstand this stone.

THE INTERPRETATION

Nebuchadnezzar was satisfied that Daniel had told him the correct dream, the one he had previously had but could not remember. In this, Daniel surpassed the ability of all the wise men of Babylon. He did not attribute this to his own intelligence or skill. He freely pointed to the wisdom, power, and knowledge of the God he served. God had revealed the dream to Daniel (vss. 28, 47). His confidence that Daniel had related the dream correctly, now gave Nebuchadnezzar confidence that Daniel could also interpret it correctly.

Daniel began his explanation of the image starting from the top. "Contrary to what you would normally expect, O King, this is not an image of a god. It is, rather, a symbol that stands for something else. And you are part of it. You are the head of gold" (see vss. 37, 38). Clearly, Daniel was not talking just about Nebuchadnezzar; he was referring as well to the empire that Nebuchadnezzar had built. This becomes clear when Daniel comes to the second metal in the image, representing the next world kingdom. "After you, another kingdom will rise, inferior to yours. Next, a third kingdom" (vss. 39, 40). Thus we are dealing here with kingdoms, not just kings. Still, it was appropriate to identify the Neo-Babylonian kingdom with Nebuchadnezzar. He was the one who had built this empire militarily; he was the one who had vastly expanded the city of Babylon architecturally; and he ruled that empire forty-three of the sixty-six years it existed. The direct connection of Nebuchadnezzar with the Neo-Babylonian Empire was quite fitting and appropriate.

Following Nebuchadnezzar's Babylon, another kingdom would arise that would be inferior to Babylon. Extrabiblical history and the books of Daniel, Ezra, and Nehemiah tell us that Media-Persia followed Babylon. In this volume, we have already looked at Daniel 5 and 6 which recount the Persian conquest of Babylon and how the Persians set up their government in the former Babylonian territory. We saw there, too, how Daniel referred obliquely and symbolically to the transition from Babylon to Media-Persia when he described "the gods of silver and gold, of bronze, iron, wood and stone" (5:23), reversing the order found here in chapter 2 and placing the silver before the gold on the very night that the silver kingdom of the Persians took over from the golden kingdom of Babylon.

Historically, in what sense was the Persian kingdom inferior to that of Nebuchadnezzar? After all, the Persians conquered Babylon, and Media-Persia actually came to include more territory than the Babylonian Empire. But superiority can exist in other areas besides mere square miles.

The culture of Babylon was renowned throughout the ancient world while that of the Medes and Persians was looked down upon as rustic and primitive. The Persians had no written language until the time of their empire. Old Persian was created as a written language by the Persian kings to use in inscribing monuments. They more commonly used the Elamite language for keeping their own records. On the other hand, the written Babylonian language went well back into the third millennium B.C., and that rich heritage of language brought with it all of the science, religion, and culture of the Babylonian Empire. So there were various ways in which Babylon was superior to Persia even though the Babylonians did not conquer as much territory as the Persians did.

The third kingdom depicted by the image was symbolized by bronze (2:39). The Greeks followed the Persians. Although earlier commercial and cultural contacts had taken place, the great intrusion of Hellenism (Greek thought and culture) into the Near East came with the invasions of Alexander the Great. Not only did he defeat Darius III, the last Persian king, but he also marched all the way to the Indus Valley of northwestern India in his wide-ranging conquests. Alexander's kingdom did not last as long as either that of the Babylonians or the Persians, however, for after his death it soon splintered into a number of pieces which were taken over by the generals who had served under him.

These pieces of the Greek Empire were picked up by Rome and absorbed into that empire. The process took a century and a quarter—from the time Rome defeated mainland Greece in the early second century B.C. until Julius Caesar conquered Egypt in the late first century

B.C. By that time, the Greek Empire had disappeared, having been absorbed by the next power on the scene of action, the iron kingdom of Rome. With this conquest, the four main metal symbols of the image were complete. Thus, in historical order, the gold represents Babylon; the silver represents Media-Persia; the bronze represents Greece; and the iron represents Rome.

What comes next? Are these all of the great Mediterranean world powers to come on the scene of action? Will there be other kingdoms greater than Rome? The prophecy takes an interesting turn at this point for there are no more metals. There is, however, another element in the image; the symbol of clay (vs. 33). The iron continues, indicating that what follows after Rome will be Romelike, but it will not be solid like Rome. It will be divided. These divisions are accentuated by the mixture of iron and clay. This is not the right way to build a strong image. To build a strong image another metal should have been used or more iron should have been added to the image. That was not the case. Instead, the weakening element of clay was added to the iron, thus taking away its strength.

The mixture of iron and clay represented the divisions and disunity that came to the Roman Empire:

> So this will be a divided kingdom. . . . As the toes were partly iron and partly clay, so this kingdom will be partly strong and partly brittle. And just as you saw the iron mixed with baked clay, so the people will be a mixture and will not remain united, any more than iron mixes with clay (vss. 41–43).

The emphasis here is upon disunion and disunity—a stark contrast with the iron that went before it. Iron was the hardest and most unified metal known to the ancient and classical worlds. From the strongest and most unified nation, the territory that had made up the Roman Empire would go to being the weakest and most divided. Such was the fate of Rome as described by the prophecy.

Historically, did the predicted disunity and mixing take place?

It is easy to see what happened to the Roman Empire under the onslaught of barbarian tribes. Under their impact, the city of Rome itself fell in A.D. 476. From that time forward, the Italian peninsula came under the control of the Ostrogoths for the better part of a century until their final defeat in A.D. 555. Historians commonly use the sixth century A.D. to mark the transition from Imperial Rome to Medieval Rome. When Rome entered that century, it was still powerful militarily and politically; it was a populous and prosperous city that was still beautiful in its architecture and monuments. When Rome came out of that century, it was a broken-down, depopulated center that controlled virtually nothing. The clay had been introduced into the iron.

This state of affairs was to continue until the end (vss. 33–35). In spite of the military conquerors of the past and the political leagues of the present, the nations of Europe (not to mention the rest of the Roman Empire) have not cleaved one to the other. Will the European Common Market and the political affiliation of European countries negate this picture? They may, with difficulty, agree upon certain political principles, and they may enter into agreements to facilitate trade and commerce, but each of these countries may be expected to retain control of its cultural, linguistic, and territorial properties. They may join together for certain common purposes, but according to Daniel's prophecy, they will never be joined into one complete political entity as was the Roman Empire.

It is interesting to see how the events tearing at the fabric of Roman society looked to a contemporary commentator on prophecy. The church father, Jerome, lived through the late fourth century and the early fifth century A.D., so he saw some of the breakup of the Roman Empire taking place. His commentary on Daniel was dedicated in the year 407. As he read through the prophecy of Daniel 2, he saw these events taking place before his very eyes. Even though the worst was yet to come, he still could write:

> Moreover the fourth kingdom, which plainly pertains to the Romans, is the iron which breaks in pieces and subdues all things. But its feet and toes are partly of iron and partly of clay, which at this time is most plainly attested. For just as in its beginning nothing was stronger and more unyielding than the Roman Empire, so at the end of its affairs nothing is weaker. *Commentary on Daniel,* comments on 2:40, column 504.

This is not the end of the vision, however, for there is one more stage in the image's career—its destruction and the scattering of its fragments to the four winds. In symbol this is accomplished by the great stone which strikes the image on the feet of iron and clay. It smashed them, and

> then the iron, the clay, the bronze, the silver and the gold were broken to pieces at the same time and became like chaff on a threshing floor in the summer. The wind swept them away without leaving a trace. But the rock that struck the statue became a huge mountain and filled the whole earth (vs. 35).

In other words, all the kingdoms of this world will eventually be destroyed and swept away, and there will be no further human kingdoms to succeed them. The kingdom that would follow would be of an entirely different nature, represented not by a metal, but by a rock cut out without human hands (vs. 34). It was to be a kingdom of an entirely different order from those preceding it. According to Daniel's divinely inspired interpretation: "In the time of those kings, the God of heaven will set up a kingdom that will never be destroyed, nor will it be left to another people. It will crush all those kingdoms and bring them to an end, but it will itself endure forever" (2:44).

This is the central fact of the conclusion to this dream-vision: that the God of heaven will one day set up a kingdom that will never be destroyed. It will never be displaced by another metal kingdom that will come down the road of history, for history itself will end in that kingdom of God. It will be history's great climax. This is the goal toward which history is moving.

THE RESULTS

Several results occurred from Daniel's recitation before the king of the dream and its interpretation. First, there was a result for Nebuchadnezzar. He recognized that this was the very dream he had dreamed and that Daniel had recalled it correctly. This had a tremendous impact upon the king. Just as he would have fallen down to worship the image that he saw in the dream, he virtually fell down to worship Daniel who brought him a knowledge of the dream. "Then King Nebuchadnezzar fell prostrate before Daniel and paid him honor and ordered that an offering and incense be presented to him" (vs. 46). He recognized, however, the source of Daniel's wisdom did not come merely from Daniel's own intelligence. He realized it came from Daniel's God. His act of respectful recognition of Daniel took careful note of this distinction. "Surely," the king declared, "your God is a God of gods and the Lord of kings and a revealer of mysteries, for you were able to reveal this mystery" (vs. 47).

At this point in his experience, Nebuchadnezzar could still be classified as a polytheist, but he was moving, under the influence of Daniel and his true God, toward henotheism—a belief in the superiority of one god, without denying the existence of other gods. Nebuchadnezzar still recognized the existence of the gods of Babylon, but he acknowledged the superiority of Daniel's God, Yahweh. A knowledge of the true God of heaven was beginning to dawn upon his understanding. The picture was certainly not complete on this particular day, but Nebuchadnezzar had begun a spiritual journey that would not end until he finally came to an adequate knowledge of the true God as described in Daniel 4.

For Daniel and his friends, the dramatic turn of events in connection with the king's dream resulted in advancement up the ladder of the Babylonian bureaucracy. Nebuchadnezzar lavished gifts upon Daniel and made him ruler over the entire province of Babylon (vs. 48). He also placed Daniel in charge of all the wise men of Babylon. This seemed only fitting—especially since Daniel's success in interpreting the dream had just saved all their lives. Human nature being what it is, however, this probably did not endear Daniel to them. They remained at odds with him over a number of points. He had shown them up with his superior wisdom. Now he had authority over them, and he had carried out his search for wisdom in a way entirely different from their techniques. Daniel did not need to search sheep livers for anomalies or study the stars. He could pray directly to the true God who revealed deep mysteries to His servants. Undoubtedly, it didn't help relations between Daniel and the other wise men when Daniel requested—and secured—promotions for his three friends,

Shadrach, Meshach, and Abednego, as administrators over the province of Babylon (vs. 49).

The king's dream and its interpretation not only had results for Nebuchadnezzar, Daniel, his friends, and the other Babylonian wise men. It continues to have implications for us some 2,500 years later.

How does it affect our lives today? It is a remarkable evidence of the foreknowledge of the true God. It demonstrates to us in a very real and concrete way—through the events of history—that there is a God in heaven and that He is concerned with human affairs. We can see His hand in history, and we can recognize His divine foreknowledge in this prophecy. We can actually check the interpretation to determine its accuracy. We can look back over the 2,500 years of history that have elapsed since Daniel's interpretation and see if those events really happened.

What of those, however, who believe that there is no supernatural element in Daniel's prophecies, that Daniel was simply thrown on his own resources in his attempt to give the king a plausible interpretation of his dream?

In evaluating such a possibility, we need to ask ourselves: If there is no supernatural source of information about the future, if Daniel simply had to hazard a human guess when he interpreted the king's dream, what kind of interpretation would he likely have given? What probable scenarios would have presented themselves to him?

First, he might well have tried to curry favor with Nebuchadnezzar. It would have been tempting to have told the king that the image was made entirely of gold and that it represented Babylon which would stand forever. But Daniel did not bring that popular message to the king. Instead, he told Nebuchadnezzar that his kingdom was going to be succeeded by another. If Daniel 3 is any indication, such a message was not popular with the king! Under other circumstances, Daniel's life might have been endangered for bringing such a message to the king.

Second, it would have been natural for Daniel, unaided by divine revelation, to have drawn on a picture of history that was popular in the ancient world—a picture of a history that was cyclical and that would continue without end. There would not be just four world kingdoms followed by an end to human history. Rather, there would be five kingdoms, six, seven, eight, etc. Since human beings had acted in a certain way in the past, they should continue to act that way in the future, leading to an endless sequence of kingdoms.

Daniel chose to neither curry favor with the king nor engage in historical philosophical speculations. He chose, instead, to declare that there would be exactly four world kingdoms that would follow each other in succession—not one, two, or three, but four. And the fourth would not signal an end to human history, but would disintegrate and be followed by another period of history marked by this divided condition. He predicted precisely four kingdoms followed by divisions that would not be put back together again. How did Daniel know that there would be exactly four kingdoms—Babylon, Media-Persia, Greece, and Rome—followed by a divided condition representing the breakup of Imperial Rome?

How did Daniel know this? He tells us. "There is a God in heaven who reveals mysteries. He has shown . . . what will happen in days to come" (vs. 28). His wisdom is available to man, to His servants the prophets such as Daniel. Through Daniel, it has been revealed to us. As we meet the 2,500-year-old word of Daniel, we meet the word of the living God today. He cared enough to speak this truth to one individual, Nebuchadnezzar, and He still cares enough to speak that truth to each of us today.

One final point regarding this dream and its interpretation should concern us: Where in the course of history, as outlined by this symbolic dream, do we live? We do not live back in the time of Babylon and Media-Persia with Daniel. We do not live in the time of the Roman Empire. We live at the very bottom of the image, in the divided times of the feet and toes.

What happened next in Nebuchadnezzar's dream? The stone struck the image, smashing it to pieces which the wind blew away. The stone then became a great mountain and filled the whole earth (vss. 34, 35). That means the God of heaven is going to set up His kingdom soon. We can prepare to enter it by giving our hearts to the same God that provided divine wisdom to Daniel. We can praise Him and honor Him and glorify Him in the same way that Daniel did. When we do, we will be prepared to enter into that same kingdom with Daniel. There, with him, we can cast our crowns of salvation before the Lord and praise Him for His glorious love to us.

THE SETTING OF DANIEL 7

Daniel 2 begins with a long historical recital of the circumstances under which the dream-vision of Daniel 2 was first given and then recovered and interpreted. It tells of the experience of Nebuchadnezzar, Daniel, and the wise men at court in Babylon in the sixth century B.C. In that sense, chapter 2 stems from a historical experience and recites that experience to us. At least half of chapter 2 is historical narrative; the remainder is prophecy.

Daniel 7 is different. It gives only a simple, short historical setting (vs. 1). It tells us little more of the local, contemporary historical setting than the date (Belshazzar's first year) and where Daniel was when he received this vision. With that minor exception, Daniel 7 is directly and completely prophetic throughout. Daniel 2 is approximately half history and half prophecy; Daniel 7 is nearly all prophecy. In this, it sets the tone for the rest of Daniel which is all prophecy.

When we compare the way the prophecy of chapter 7 was given with that of chapter 2, we find both similarities and differences. Both Nebuchadnezzar (chapter 2) and Daniel (chapter 7) were asleep on their beds when they received their respective visions. Thus the mode of revelation in these two cases was the same. The recipients, however, were quite different. The dream of chapter 2 was given to a pagan king initially for his own personal benefit; the dream of Daniel 7 was given directly to the prophet Daniel to communicate to God's people.

The different recipients also emphasize the different roles Daniel played in these two experiences. In chapter 2, he eventually received the vision and its interpretation from God, but his function was primarily that of an inspired wise man to explain the dream to the king. In chapter 7, Daniel received the dream directly from God. *Chronologically,* this is the first such occurrence in the book of Daniel. (Remember that the chapters as they presently appear in Daniel are not arranged in chronological order.) So the vision of chapter 7 actually constitutes Daniel's call to the office of prophet in his own right, being the first time he received a vision directly from God.

THE DREAM

The vision of Daniel's dream began with a view of "the great sea" (vs. 2). Winds were blowing upon the sea, churning it into an agitated state. Daniel saw four beasts come up out of the sea, one after another (vs. 3). Geographically, this great sea can be identified with the Mediterranean because each of the four nations which Daniel saw portrayed were Mediterranean world powers—either located in the Mediterranean area or conquering territory to its shores.

The successive visions of Daniel's book show a progression in the degree of activity they involve. In Daniel 2, the great image just stood there. Here in Daniel 7, the beasts Daniel saw emerge from the water demonstrate different characteristics, but their actions still are not directed toward a specific goal. In Daniel 8, the actions of the ram and the goat become directional. The ram charges west, and the goat charges east toward the ram and challenges it. This directional activity is not yet developed in the vision of Daniel 7, however, and we need to rely for understanding more upon the characteristics the animals manifest than those they act out.

As Daniel describes the vision of chapter 7, he says the first beast he saw emerging from the sea looked to him "like a lion" (vs. 4). It was an animal he could recognize, but at the same time, it was not a completely normal lion because it had wings on its back. Daniel watched as those wings were plucked off. It stood up on its two hind feet like a man, and a man's heart was given to it (vs. 4). The interpretation given by the angel later in the chapter does not identify this beast-nation by name.

The second beast to come up out of the waters was a bear (vs. 5). This bear was somewhat disfigured, being raised up higher on one side than the other. It had three ribs in its mouth, representing its conquests. The bear is an animal which lives in the mountains, suggesting that the kingdom represented by this animal would come from a mountainous region.

The third beast to appear was a leopard. While it had something of the normal configuration of a leopard, it also had some unusual features. Instead of having one head, it had four. Like the lion, it also had wings on its back—four of them to match the number of its heads (vs. 6).

The fourth beast Daniel saw was not like any of the others nor like anything he had seen before. It appears to have been a composite beast made up of various features of different animals. It also appears to have been the most fierce of the four and was definitely a conquering, crushing power as it took up its activities (vs. 7).

One of the strange characteristics of this fourth beast was the fact that it had ten horns. As the vision unfolded, Daniel observed a great deal of activity going on among these horns. First, a little horn, smaller than the others, started to grow up among the ten. Although it began small, it soon became bigger than the others. As it grew and became stronger, this little horn uprooted three of the other horns (vss. 7, 8). Its activities were described in distinctly religious terms. It uttered blasphemy, and it persecuted the saints (vs. 25).

As Daniel continued to look, his view was directed to heaven where he was shown a great heavenly tribunal. The heavenly court convened and passed sentence upon the beast, the little horn, and all mankind (vss. 9–12). Following the execution of the sentence against the beast, Daniel saw God set up His everlasting kingdom. The saints of the Most High were ushered into His kingdom where the Son of Man would rule over them forever and ever. Through the ages, God's saints have been under the authority of the different world powers as they have emerged one after the other. But the ultimate destiny of the saints is to live in God's eternal kingdom under the wise, benevolent rulership of God and His Son (vss. 13, 14).

IDENTIFYING THE BEASTS

In his vision, Daniel turned to an angel standing nearby and asked him the meaning of these things (vss. 15, 16). In response, the angel gave him a brief explanation, saying, "the four great beasts are four kingdoms which will rise from the earth. But the saints of the Most High will receive the kingdom and will possess it forever—yes, for ever and ever" (vss. 17, 18). Beyond the travail of this earth's history lies God's kingdom, the ultimate answer to all of the problems created by those earthly kingdoms.

After more questioning from Daniel (vss. 19–22), the angel interpreter went on to give the prophet a longer explanation (vss. 23–27).

In neither his brief answer nor the more detailed explanation did the angel interpreter name any of the kingdoms represented by the four beasts. How, then, are we to identify them? We can do so by comparing them with the other prophecies of Daniel. A comparison with Daniel 2 provides the name of the kingdom with which this sequence begins. A comparison with Daniel 8 gives us the names of two more powers in the succession of kingdoms.

Are such comparisons legitimate? Can we be certain, for example, that chapter 2 and chapter 7 are describing the same four kingdoms? We know that the sequence in chapter 2 began with Babylon (2:38, 39) because Daniel plainly told Nebuchadnezzar so. If chapter 7 is describing the same sequence of kingdoms, then the first symbol in that chapter must likewise represent Babylon. The question, then, becomes: What evidence do we find that chapters 2 and 7 are dealing with the same broad prophetic outline?

The first link occurs on the broadest scale—literary structure. In the chiastic literary structure of the first half of Daniel's book, chapters 2 and 7 are found in corresponding, parallel locations (see the discussion of Daniel's literary structure on pages 28–31). Just as common themes link chapter 4 with chapter 5, and chapter 3 with chapter 6, so also chapter 2 is linked with chapter 7 in terms of similar content. This means that they cover the same ground and should be seen as explanatory of each other.

The second link between these two prophecies is that both contain the same number of major elements. Daniel 2 brings to view a series of four kingdoms represented by four metals; chapter 7 depicts four major kingdoms under the symbolism of beasts emerging from the sea. Chapter 2 has the fourth kingdom divided by an intermingling of clay with the iron; in chapter 7, the division of the fourth kingdom is represented by the horns on that beast and the activity going on among them. In chapter 2, the series of four kingdoms is superseded by something entirely different—a stone kingdom that lasts forever; in chapter 7, the series of powers concludes with God's eternal kingdom which the saints of the Most High will possess forever. Thus chapters 2 and 7 contain the same major elements even though they are given in different forms. Given the fact that these two chapters have similar outlines, it seems clear that the two prophecies are talking about the same kingdoms—with added enrichment in the latter chapter.

Beyond the similarity of a general outline, there is specific language in these two chapters that tell us they are dealing with the same number and sequence of kingdoms. In Daniel 2 the bronze kingdom is specifically enumerated as the "third" kingdom (2:39), and the iron kingdom is called the "fourth" kingdom (2:40). In Daniel 7, the "first," "second," and "fourth," beasts are identified with those specific numbers, and in the angel's interpretation he says that the "four great beasts are four kingdoms" that will arise from the earth (vs. 17). Daniel gives us the numbers, and the angel gives us the interpretation of those numbers. The numbers are the same as those found in Daniel 2. Since both prophecies talk about exactly the same number of kingdoms, the implication is clear that they must be referring to the same powers.

As if to cement this relationship, the fourth kingdom in both visions was represented by iron—the image's iron legs of chapter 2 and the iron teeth of the fourth beast in chapter 7. Of the four animals found in chapter 7, the fourth beast alone contained iron, thus linking it directly with the fourth kingdom in Daniel 2.

Once we know these two prophecies are talking about the same four kingdoms, it is easy to identify the lion, the first power depicted in the prophecy of chapter 7, as Babylon—since Daniel specifically identifies the first kingdom in chapter 2:38, 39 with that power. The sequence of the succeeding three beasts in chapter 7 should, therefore, be identified with the same kingdoms that we have described in the interpretation of chapter 2—Media-Persia, Greece, and Rome.

The beasts of chapter 7 can also be identified through the identifications given by name in Daniel 8. In this case, the second beast of Daniel 7 is parallel to the first beast of Daniel 8, and the third beast of Daniel 7 is parallel to the second beast of Daniel 8. How so?

The bear in Daniel 7 was lifted up on one side (7:5) while the ram in Daniel 8 had one of its horns standing up higher than the other (8:3). In Daniel 8:20, this ram is identified as Media-Persia, and the dual nature of this kingdom is said to represent the two political entities out of which it was formed. Thus the bear of chapter 7 and the ram of chapter 8 represent the same power.

Likewise, the goat in chapter 8 with a "prominent horn between his eyes" (vs. 5) is identified as the power of Greece (vs. 21). This horn was uprooted, and four more horns came up in its place. This symbolism corresponds to the four heads and four wings on the leopard in chapter 7 so that the goat of chapter 8 and the leopard of chapter 7 represent the same powers.

We can diagram what we have learned thus far:

Kingdom	Daniel 2	Daniel 7	Daniel 8	Identification
1	Gold	Lion	—	Babylon, 2:38, 39
2	Silver	Bear	Ram	Media-Persia, 8:20
3	Bronze	Leopard	Goat	Greece, 8:21
4	Iron	Nondescript beast	King of fierce countenance	Rome

So, although the powers brought to view in chapter 7 are not named specifically, we can identify them with certainty as Babylon, Media-Persia, Greece, and Rome through clear connections with the powers that *are* named specifically in chapters 2 and 8. It remains to identify their various characteristics and see how they fit into history.

THE BABYLONIAN LION

The lion had wings on its back giving it the rapidity of flight. This speed was demonstrated in Babylon's early conquests under Nebuchadnezzar. But Daniel watched as the wings were plucked off. The situation in Babylon changed; speed on the battlefield declined, and conquests grew scarce as the kingdom shrunk under weaker kings such as Nabonidus. No longer did Babylon have the heart of the conquering lion; it was reduced to the heart of a man with no more taste for conquest (7:4).

A lion was a particularly apt symbol to represent Babylon. Lions were depicted on the walls of Babylon's Ishtar gate and on the outer wall of the audience chamber of the king's palace. A statue of an immense lion stood in the courtyard of the palace. In the mythology of Babylon, these lions were thought of as carrying the goddess Ishtar on their backs.

DANIEL

THE PERSIAN BEAR

We have already mentioned the twofold nature of the Medo-Persian kingdom as symbolized by the fact that the bear, the second power depicted in chapter 7, was raised up on one side (vs. 5). Through the ninth, eighth, and seventh centuries B.C., the kingdom of the Medes was a powerful force in the Near East, constantly threatening the dominant Assyrians. But in the sixth century B.C., the up-and-coming kingdom of Persia, under Cyrus, succeeded in conquering the Medes and fusing them into a combined Media-Persian Empire. The three ribs in the mouth of the bear could easily represent the conquest of Lydia in Anatolia, or ancient Turkey, in 547 B.C, the conquest of Babylon in 539 B.C., and that of Egypt in 525 B.C. The first two conquests were accomplished by Cyrus after he had put the Media-Persian Empire together; the campaign to Egypt was led by his son Cambyses.

THE GREEK LEOPARD

The outstanding characteristic of the leopard was the wings on its back (vs 6). These wings denote speed, an apt illustration of the rapidity with which the Greeks conquered the Near East. It was all accomplished essentially in three short years by Alexander the Great. By comparison, it took the Assyrians three years (725–722 B.C.) to conquer Samaria and the Babylonians three years (589–586 B.C.) to conquer Jerusalem. Yet in the same amount of time Alexander conquered the whole of the ancient Near East, from Egypt to the Indus Valley of India!

But as rapid as this conquest was, it was not destined to last. The leopard's four heads (vs. 6) represented the four divisions into which Alexander's kingdom broke up after his death. His generals picked up the pieces of that kingdom and divided them into mainland Greece, Asia Minor, Syria (including Babylon), and Egypt. This same historical division of the kingdom of Greece is represented by the four horns on the goat in Daniel 8:8, 22.

THE ROMAN BEAST

The fourth kingdom in chapter 7 represented Rome which crushed and devoured its victims, trampling underfoot whatever remained (vs. 7). Archeology has given us an excellent example of how apt a description this is of Rome's conquests. On the west side of Jerusalem there used to be a valley known as the Tyropoean Valley, or "Cheesemaker's" Valley. It does not exist today because it was filled in with the debris of the Roman destruction of Jerusalem in A.D. 70. The English archaeologist, Kathleen Kenyon, made a deep, narrow sounding into this area and found the debris was some seventy feet deep! The Romans virtually swept the site of the old city of Jerusalem clean. Roman engineers were known for their thoroughness in both destruction and construction. In this way this power "crushed and devoured" (vs. 7).

Strong as it was, however, the Roman Empire was not to last either. By the fifth and sixth centuries A.D., Rome was crumbling under the assault of the barbarian tribes. The capital of the empire had moved to the east, to Constantinople, leaving a vacuum of leadership in the Italian peninsula. For a time, the Ostrogoths took over the region. In the middle of the sixth century A.D., however, the Ostrogoths were defeated and faded from history. When that happened, the leadership of the city and territory of Rome fell into the hands of the bishop of Rome. Much of his assumption of civil power dates to this time when there was a vacuum of leadership in the region.

THE TEN HORNS AND THE LITTLE HORN

These developments connected with the division and demise of the Roman Empire are symbolized in the prophecy, first by the ten horns on the fourth beast, and then by the rise of the little horn. Of these ten horns the angel interpreter said, "The ten horns are ten kings who will come from this [fourth] kingdom" (vs. 24). The words for *king* and *kingdoms* are used rather interchangeably both in Daniel 7 and also in Daniel 2. In Daniel 7:17, where the NIV translates four "kingdoms," the original word is actually "kings." The same feature appears in chapter 2 where Daniel tells Nebuchadnezzar, "You, O *king,* are this head of gold," but, "after you shall arise another *kingdom* inferior to you" (2:38, 39, KJV, emphasis supplied). Thus the ten horns which protrude from the head of the Roman beast represent the different pieces into which the empire shattered under assault by the barbarian tribes then migrating into Europe and settling in various places. The *coup de grace* of this process occurred in A.D. 476 when the city of Rome itself fell to the

Heruli. These pagan tribes, represented by the ten horns on the fourth beast, eventually developed into the modern nations of Europe. Considerable ingenuity has been exercised trying to identify precisely ten of these tribes-turned-nations. It probably is preferable to take the number ten as a round number which may have fluctuated up or down at any given historical time, according to the political and military fortunes of those various powers.

In Daniel's vision, he saw three of these horns plucked up before the rising power of the little horn (vs. 8). These three tribes can be identified with some degree of accuracy. As the various European tribes struggled for supremacy, the wars that were fought were both political and theological in nature, often combining territorial disputes with controverted points of religious doctrine. To a degree never before employed in Christianity, the power of the state came to be used to root out heretics. Justinian, the reigning Roman emperor in Constantinople, was happy to support the bishop of Rome in these struggles both for his own political gain and for the gain of the Roman-centered church. In A.D. 534, Justinian sent his army and navy against the Vandals in North Africa and defeated them.

Following that conquest, Belisarius, Justinian's general, led his troops on an invasion of the Italian peninsula to liberate the city of Rome from the Ostrogoths. Finally, Belisarius was successful in defeating the Goths at their capital of Ravenna in A.D. 538, although they lingered on in the Italian peninsula and even retook considerable territory until they were finally wiped out in A.D. 555. The turning point, however, had come when in A.D. 538 the city of Rome stood free of barbarian control for the first time in sixty years. The bishop of Rome assumed the leadership of the city.

If it is agreed that two of the three horns uprooted by the little horn (vs. 8) were the Vandals (A.D. 534) and the Ostrogoths (A.D. 538/555), there is less agreement among historians about which was the third uprooted power. Some Adventist historians favor the Heruli, the tribe that conquered Rome in A.D. 476. The Heruli were later defeated by the Ostrogoths who were, in turn, defeated by the Roman general Belisarius. Thus the Heruli provide one possible identification for the third horn.

But the evidence seems to be in favor of the Visigoths as the third horn. For a time this tribe lived in southern France. There the Visigoths were eventually defeated by Clovis, king of the Franks around A.D. 508. Although their power was largely destroyed at this time, the survivors were pushed into Spain where they were subjugated at last by a Moslem invasion in the eighth century A.D. Because the Visigoths were not eradicated by the Franks, some Bible historians have felt they should not be identified as the third horn uprooted before the little horn in Daniel's vision. It is not clear, however, that the prophecy requires total eradication to fulfill the symbol of being uprooted.

The three horns uprooted by the little horn can be identified, then, as the Vandals, the Ostrogoths, and the Visigoths (or the Heruli). All three had been in theological opposition to Rome over the nature of Christ's divinity. Their demise and thus the removal of their theological opposition made way for the even more widespread distribution of orthodox Roman Christianity. This might be seen as a welcome development for Christianity, but internal developments within the church had a negative impact upon the form of Christianity presented. The movement went awry, and thus the prophecy depicts this power as gathering religious power into its own hands in order to persecute those who did not recognize its authority (vss 21, 25).

The four beast powers of chapter 7 all appear to be concerned with territorial expansion. The little horn, on the other hand, is clearly a religious power and is interested in distinctly religious issues. Bible students have long identified this little horn as the second phase of Rome, the first phase being the terrible beast of vs. 7. What characteristics of this little horn does Daniel 7 give that would lead to such an interpretation?

CHARACTERISTICS OF THE LITTLE HORN

First, the little horn grows out of the fourth beast—among the ten horns. It comes out of the Roman beast (vss. 7, 8, 24), and therefore it must be in some way a continuation of the Roman Empire.

Second, the time of the little horn's appearance and the events which occurred at that time help to identify it. The ten horns of the Roman beast represent the divisions into which the Roman Empire fell. The little horn grew up among these ten horns, thus it grew up to its height of power *after* the barbarian tribes had divided the Roman Empire into pieces, that is, by the fifth or sixth centuries A.D. We have already seen how three horns, or powers, were uprooted by the power of the Roman emperor Justinian and the Franks, working together with the bishop of Rome.

A third characteristic of the little-horn power is that it was to speak great or "boastful" words against the Most High God (vss. 8, 11, 20, 25). In addition to taking some of the titles previously carried by the Caesars, the bishop of Rome assumed religious titles and prerogatives that can be described only as "boastful" words.

What were some of these titles and functions assumed by the bishop of Rome?

He took the title, "Vicar of the Son of God," meaning that he stood in place of the Son of God to represent Him here on earth. Compare also the title of "holy father" with Jesus' comments about the use of that title in a religious setting (see Matthew 23:9). Note, too, the claim to be able to forgive sins through the rites of the confessional whereas the Jews in Jesus' time considered His claim to forgive sins was blasphemy (see Matthew 9:2–6).

The claim is made in a training manual for priests, *Dignities and Duties of the Priest;* or *Selva,* that God is obligated to come down upon the altar at the time of the mass regardless of the spiritual state of the priest who officiates in that service! Thus man is not serving God, rather, God is under the control of man! (See pp. 26, 27.) In a number of respects the theological and titular claims of this religious power have exceeded those which are enjoined by Scripture.

A fourth characteristic is that the saints of the Most High were to be given into the power of the little horn and be oppressed by it. Thus the little horn would be a persecuting power (vs. 25). The Roman Church has upheld the principle of its right to persecute those who deny its religious authority. The *New Catholic Encyclopedia* states in its article on "Torture":

> Under the influence of Germanic customs and concepts, torture was little used from the 9th to the 12th centuries, but with the revival of Roman law the practice was reestablished in

the 12th century. . . . In 1252 [Pope] Innocent IV sanctioned the infliction of torture by the civil authorities upon heretics, and torture came to have a recognized place in the procedure of the inquisitorial courts.

Writing from a strongly anti-Catholic position, the nineteenth-century historian W. E. H. Lecky wrote:

> That the Church of Rome has shed more innocent blood than any other institution that has ever existed among mankind [up through the end of the nineteenth century], will be questioned by no Protestant who has a competent knowledge of history. The memorials, indeed, of many of her persecutions are now so scanty, that it is impossible to form a complete conception of the multitude of her victims, and it is quite certain that no powers of imagination can adequately realize their sufferings. Llorente, who had free access to the archives of the Spanish Inquisition, assures us that by that tribunal alone more than 31,000 persons were burnt, and more than 290,000 condemned to punishments less severe than death. The number of those who were put to death for their religion in the Netherlands alone, in the reign of Charles V., has been estimated by a very high authority at 50,000, and at least half as many perished under his son (Lecky, 2:40, 41).

At the other end of the scale are the writings of Robert Kingdom, who has attempted to downplay the effects of the St. Bartholomew's Day Massacre in France. In spite of his aim he admits:

> The massacre did not stop with these killings. It spread to the general populace of Paris, as fanatical mobs killed hundreds, probably thousands, of Protestant residents of the city. The violence did not even stop in Paris; as news of what had occurred in the capital spread throughout the kingdom there were popular uprisings and massacres of Protestants in about a dozen other cities. Their aim was evidently to extirpate the entire Protestant movement, root and branch (Kingdom, 35).

As for the outcome of those massacres, Kingdom concludes:

> The massacres unleashed by the assassination of Coligny did not unify France religiously or even end violence between the religious communities. The royal government next turned to more concerted and calculated action, mobilizing royal armies to reduce the communities that remained under the control of defiant Protestants. That only moved the conflict to a different plane and created new types of martyrs for Goulart and other Protestant writers to memorialize (Ibid., p. 50).

One can also think of the crusades against the Waldenses of the Piedmont Valleys of northwestern Italy (see E. Comba, *History of the Waldenses of Italy*) and the Albigenses of southern France (see E. Ladurie, *Montaillou: The Promised Land of Error*). This is a bloody record, but one which is sometimes excused by saying that the power of the state did this.

A fifth characteristic of the little-horn power is that it would "try to change set times and the laws" (Daniel 7:25). The Aramaic word for "times" is *zimnin,* the plural form of *z^e^man*. When used in the singular, this word refers to a point in time, but as a plural, it refers to repeated points in time. These repeated points in time are connected in the very same Bible verse with God's law.

What law is this?

God has given various laws in the Old Testament, but the law of God *par excellence* is the law of the Ten Commandments (see Exodus 34:28; Deuteronomy 4:13; 10:4). The only provision regarding time in this most special law of God appears in the fourth commandment which deals with the Sabbath, the seventh day (see Exodus 20:8–11). Earthly religious powers have endeavored to alter that commandment by transferring the obligation of the Sabbath to Sunday, even though there is no biblical command to do so. But the original divine precept remains unchanged, so these earthly powers only "think to change" (Daniel 7:25, KJV; "try to change," NIV) this law and its specification about time.

Not only have these earthly powers attempted to make this change, but they have also considered it to be a mark of their authority. The

Roman Church says that it has received the *magisterium,* or teaching authority, from God and that this has enabled it to make this transfer.

Listen to John A. O'Brien, professor of theology at the University of Notre Dame from the 1940s to the 1960s on this point:

> The Bible does not contain all the teachings of the Christian religion, nor does it formulate all the duties of its members. Take, for example, the matter of Sunday observance, the attendance at divine services and the abstention from unnecessary servile work on that day, a matter upon which our Protestant neighbors have for many years laid great emphasis. Let me address myself in a friendly spirit to my dear nonCatholic reader:
>
> You believe that the Bible alone is a safe guide in religious matters. You also believe that one of the fundamental duties enjoined upon you by your Christian faith is that of Sunday observance. But where does the Bible speak of such an obligation? I have read the Bible from the first verse of Genesis to the last verse of Revelations, [sic] and have found no reference to the duty of sanctifying the Sunday. The day mentioned in the Bible is not the Sunday, the first day of the week but the Saturday, the last day of the week.
>
> It was the Apostolic Church which, acting by virtue of that authority conferred upon her by Christ, changed the observance to the Sunday in honor of the day on which Christ rose from the dead, and to signify that now we are no longer under the Old Law of the Jews, but under the New Law of Christ. In observing the Sunday as you do, is it not apparent that you are really acknowledging the insufficiency of the Bible alone as a rule of faith and religious conduct, and proclaiming the need of a divinely established teaching authority which in theory you deny? (O'Brien, 138, 139).

A bit further in his treatment, O'Brien reinforces that argument and makes it even more explicit:

> The third [fourth in the thinking of most Protestants] commandment is: "Remember thou keep holy the Sabbath Day."

> Like the first two commandments, this one also concerns our duties to God, Particularly the duty to worship Him on a designated day. The word "Sabbath" means rest, and is Saturday the seventh day of the week.
>
> Why then do Christians observe Sunday instead of the day mentioned in the Bible? . . . .
>
> The Church received the authority to make such a change from her Founder, Jesus Christ. He solemnly conferred upon His Church the power to legislate, govern and administer . . . the power of the keys. It is to be noted that the Church did not change the divine law obliging men to worship, but merely changed the day on which such public worship was to be offered; thus the law involved was merely a ceremonial law.
>
> But since Saturday, not Sunday, is specified in the Bible, isn't it curious that non-Catholics who profess to take their religion directly from the Bible and not from the Church, observe Sunday instead of Saturday? Yes, of course, it is inconsistent; but this change was made about fifteen centuries before Protestantism was born, and by that time the custom was universally observed. They have continued the custom, even though it rests upon the authority of the Catholic Church and not upon an explicit text in the Bible. That observance remains as a reminder of the Mother Church from which the non-Catholic sects broke away—like a boy running away from home but still carrying in his pocket a picture of his mother or a lock of her hair (O'Brien, 406–408).

These claims stand in opposition to the plain and simple truth of the Word of God that "the seventh day is the Sabbath of the Lord thy God" (Exodus 20:10, KJV).

Daniel 7:25 says that the religious power identified by the various characteristics of the little horn would make an attempt to change a particular type of time—a repeated point in time that is connected with God's law. This prediction fits precisely with the role of the little horn in regard to God's seventh-day Sabbath. Thus this characteristic of the little horn can be added to those other characteristics listed above.

The final characteristic of the little horn found in the prophecy is noted in Daniel 7:25: "The saints will be handed over to him for a time, times, and half a time." What is a "time"?

In Daniel 4, as we have seen, a "time" refers to a year. Seven "times" were to pass over Nebuchadnezzar until he regained his sanity (4:16, 23, 25, 32). The "time, times, and half a time" of Daniel 7:25, then, equal three and a half prophetic years. Each year is made up of 360 days, making a total of 1,260 days. The year-for-a-day principle gives us 1,260 actual years (see Ezekiel 4:6; Numbers 14:34). A fuller discussion of the year-for-a-day principle is found in chapters 6, 7 of this study on Daniel). Revelation 12:6, 14 confirms this calculation. There, verse 6 refers to 1,260 days which are equivalent to "a time, times, and half a time" in verse 14.

The question then becomes: Where in the course of the history of the little horn, or papacy, should we place these 1,260 years? To what period do they best correspond?

As noted above, the transition from Imperial Rome to Medieval Rome took place in the sixth century A.D. With that transition, Imperial Rome faded away, and the papacy came to the forefront, occupying the position of leadership in Rome vacated by the political power. The particular point at which the papal power began to be realized was when the Ostrogoth's control of Rome was lifted in A.D. 538. Prior to that time, the bishop of Rome had been under the control of barbarian tribes for more than sixty years. Now, free of that encumbrance, his authority, both civil and religious, began to increase until the medieval papacy reached its zenith in the eleventh through the thirteenth centuries.

In A.D. 533, the events of A.D. 538 had been foreshadowed by a decree which the emperor Justinian issued from Constantinople proclaiming the bishop of Rome head of all the churches. This decree arose out of certain theological controversies and resulted in the emperor confirming to Pope John II the headship of all the churches. All the correspondence relating to this decree was codified as *Corpus Iuris Civilis* (book 1, title 1, 7). It was reconfirmed by Justinian's Novella 9 in A.D. 535 and again in Novella 131 in A.D. 545. (A text of all three of these decrees can be found in L. E. Froom, *Prophetic Faith of Our Fathers,* vol. 1.)

In A.D. 538, thanks to the emperor's troops, the Roman bishop was in a position to assume the headship of the church in fact and not just on paper. Another decree by Justinian given in 555, the year of the final defeat of the Ostrogoths, cemented both the religious and political authority of the papacy. Since the military liberation of the papacy was a central event in this series of events, without which the other decrees would never have become effective, it is appropriate to date the "time, times, and half a time" (Daniel 7:25) of papal authority as beginning in A.D. 538.

The endpoint is even more sharply defined. It came on February 15, 1798, when the French general, Berthier, deposed Pope Pius VI and exiled him to France where he died in July 1799. Not until 1801, when Napoleon signed a concordat with Pius VII, did the first stirrings of a revived papacy take place. For a time it appeared as if the papacy had received a "deadly wound," in 1798, but from that nadir in its experience it has gradually arisen to a new state of prominence in the world (see Revelation 13:3).

SUMMARY

The characteristics of the little horn as given in the prophecy of Daniel 7 may be summarized as follows.

First, the little horn comes out of the Roman beast, therefore it is Roman in character. Second, it comes up after the divisions of Rome, represented by the ten horns, had taken place. Third, three of those horns were to be plucked up before it. Fourth, growing from smallness, this power came to speak boasting words against the Most High, fulfilled in the presumptuous claims of this religious power. Fifth, it was also to be a persecuting power, as amply attested by the various crusades and inquisitions that it has conducted. Sixth, it would also make an attack upon God's law, especially that part which has to do with a repeated point in time such as the Sabbath.

Regarding this last point, the church claims the change of the Sabbath to Sunday to be a mark of its authority. The 1957 edition of

Peter Geiermann's *Convert's Catechism of Catholic Doctrine* makes this claim:

> Q. *Which is the Sabbath day?*
> A. Saturday is the Sabbath day.
> Q. *Why do we observe Sunday instead of Saturday?*
> A. We observe Sunday instead of Saturday because the Catholic Church transferred the solemnity from Saturday to Sunday (50).

Geiermann's catechism simply reiterates a claim made at the Council of Trent in the late sixteenth century A.D. in response to the charges of the Protestant Reformation. The Council decreed: "The Church of God has thought it well to transfer the celebration and observance of the Sabbath to Sunday" (McHugh and Callan, 402).

The Catholic historian V. J. Kelly has also made this point:

> Some theologians have held that God likewise directly determined the Sunday as the day of worship in the New Law, that He Himself has explicitly substituted the Sunday for the Sabbath. But this theory is now entirely abandoned. It is now commonly held that God simply gave His Church the power to set aside whatever day, or days, she would deem suitable as Holy Days. The Church chose Sunday; the first day of the week, and in the course of time added other days, as holy days (Kelly, 2).

He continues:

> The fact, however, that Christ until His death, and His Apostles at least for a time after Christ's Ascension, observed the Sabbath is evidence enough that our Lord Himself did not substitute the Lord's day for the Sabbath, during His lifetime on earth. Instead, as most agree, He simply gave His Church the power to determine the days to be set aside for the special worship of God. . . . It is easy to surmise that this preference of Christ for the first day of the week greatly influenced the

> Apostles and the early Christians to keep that day holy, and eventually moved them to make a complete substitution of the Sabbath for the Sunday. There is no conclusive evidence, however, that the Apostles made this change of days by a definite decree (ibid.).

As a final characteristic of the little-horn power, the prophecy allots it a certain period of time—three and a half "times"—for the exercise of its authority. This symbolic time period, interpreted according to the year-for-a-day principle, extended from A.D. 538, when Rome and its bishop were liberated from the stranglehold of the Ostrogoths, to A.D. 1798 when the pope was taken prisoner and exiled from Rome, thus temporarily ending his dominion and authority.

Thus, all seven of the characteristics given in the prophecy fit the Roman Church and no other power, identifying it firmly with the symbol of the little horn. By way of caution, we must be careful to maintain a distinction between a theological system and the administrative center of a church, on the one hand, and the conscience of the individual Christian, on the other. Only God knows the motives of an individual, and He alone can read the human heart. As the great Judge, He will determine each person's sincerity and devotion in His great final judgment. The focus in Daniel's prophecy is not on individual Christians, but on a religious system that has gone awry—a system that has adopted unbiblical theological principles rooted in Greek philosophy. It is this system that the prophecy identifies and from which it calls for separation (see Revelation 18:1–4). An individual Christian can still act in good conscience within that communion, but once light becomes known, it is time for him or her to act accordingly.

The prophecy of Daniel 7 does not end with the career of any of the four beasts that it portrays. Nor does it conclude with the actions of the little horn. Dark though the picture is, God has an answer to all this sinful human history. It is God's answer; it is not of human devising. God's answer lies in the process whereby He leads His people into His kingdom—the divine judgment, the coming of the Son of Man, and the vindication of God's saints. These topics, as described in the prophecy of chapter 7, fit best with the prophetic themes to be discussed in later chapters of this study on Daniel and will be treated fully there.

THE RESULTS

We need to keep in mind that this prophecy was written by Daniel in the sixth century B.C. at the time God gave it to him. With the exception of Babylon, none of the world kingdoms brought to view were yet on the stage of world history as the superpowers they would become. Yet the history subsequent to Daniel's time has fulfilled the prophecy precisely. There have been four, and only four, world powers that arose on the scene of action—not two or three or five or seven, but four. Each of these four powers can be identified, and it can be demonstrated that they did indeed manifest the characteristics depicted in the symbolic prophecy. The prophecy predicts with precision the onward march of Babylon, Media-Persia, Greece, and Rome. Looking back through the centuries from our vantage point in history, we can trace the fulfillment of Daniel's prophecy and see how the specifications are matched evenly by the procession of kingdoms that arose and fell in the Mediterranean region. Following the succession of these four kingdoms, the little horn, representing the medieval papacy that arose out of the ruins of Imperial Rome, appeared as foretold. It, too, acted out the activities predicted in the prophecy until the end of the time allotted to it. Shortly after that time, according to the prophecy, God was to take up His work of judgment in response to this procession of human powers (see 7:22, 26). The reality of the judgment and the establishment of God's everlasting kingdom is just as certain as has been the fulfillment of the earlier stages of the historic panorama of Daniel 7. The procession of human powers expressed by the beasts and the horns sets the stage for God's final and decisive action in history.

One way to study the Bible and understand it better is to look for key words—words that appear over and over in a biblical narrative. In Daniel 7, such a key word is repeated and repeated—the Aramaic word translated "dominion." This word occurs seven times in chapter 7 (vss. 6, 12, 14, 26, 27). The NIV translates this word more broadly as "authority" (vss. 6, 12), "dominion" (vs. 14), "power" (vss. 26, 27), and "rulers" (vs. 27). This variety of translational equivalents weakens the impact of the repetition of this key word. When we realize that the word "dominion" is repeated over and over again in this chapter, it becomes evident that it provides a key to understanding this chapter.

In terms of ordinary human political entities, dominion, or authority, appears to be rather transitory. Babylon had it for a while, but then it lost it to Persia. Persia had it for a little longer time, but still lost it to Greece. Strong as Greece first appeared under Alexander the Great, it soon lost dominion too. Rome, which looked like an eternal kingdom, did not last nearly as long as expected, and it, too, lost its dominion. At the noontide of the papacy in the twelfth century it looked as though it might maintain an eternal dominion, but it, too, came to a loss of dominion.

Is this all that human beings have to look forward to? Is the eternal fate of humanity to be subject to this constant change in the cycle of earthly rulers, most of whom are self-serving and oppressive?

God's answer is, No! There will come a time when He will set up His kingdom, and His kingdom is going to be different from any that humanity has seen previously (vs. 27). Not only will it be different in character, being based upon love and justice and grace, but it will also be different in terms of time. It will not be temporary and transitory like all the earthly entities that have gone before it. This kingdom will be eternal; its dominion will go on forever. Thus there is a contrast in the way the word *dominion* is used in this chapter. When it is used of earthly human governments, it refers to something temporary and transitory. But when it is used of God's government, it is eternal. The dominion of God and His kingdom will last forever and ever. That is one of the precious promises of this prophecy. And that kingdom will soon come for we have almost reached the end of the line of history depicted in the prophecy of this chapter.

Daniel 7 marks a transition point in Daniel's book. It marks the transition from the mostly historical first half of the book to the fully prophetic section in the second half. That is why chapter 7 contains both history and prophecy—although more prophecy than history. It foreshadows the prophetic last half of Daniel's book. The transition to apocalyptic prophecy begins in this chapter without waiting for the second section of the book.

But chapter 7 also has ties to the historical half of Daniel. It is anchored in that section by its language, being the last chapter written in Aramaic. It is anchored there by its location in the book, integrated into the literary structure of that portion of the book.

Now that the study of all of the historical section of Daniel's book is complete, it is appropriate to again review the chiastic outline of that section as a whole:

A. Daniel 2—Fallen kingdoms (the great image)
B. Daniel 3—Kingly persecution (the fiery furnace)
C. Daniel 4—Fallen king (Nebuchadnezzar's madness)
C. Daniel 5—Fallen king (Belshazzar's last night)
B. Daniel 6—Kingly persecution (the lions' den)
A. Daniel 7—Fallen kingdoms (beasts rise and fall)

In this outline, we can see visually that similar content ties together chapters 4 and 5, chapters 3 and 6, and chapters 2 and 7. That is why we have discussed them in this order. Thus the literary structure has a bearing on our interpretation and shows that Daniel 7 is indeed a further and more detailed explanation of what has already gone on before in more simple terms in Daniel 2. Daniel 2 and 7 are complementary in content and complementary in literary structural location.

CHAPTER SIX

INTERPRETING PROPHECY

Among the interpreters of Daniel's prophecies there is considerable disagreement about how the task of interpreting prophecy should be carried out. Three basic schools of thought exist.

The *preterist* view wants to put the fulfillment of all of Daniel's prophecies in the past, ending with the second century B.C. In this case, none of the prophecies would extend to Rome or beyond.

The *futurist* view considers much of Daniel's prophetic section as still future and as yet unfulfilled. Futurist interpreters begin in the past, starting Daniel's prophecies with the historical sequence of Babylon, Media-Persia, Greece, and Rome. But then they jump over the entire Christian era and place the main fulfillment of most of these prophecies in the last seven years of earth's history.

The *historicist* view sees the prophecies of Daniel as being fulfilled throughout history, extending from the past through the present to the future. Because of the flow of history that is involved in this view, it is sometimes called the "continuous historical" view.

As an example of how these different methods handle the prophecies of Daniel, let's look briefly at what each does with the prophetic symbol of the little horn of Daniel 7 and 8. For the preterist, the little horn refers to the Seleucid king, Antiochus Epiphanes. Antiochus ruled Syria from Antioch during the Hellenistic period of history from 175–163 B.C. He was noted for his persecution of the Jews.

The futurist also concentrates on one central figure when interpreting the symbol of the little horn. But instead of the historical figure of Antiochus Epiphanes, the futurist identifies the little horn with a personal antichrist who will arise in Israel at the end of time and who will persecute the Jewish people. The Christian church, however, will have been raptured out of the world and will not have to endure this persecution, according to this view.

The historicist takes Daniel's symbol of the little horn to be corporate, not individual. The historicist view is that the little horn stands for an institution, the religious phase of Rome, that is, the papacy. This institution stands at the end of a series of nations outlined by the prophecy and, according to the time specification, was to be a central prophetic figure through the medieval period.

Obviously, these three schools of thought—preterist, futurist, and historicist—must be using widely differing rules of interpretation in order to reach such widely differing conclusions. Let's look at some of the more important of these rules of interpretation, known technically as *hermeneutics,* and see how they stand up against the biblical text and the rules which it proposes for interpreting itself.

When interpreting the prophecies of Daniel, we need to ask four basic questions:

- What is a symbol, and when does it operate?
- What is the basic outline of the nations involved in these prophecies?
- How prominent a place should be given in these prophecies to the role of Antiochus Epiphanes?
- How should prophetic time in Daniel be understood?

SYMBOLS

The prophecies of Daniel contain numerous symbols. In fact, this is one prominent characteristic of apocalyptic prophecy such as we find in Daniel and Revelation. Symbols are also used in classical prophecy such as is found in the books of Isaiah, Jeremiah, Hosea, and others. (For a discussion of the differences between apocalyptic prophecy and classical prophecy, see the Introduction to this volume, pages 11, 12). However, apocalyptic prophecy employs symbols to a much greater degree ,than does classical prophecy. That is why we find such a large cast of symbols in Daniel—metals, beasts, horns, winds, seas, etc.

It is a relatively simple task to sort out what is literal and what is symbolic in chapters 2, 7, and 8 of Daniel. The text itself makes sharp distinctions between the two. Daniel clearly tells us when he was in vision and what he saw in those visions. Here we find the symbolic elements. Following the vision, the prophet also clearly lets us know when he is literally talking with an angel interpreter and the content of that conversation. These divisions are straightforward and clear. In Daniel 7, for example, the vision ends with verse 14, and the explanation begins with verse 15. In Daniel 8 the vision also ends with verse 14, and the angel's explanation takes up the rest of the chapter. Even in Daniel 2 these divisions are clear. Although Daniel himself recites the dream (vss. 31–35) and also gives the interpretation (vss. 36–45), the transition between the symbolic dream and its explanation in chapter 2 is quite distinct.

The situation is somewhat different in chapters 9 and 11. In these two prophecies, no symbolic vision precedes the explanation. Rather, these two chapters consist of further prophetic information given to Daniel by the angel Gabriel, based on the earlier vision given in chapter 8. Gabriel makes this connection clear in Daniel 9:23, and Daniel himself notes this relationship in Daniel 10:1. So in chapters 2, 7, and 8 we have symbolic visions followed immediately by their explanations, while in chapters 9 and 11 we have only explanations referring back to a previously given symbolic vision in chapter 8.

The distinction made here between symbolic visions and literal interpretations should not be understood as meaning that, in Daniel, the visions are 100 percent symbolic and the explanations are 100 percent literal. There is some overlap. For example, Daniel's vision of the heavenly court scene (7:9–14) is essentially literal although it is part of the vision. The beings Daniel sees there—God the Father ("the Ancient of Days"), God the Son ("the Son of man"), and the angels—are all literal beings. There is no need to make them into symbols. Likewise, occasional symbolic elements may occur in the more literal interpretations of a vision. An example would be the time elements appearing in both the symbolic visions (8:14) and their interpretations (7:25), where they still retain their symbolic value. Thus we should say that the visions are *predominantly* symbolic and the interpretations are *predominantly* literalistic, but they are not exclusively so.

KINGDOMS

The commentaries on Daniel generally agree on what is symbolic and what is literal in the book, largely because the book of Daniel itself makes a rather clear distinction between the two. However, there is no general agreement at all on how these symbols should be interpreted. For example, interpreters have significant differences of opinion regarding the identity even of such a major symbolic element in Daniel as the four-nation sequence of chapters 2 and 7. Yet, if we cannot correctly interpret such basic prophetic symbols in Daniel, there is little hope that we will be able to correctly interpret lesser symbols. If we cannot identify the kingdoms involved, how can we understand the prophetic details given regarding these kingdoms?

Here is how the different schools of prophetic interpretation have identified the four kingdoms outlined in Daniel 2 and 7:

School of Interpretation	Gold/ Lion	Silver/ Bear	Bronze/ Leopard	Iron/ nondescript beast
Preterist	Babylon	Media	Persia	Greece
Historicist	Babylon	Media-Persia	Greece	Rome
Futurist	Babylon	Media-Persia	Greece	Rome

There is general agreement that the first kingdom represents Babylon. The golden head of the image in chapter 2 is specifically said to be the kingdom of Babylon (2:38), and all the different interpretive schools of thought accept this identification.

The major difference of interpretation involves the identity of the second kingdom. Preterists identify the silver in the image of Daniel 2 and the bear in the vision of Daniel 7 as the Median kingdom alone; historicists and futurists see these symbols as representing the combined kingdom of Media-Persia. The effect of this different view of the second beast is to upset the identification of the rest of the sequence. As the diagram indicates, preterists conclude the four-nation sequence with Greece, but futurists and historicists see the sequence ending with Rome.

Thus, three of the four kingdoms listed are given different identities with the result that their individual characteristics are identified differently as well.

The biblical symbols for the second kingdom clearly favor identifying it with the dual kingdom of Media-Persia, rather than with the kingdom of Media alone. For example, in chapter 7, the second kingdom is represented by a bear that is raised up on one side (vs. 5). The bear's bi-form nature is of major importance in properly identifying the kingdom represented because it establishes a parallel with the symbol of the ram in chapter 8. The bear raised up on one side in chapter 7 is mirrored in chapter 8 by the symbol of a ram with two horns, one of which is higher—some Bible versions say "longer"—than the other (vs. 3). Verse 20 clearly identifies this ram as representing the dual kingdom of Media *and* Persia. Thus the bear of chapter 7 also represents the combined, Medo-Persian kingdom.

With this clear identification, why do preterist interpreters divide these two kingdoms, identifying the second kingdom in the sequence with Media and the third with Persia?

The answer is that they feel the book of Daniel itself makes a distinction between Media and Persia in chapter 5 when it identifies the king mentioned there as Darius *the Mede* (vs. 31). This indicates, they argue, the existence of a separate Median kingdom in Daniel's thinking.

We have already mentioned briefly the special historical problem of identifying Darius the Mede and have cited some specialized literature on the subject (see chapter 4). Beyond that, however, there is further evidence in Daniel 5 and 6 that the author considered Media-Persia to be a single, combined kingdom. Daniel 5:28 indicates that Babylon was to be conquered contemporaneously by the Medes *and* the Persians, and Daniel 6:8 indicates that Darius was under the law of the Medes *and* the Persians. These two chapters, describing events contemporaneous to the fall of Babylon, give direct evidence in harmony with Daniel 8:20 that the writer knew the power that overthrew Babylon was the combined kingdom of the Medes and Persians. The internal evidence of the book of Daniel invalidates the preterists' attempt to divide the second kingdom in the series into separate Median and Persian kingdoms, symbolized by different metals and beasts.

Preterists have interpreted this major symbol—and thus the entire series of kingdoms—incorrectly. Historicists and futurists have correctly interpreted the sequence of kingdoms as Babylon, Media-Persia, Greece, and Rome.

THE LITTLE HORN

The little horn is another major symbol to interpret in Daniel 7 and 8. It is described as "little" only in its formative stage; it quickly grew and became great. All three schools of prophetic interpretation—preterist, futurist, and historicist—agree that this horn is a symbol, but they disagree about what it represents. The preterist school holds that the little horn should be identified with Antiochus Epiphanes (175–163 B.C.), a Greek king who ruled Syria and Judea from Antioch. Historicist interpreters since the Reformation have identified this power as the papacy, the religious power to emerge supreme from the breakup of the Roman Empire. Futurist interpreters see the little horn as representing an individual person who will arise in Israel and persecute the Jews in the last days. Thus for futurists, there is a gap in the prophecy from Imperial Rome down to these future, final events—an intermediate period not covered by any elements present in the prophecy.

Since Antiochus Epiphanes has played such a large part in the history of the interpretation of the little horn, we need to examine his historical career in the light of the characteristics of the little horn as given in the prophecy. How well does Antiochus fit the prophetic details?

Since the little horn emerges from the fourth beast (Daniel 7:7, 8), it is clear that little horn's identity depends upon the identity we give to the fourth beast. That actually is the preterist's motivation for shortening this series to end with Greece, not Rome. Since Antiochus emerged from the breakup of Alexander's Greek kingdom, the preterist can identify the little horn with Antiochus only by identifying the fourth kingdom with Greece. But as we saw above, preterists are in error to identify the fourth beast as Greece. The fourth beast is Rome, not Greece. And since preterists have misidentified the fourth beast in the series, they have also gotten the identification of the little horn wrong. Clearly, the Greek king Antiochus cannot come out of Rome!

Another consideration militates against the little horn being Antiochus. In Daniel 8, we see a progression in the power of the kingdoms pictured. The ram (Media-Persia) magnified himself (vs. 4). Then came the goat (Greece) who magnified himself exceedingly (vs. 8), followed by the little horn which magnified itself to heaven (vss. 9, 10, 11). Such a progression fits much better if the little horn is seen as Rome rather than Antiochus. Rome's power was greater than that of Greece. But if we identify the little horn as Antiochus, the progression does not match because the power of Antiochus was far less than that of Alexander the Great, represented by the first great horn on the goat (vss. 5, 21).

Verse 9 states that the little horn pushed its conquests "to the south and to the east and toward the Beautiful Land." These directions fit Rome perfectly as it picked off the four main pieces of the Greek Empire—Macedonia and Pergamum to the east in 168 and 133 B.C., the "Beautiful Land" of Judea in 60 B.C., and Egypt to the south in 33 B.C.

Antiochus, on the other hand, did rather poorly in these three directions. He had some success to the south in 169 B.C., capturing the eastern half of the Egyptian delta. But when he returned the next year, the Roman ambassador drew a line in the sand and threatened Antiochus with the power of Rome if he did not turn back. Antiochus turned around and went back to Syria without firing an arrow, which shows where the real power of the time was located.

Antiochus had some initial success on his eastern campaign, but then died during the expedition. His record was even worse with the "Beautiful Land" of Judea. Not only did he not conquer it, he was the one who was responsible for losing it. Chafing under his persecutions, the Jews rose up and liberated Judea from Syria! Thus Rome fits this specification of the prophecy far better than does Antiochus.

A final point regarding the identification of the little horn has to do with prophetic time in Daniel's book. None of the prophetic time periods in Daniel—the 2,300 days (8:14), the three and a half times (7:25; 12:7), the 1,290 days (12:11), or the 1,335 days (12:12)—fit Antiochus Epiphanes. The book of I Maccabees says that Antiochus's desecration of the temple in Jerusalem lasted exactly three years to the day. Even if measured in literal, not symbolic, years, it's obvious that all the prophetic time periods in Daniel exceed three years.

Preterist commentators are aware of this difficulty and have endeavored to resolve it by dividing the 2,300 days, literally 2,300 "evenings-mornings" in half to arrive at 1,150 days, or symbolic years. However, this does not solve the problem because three complete luni-solar years equal 1,092 days (354 + 354 + 384).

Thus we should reject the interpretation that sees Antiochus Epiphanes as the fulfillment of the little-horn symbol. In chapter 7, the little horn represents the religious phase of Rome which came up after the divisions of Imperial Rome (vss. 7, 8; cf vs. 24). And in chapter 8, the little horn initially represents the imperial phase of Rome that came on the scene of action after the division of Greece (vss 9, 23). These identifications fit the historical facts far better than does the view that sees Antiochus Epiphanes as the fulfillment of the little horn.

PROPHETIC TIME

How shall we understand the time periods brought to view in the prophecies of Daniel? When the prophecy speaks of "2,300 evenings and mornings" (8:14) or "1,290 days" (12:11), should we understand that to be literal days or symbolic time?

One clue lies in the point just made that the little horn is best identified with Rome. If this identification is correct, then the prophetic times associated with the little horn's activity should also fit with the time periods covered by Rome. Imperial Rome lasted a number of centuries, and Papal Rome continued on through the Middle Ages. Taken in terms of literal time, the prophetic periods of Daniel would not span even a small portion of that history. This correlation indicates that the prophetic periods should be understood as symbolic time in harmony with their contexts.

Preterist and futurist commentators, however, hold that these periods of time should be taken as literal time—with the exception of some references in Daniel 9. Preterists, of course, place that literal time in the past, while futurists place it in the future. Historicists, on the other hand, understand these prophetic periods as symbolic time, fulfilled, like the larger content of the prophecies in which they occur, through the course of centuries of history.

What evidence is there that these prophetic times should be understood symbolically? And if they are to be so interpreted, what rules of interpretation should be followed?

The first feature of these time periods which points to their symbolic nature is their symbolic context. For example, the 2,300 evenings and mornings are found in the vision of Daniel 8 in a setting containing various other symbols such as a ram, a goat, four horns, and a little horn.

In Daniel 7:21, the prophet says, "As I watched, this horn [the little horn] was waging war against the saints and defeating them." This is clearly symbolic imagery. Verse 25 indicates how long ["a time, times, and half a time"] this persecution of God's people would continue. Since the entire context of what is said about this persecuting power is symbolic, it seems logical that the time periods given would likewise be symbolic.

The fact that these prophetic time periods should be understood symbolically is also indicated by the symbolic nature of the units in which they are given. Daniel 8:14 uses "evenings and mornings" which is not a normal unit of expressing time in the Old Testament. Similarly, the "time, times and half a time" of Daniel 7:25; 12:7 is not the word for "years." These times have to be interpreted as years through Daniel 4:16, 23, 25, 32 along with Revelation 12:6, 14; 13:5. Again, in Daniel 9 the time unit is "weeks" or "sevens" (vss. 24–27) even though as the content of the prophecy shows, these are not normal weeks of seven twenty-four hour days.

Another point to note is that the time periods are expressed in quantities that emphasize their symbolic nature. A Hebrew would not normally date some event as being 2,300 days in the future. He would say six years and four months. Nor would he date something by referring to seventy weeks. Instead, he would say one year and four and a half months. The 1,260 days, the 1,290 days, and the 1,335 days would have more commonly been spoken of as three and a half years, three years and seven months, or three years and eight and a half months.

All these considerations indicate that we are not dealing with literal time in the prophetic portions of Daniel, but with symbolic time.

If so, by what standard should we evaluate these symbolic times in terms of actual historical time? This brings up the day-for-a-year rule in prophecy. It is found first of all in Numbers 14:34 and Ezekiel 4:6—two classical, not apocalyptic, prophecies. Numbers 14:34 sets forth a rule to be utilized as a basis for the future judgment of Israel. The forty days spent scouting the land by the spies who brought back a bad report provided a scale for the forty years during which the Israelites would wander in the wilderness.

In Ezekiel 4:6, the prophet was to symbolize the past years of iniquity in Israel and Judah by lying on his side for a corresponding number of days on the basis of the year-for-a-day rule. Thus Ezekiel, who prophesied at the same time as Daniel, knew and used this rule regarding prophetic time.

There is also evidence right in Daniel's book that this day-for-a-year rule should be utilized in his time prophecies. Daniel 9:24–27 refers to a prophetic period of seventy weeks. Because of all the events that were to occur within these seventy weeks it is clear that they must be understood symbolically. Within these seventy weeks, Judah was to return to its own land and rebuild Jerusalem and the temple. Then, sometime later within this time period, the Messiah would come and minister to the people, but he would be cut off, or killed. Obviously, all of this could not have been accomplished in a literal year and a half. These "weeks" must be symbolic.

The pragmatic test of history shows that the symbolic unit of one week is equivalent to seven literal years—a day for a year. Using this standard, the events of this prophecy work out correctly. The period was to begin with "the issuing of the decree to restore and rebuild Jerusalem" (vs. 25) and end with the Messiah confirming the covenant with many (see vs. 27). Jerusalem was to be restored at the end of seven "sevens" or weeks (vs. 25), and Messiah was to come sixty-two "sevens" later (vs. 26). If we use the rule of a day for a year and begin the seventy weeks (or 490 years) in 457 B.C. when Artaxerxes issued a decree which resulted in the rebuilding of Jerusalem, the predicted dates all fall into place with the time period ending in A.D. 34. We will be examining the details of this precisely fulfilled prophecy in the next chapter.

Although both preterists and futurists believe the prophetic time periods of Daniel are literal rather than symbolic, they implicitly acknowledge the validity of the year-for-a-day rule when it comes to the seventy weeks in Daniel 9. They do not use the precise dates given above (457 B.C. and A.D. 34), but neither do they try to fit the prophecy into a literal seventy weeks—or about a year and a half. Futurists often date the beginning of the period around 444 B.C. and end the sixty-ninth week with a date for Christ's crucifixion of A.D. 33 or 34. Preterists often begin the seventy weeks in 593 B.C. and bring it down to the time of Antiochus Epiphanes c. 165 B.C. But despite such variations, both futurists and preterists commonly see the seventy weeks in Daniel 9 as referring to a period of time that clearly extends far beyond a literal "seventy weeks" thus implicitly admitting that the year-for-a-day rule has value for this prophetic time period at least.

Earlier in this chapter, we made the point that chapter 11 consists of further prophetic information given to Daniel by the angel Gabriel, based on the earlier vision given in chapter 8. Daniel 8 provides the symbols, and Daniel 11 provides their literal interpretation. This fact gives us an additional reason for seeing the prophetic time periods in Daniel as symbolic.

For example, in chapter 8 Daniel sees symbolic entities (kingdoms), but in chapter 11 these are presented as literal persons (individual kings). In chapter 8, Daniel sees symbolic actions taking place (casting down stars, etc.); in chapter 11, we have literal actions (recognizable battles). And in chapter 8, Daniel is given symbolic time periods (evenings-mornings); in chapter 11, we find literal time (years).

For example, in chapter 11, verses 6, 8, and 13 refer to "years." In each case, these years measure (although without specifying a particular number) some of the activities of the Greek kings in Egypt (the Ptolemies) or in Syria (the Seleucids). These Greek kings belong to the time period covered by the four horns that came out of the head of the goat (8:22). That same time period of the goat and its four horns is also covered by some of the 2,300 evenings-mornings (8:14). Thus when we utilize Daniel 11 to interpret Daniel 8, we find that the evenings-mornings in chapter 8 correspond to literal, historical years in chapter 11. It is clear, then, that the time period in chapter 8, the 2,300 evenings-mornings, must be symbolic. If they were literal time, they would extend only for less than six and a half years—not nearly enough time to encompass the activities presented as their counterpart in chapter 11. Thus the book of Daniel itself teaches the year-for-a-day principle.

SUMMARY

The book of Daniel contains a type of specialized prophecy known for its intense use of symbols. In Daniel, the symbols are found mainly in the recorded visions, while their literal, historical equivalents are found mainly in the interpretations given by the angel. The distinctions between the symbols and the interpretation is fairly sharp in chapters 2, 7, and 8. But in chapters 9 and 11 there is no symbolic vision. Rather these chapters refer back to the symbolic vision in chapter 8 and provide interpretations of certain aspects of that vision.

Foundational to the prophetic portions of Daniel is the outline of successive world powers found in chapters 2, 7, 8, and 11. The basic work of interpretation involves identifying the kingdoms presented by the symbols in these chapters. Using correlations found within the book of Daniel itself, I have taken the position in this volume that the sequence should be identified as Babylon, Media-Persia, Greece, and Rome. The little horn of Daniel 7 and 8 follows the fourth of these kingdoms, indicating that it comes on the scene of action as a new phase of Rome, a religious phase. Thus the position taken in this book is that the little horn represents the papacy, not Antiochus Epiphanes. The events of recorded history confirm this identification.

Several of the prophecies of Daniel include time periods, raising the question of whether these should be understood as literal or symbolic. The context, the units of time measurement used, and the numbers themselves all indicate that these prophetic time periods should be understood symbolically and that they stand for long periods of actual, historical time. Numbers 14:34; Ezekiel 4:6; Daniel 9:24–27; and Daniel 8:14 compared with Daniel 11:6, 8, 13 demonstrate that the rule for interpreting prophetic time in apocalyptic prophecies should be the day-for-a-year principle.

These are the basic interpretive principles that we will apply to the book of Daniel as we examine its prophecies. Others will be presented as the need arises in the context of specific prophecies.

CHAPTER SEVEN

Christ as Sacrifice

The prophecy of Daniel 9 begins with one of the longest prayers recorded in the Bible. It is also a beautiful prayer because it is so unselfish. Daniel prays—not for blessings for himself, but for his people. He intercedes with God for the remnant of Judah which is still living in exile in Babylon.

As he prayed, Daniel had the scroll of the prophet Jeremiah in mind, especially the portion we call chapter 25. There Daniel read Jeremiah's prophecy that the exile of Judah in Babylon would last seventy years (see Jeremiah 25:10–14; Daniel 9:1–3). He knew those seventy years were almost over.

Three different times Nebuchadnezzar of Babylon had besieged Jerusalem—first in 605 B.C., then again in 597, and finally in 589–586. Each time he took captives back to Babylon. Daniel went with the first group in 605 B.C. By the time Babylon fell to the Persians, Daniel himself had been in Babylon almost seventy years. No wonder his prayers took on a note of urgency as he saw the predicted time period drawing rapidly to a close.

In response to Daniel's prayer, the angel Gabriel was sent to reassure the prophet that God's answer was yes! "Yes," Gabriel promised Daniel, "your people will go home to their own land. Yes, they will rebuild Jerusalem and its temple."

But God's answer to Daniel went beyond the immediate future. "God is telling you more," Gabriel continued. He wants to tell you what is going to happen to your people a long time after that restoration. He wants to tell you about the Messiah—when He will come, what He will do, and what will happen to Him. God wants to tell you how your people will respond to the Messiah who will come and what will happen to them as a result."

All this God made known to His prophet Daniel, and that revelation is the content of the prophecy of chapter 9.

A PRAYER FOR UNDERSTANDING

Daniel dates his prayer as taking place in the first year of Darius and then goes on to identify Darius by his father, his ethnic affiliation, and his political office (9:1). Then he repeats the date (vs. 2). What are we to make of this?

It should tell us that prayer ought to be tied to specific, concrete situations in our lives. It is not something vague and unconnected to the real events that are taking place in our experience. Like Daniel, we need to pray about things that deeply concern us. With Babylon's conquest by the Medes and Persians, exciting changes had taken place. This was the first full calendar year under the new government, and Daniel was eagerly anticipating coming events as he prayed.

He knew from the prophecy of Jeremiah (25:10–14) that the Jewish captivity in Babylon was to last for seventy years. He also knew the end of that period was drawing near; he himself had lived in Babylon almost seventy years. He had come to Babylon in 605 B.C., and now it was 538/537 B.C. Daniel was praying over an open Bible (vs. 2), as he thought about these things. This is an example we would do well to follow. We find precious promises in God's Word; it's fitting, then, for us to take these to Him in prayer, pleading for their fulfillment in our lives and in the church.

Daniel began his prayer by addressing God as "the great and awesome God, who keeps his covenant of love with all who love him and obey his commands" (vs. 4). This introduction says much about Daniel's understanding of God and the experiences he had had with Him during his long life. In our prayers, we, too, should express our feelings about God based on the experiences we have had with Him and our understanding of Him. Daniel's description of God as "great and awesome" expresses God's transcendence. His very nature is deserving of reverential awe—an appreciation of His holiness and almighty power. This is what the Bible means when it speaks of "fearing" God.

Daniel's reference to God as a covenant-keeping God emphasizes the fact that God is faithful to keep His promises to us. As surely as did ancient Israel, we today have likewise entered into a covenant agreement with Him. This covenant imposes certain obligations on us and on God, but on neither side are the obligations carried out merely from a sense of obligation. As Daniel points out, love is the motive that both originates the covenant and sustains it. It is based on love—God's love expressed toward us, and our love for Him. The Hebrew word used for this idea of covenant love is *chesed.* This is a word rich in meanings that are difficult to translate adequately. It contains the idea of faithfulness—that God will always fulfill His part of the covenant. But it also conveys the idea of the deep love from which that faithfulness stems. The English Bible sometimes translates these concepts as "loving kindness." It reminds us here that we can approach God in prayer expecting that He will hear and answer us because He loves us.

The idea of God's loving kindness is particularly startling in the context of Daniel's prayer. After nearly seventy years of exile in a foreign land, the natural question would be, "Where are You, God?" Was God really working through all the calamities that had overtaken them? The natural inclination would be to feel that God had abandoned His people. But Daniel says otherwise. "God," he prays, "You have not abandoned us, rather, we have abandoned You." That perception is just as valid today as it was in Daniel's time.

In his prayer, Daniel goes right to the heart of the matter. Verses 5 and 6 repeat one central idea many times—"We have sinned." "You gave us good laws," Daniel says, "but we broke them. You sent Your servants to us, but we would not listen to them." Daniel had the book of one of these prophets open before him. The people had refused to listen to Jeremiah; if they had been willing to pay attention to him, they could have saved themselves, the city of Jerusalem, and their nation.

We marvel today at their stubborn refusal to listen to God through His prophets. But do we act any differently? How carefully do we listen to God's voice through His modern-day servants and through His written Word? If we had lived in Jeremiah's time, would we have listened to him any more than did the people of Jerusalem then?

Daniel reaffirms the view of God as unchangingly righteous. "You are righteous" (vs. 7). The people are not righteous, but God is. Even when the people persist in their unrighteousness, God continues to be righteous. He changes not. Today, we have to do with the same unchanging, ever-righteous God. Like Daniel, then, we should serve Him in righteousness. We should ask Him for the gift of His righteousness through Jesus Christ.

According to verse 7, the result of the people's unrighteousness was clearly evident. They had been scattered in exile throughout the nations of the ancient world. And worse, the inhabitants of these pagan lands knew why God's people had been scattered. The Hebrews and their God had become a byword for shame in the ancient world.

Our failures and sins have repercussions as well—on ourselves and on our God. We have to face that reality. But there is a remedy. Daniel shows us the way. We need to surrender to God our waywardness and the sad results it has produced. He is the great Restorer. He can forgive and bring us back to our original state. Just as God could restore the sanctuary, He can restore our lives to righteousness if we are willing to have Him do so.

More so than people do today, persons in ancient times identified quite directly with their ancestors. This is what Daniel is talking about in verse 8. "O Lord, we and our kings, our princes and our fathers are covered with shame because we have sinned against you." Daniel felt the need for a forgiveness that would cover the collective sins of himself and his countrymen, wiping out the shame of the past and restoring God's favor to His people. For this, he relied, again, on God's "merciful and forgiving" character (verse 9). He freely admits that neither he nor the people nor their forefathers deserve mercy. But he trusts a God who forgives even when we don't deserve to be forgiven.

In verses 10 and 11, Daniel once more goes over the list of sins, summarizing them by saying, "All Israel has transgressed your law" (verse 11). This is similar to Paul's summary of the human condition, "There is no one righteous, not even one" (Romans 3:10).

The next element in Daniel's prayer (verses 11, 12) is an acknowledgement of a more specific reason why the exile came upon the people of Judah. Their unfaithfulness had laid them open to receive the curses contained in the law of Moses for those who fail to obey. These are found especially in Deuteronomy chapters 26 through 33. Moses pointed out that the people would be blessed in obedience to these laws, but that the curses would fall upon them as a result of disobedience. This is the outworking of the principle that there are natural consequences that result from disobedience. But it is also a function of God's judgment against sin. Daniel saw the inexorable outworking of these principles in the fate of the people of Judah as they suffered exile in foreign lands.

We, too, receive the results of our disobedience today. As an example, lung cancer can be traced directly to smoking in the vast majority of cases. By smoking, one runs the risk of developing cancer because he or she is introducing a carcinogen into the bronchial tree. Similar effects operate in the spiritual realm as well. In other cases, such as Job's, no direct cause can be determined for calamities that befall us. But regardless of the situation, we can know that a loving and forgiving God waits for us to return to Him in repentance.

It was clear to Daniel where the spiritual cause for the exile lay. It lay with the disobedience of the people themselves. In this intercessory prayer, he seeks forgiveness for them. As their intercessor, Daniel once again draws on God's mighty acts as the ground for his appeal (verses 15, 16). He reflects back on the experience of the Exodus from Egypt in which God brought His people out with a mighty hand. Covenant making in the ancient world always began with an introduction that recounted the story of past relations between the two covenanting parties. Following this structure, Daniel "reminds" God of these events. He admits that such gracious acts by God in the past should have motivated the people to loving obedience. He admits their ingratitude and faithlessness in the light of God's great love for them and their fathers.

As we look back on the loving, gracious way God has led us in our personal lives, we should be motivated as well to serve Him and love Him. We need to express in our prayers a recognition of all that God has done for us and admit how often we have failed to respond in love.

Daniel's final appeal to God is based on the honor of His name (verses 17–19). By forgiving the unworthy, undeserving people of Judah, God would cause His name to be honored among all the nations of the world. People everywhere would realize how great and merciful He really is.

The honor of God is at stake in the world in our day as well as in Daniel's. We all play a part in the great controversy, and we have an obligation to bring praise and glory to our heavenly Father. It is difficult to avoid selfish prayers, but we need to have a larger view, praying not just for ourselves and our families, but for the honor of God. Jesus put it this way in His Sermon on the Mount: "Let your light shine before men, that they may see your good deeds and praise your Father in heaven" (Matthew 5:16). Our lives should be lived in such a way that God's name is praised.

The language with which Daniel closes his prayer indicates the earnestness of his feelings. His words breathe with the intensity of his desire. "O Lord, listen! O Lord, forgive! O Lord, hear and act! For your sake, O my God, do not delay, because your city and your people bear your Name" (verse 19). Too often our prayers are offered up in a listless fashion with much repetition and hackneyed phrases. Like Daniel's prayer, they ought to breathe with an intensity of interest. Daniel's prayer was no sleepy repetition of standard, trite phrases. This was a prayer into which Daniel immersed himself with emotional intensity. If we prayed in a similar way, we would no doubt see more answers to our prayers because we would be demonstrating to God that we are serious about what we are praying for.

Finally, in response to Daniel's earnest prayer, God's initial response was to send Gabriel to the aged prophet. Gabriel brought God's answer to Daniel, and that answer relates to the prophecy given in chapter 8 and discussed further in the following chapters.

We can see from Daniel's prayer something of what Daniel thought about God. But what did God think about Daniel? We get an idea in some of Gabriel's introductory words to the prophet. "You are highly esteemed" (verse 23), he told Daniel, addressing him in terms of respect and endearment. "You are greatly beloved" is how it is translated in the RSV, which conveys more emotion.

Daniel was an aged warrior for God. He was almost ninety years old at this time. One might think he was of little usefulness to God at such an age. On the contrary, he was still "highly esteemed." This should give encouragement to those who are advanced in years. God still takes note of the elderly and cares for them. He holds us each in high esteem; we are greatly beloved by the God of the universe!

GABRIEL SENT TO ANSWER DANIEL'S PRAYER

In answer to this earnest prayer regarding the captivity of Daniel's countrymen and the desolation of their city and sanctuary, God sent the angel Gabriel to give Daniel an answer (9:21). This answer is contained in verses 24–27. Basically, Gabriel assured Daniel that his prayer for the deliverance of the people would be answered. The Hebrews would return to their land. They would rebuild the temple, and they would reconstruct the city.

But Gabriel went on to tell Daniel more about the future of God's people beyond these initial events. The prophecy looked to events beyond with a special focus—the Messiah. Verses 25 and 26 specifically mention the Messiah, and verse 27 describes further Messianic activities. Gabriel's prophecy (verses 24–27) basically revolves around two poles: One pole is the people, the city, and the sanctuary; the other is the Messiah. And a considerable part of the story here is the working out of the relationship between the two.

A third party intrudes into the picture, however, bringing storm clouds that darken the sky over this picture. That third party is known as the desolater (verses 26, 27). The desolater brings desolation to the city of Jerusalem and to its temple. This we know was historically accomplished by the power of Imperial Rome, the forces of which eventually conquered and destroyed Jerusalem in A.D. 70. Thus, despite the bright spots of this prophecy—the restoration of the people and the coming of the Messiah—it ends with the somber note of another destruction.

THE PRELIMINARY ANSWER—DANIEL 9:24

For modern readers, the prophecy begins in a somewhat unusual way. It begins with a summary or conclusion (verse 24). Then it goes on to give the details that fill in or support that conclusion (verses 25–27). Modern thought, influenced by the scientific method, would first collect the data, or details, and then work out a summary. Gabriel did it the other way around because people in Daniel's time commonly reasoned from the effect back to the cause. Daniel and other Old Testament books contain other examples of this approach.

The opening phrase of verse 24 specifies the time element involved and the special focus of that time element—the people: "Seventy 'sevens' are decreed for your people and your holy city." In the margin, the NIV gives "weeks" as an alternate reading for the word translated "sevens." Most other English versions of the Bible also prefer some variation of the word "weeks" instead of "sevens." Although the word for "week," *shabua,* was built upon the root word for "seven," *sheba,* it was given different vowels so that there is no mistaking the difference between the two. Nor should we add the word "years" (weeks of years) here as does the RSV, because that word is not in the original text. The word used here should simply be translated "weeks"—that, and nothing more.

Obviously, however, the use of the word "weeks" brings with it the clear idea that symbolic time is involved here. No commentator holds that all of the predicted events could have taken place in a literal year and a half. That was hardly time enough to rebuild the altar of the temple, much less the rest of the temple and the city (see Ezra 3). Clearly, we are dealing here with symbolic time. Seventy weeks of seven days each equals 490 days. If each day stands for a year of actual time (see Numbers 14:34; Ezekiel 4:6), this prophecy spans almost five centuries—a long-range prophecy indeed!

Basically, all commentators agree that some form of the year-for-a-day principle must be employed in Daniel 9 because it is impossible to squeeze all of the predicted events into a literal seventy weeks—approximately a year and a half. This matter becomes even more acute in the time prophecies of Daniel 7, 8, 11, and 12. Arguments for the application of this principle can be drawn from Old Testament passages outside of Daniel, but a comparison of the symbolic time unit, "evenings-mornings," of Daniel 8:14 with the literal "years" of Daniel 11:6, 8, 18 indicates that the former should be interpreted by the latter. This connection is supported by the fact that Daniel 11 is the closest and most direct explanation of the symbolic prophecy of Daniel 8. (Some specialized reading on the subject of the year-day principle has been suggested at the end of this chapter. See also chapter 6 for further discussion of this topic.)

The time-range of this prophecy was extensive, yet its geographical focus was narrow. It focused especially upon "your people and your holy city" (verse 24), that is, Jerusalem and the people of Judah. This is a very different focus from that of the other major lines of prophecy in the book of Daniel. The prophecies in Daniel 2, 7, 8, and 11 outline the rise and fall of world nations and their rulers as they come on the scene of action and disappear. But in Daniel 9 we do not see the onward march of Babylon, Media-Persia, Greece, and Rome. Some of these nations formed the historical backdrop against which the fate of Judea played out, but Daniel 9 focuses more specifically upon the people of God.

The verb in the phrase, "seventy 'sevens' are decreed for your people," (verse 24) is also commonly translated "determined." More literally, it means "to be cut off." This meaning forms a definite connection with the prophecy of Daniel 8. That connection is discussed further at the end of the next chapter.

The opening phrase of this prophecy proceeds to list a series of six events, or actions, that are to be accomplished by the end of the specified seventy weeks allotted to the Jewish people. It does not yet say precisely when each of these events is to be accomplished; that awaits the more detailed portion of the text. Remember, this is only the opening summary which will be given more substance in subsequent verses.

These six actions come in three pairs. The first pair is addressed especially to the people of Judah and describes what they were to accomplish within this time frame of seventy weeks. The second pair describes actions that God would take upon Himself as His own responsibility. The final pair points to the results that would flow from the combination of the previous four actions.

The two actions that were the responsibility of God's people were "to finish transgression, [and] to put an end to sin" (verse 24). The Hebrew language has quite a few words for sin, each with its own shade of meaning. The meaning of "transgression" (in the phrase "to finish transgression") is sin as rebellion against God. The second phrase ("to put an end to sin"), uses the common word for sin, meaning to miss the mark, the goal, or standard which God has set up. Thus, Gabriel charges the Jewish people with the responsibility of putting away sin and developing a righteous society. Like ancient Israel in the wilderness, they were to purify the camp in order to prepare conditions which would be right for the Messiah to come.

God's responsibility, as reflected in the second pair of actions in verse 24, was "to atone for wickedness, [and] to bring in everlasting righteousness." Atonement was a central feature of the sacrificial system in the Hebrew sanctuary (see Leviticus 4 and 16). But the atonement mentioned here goes beyond what that system could accomplish. As the book of Hebrews points out, there was a problem with the old system. The problem was that the atonement provided was temporary. A sin was dealt with by offering a sacrifice, but when another sin was committed, it required another sacrifice. Round and round the system went (see Hebrews 7:11; 10:4). But what Daniel 9:24 looked forward to was *one great final atonement.* That was provided for us by Jesus Christ in His death on the cross. Since that great all-encompassing sacrifice has taken place once for all people, no more ongoing round of sacrifices is necessary (see Hebrews 7:27; 9:12, 25; 10:10, 12, 14).

This marks the transition from a temporary, transitory righteousness to one that is permanent and everlasting. And that is exactly the next action referred to in Daniel 9:24—"to bring in everlasting righteousness." The righteousness that flows from Christ's death continues until today, almost 2,000 years later, and it will continue to flow unabated into eternity.

The final pair of events in verse 24 are results of the first four actions. The first was "to seal up vision and prophecy." The word translated *prophecy* here is actually the word for "prophet." There would come a time when both vision and prophet would be sealed up. This is in the context of what would happen to the people of Judah. This prophecy would be dramatically fulfilled with the stoning of Stephen (see Acts 7). One may reasonably ask what there is about Stephen's martyrdom that makes it more special than others. Several features show it to be especially significant in a spiritual sense.

First, there is the setting of Stephen's speech. He gave his defence before the Sanhedrin, the highest religious body of the people and the religious representatives of the nation (see Acts 6:15). Second, there is the nature of Stephen's speech. To a modern reader, it is rather long and not very interesting, because it goes through a lot of history. It starts with Abraham (7:2); it continues with Isaac, Jacob (verse 8), and Joseph (verse 9) to explain how the Israelites happened to be in Egypt. Then it takes up the story of the deliverance under Moses (verse 20) and the rebellion under Aaron at Sinai (verse 40). Joshua brings the people into the land of Canaan (verse 45). Then Stephen mentions David (verse 45) and Solomon (verse 46) who built the temple. At that point, Stephen breaks off his speech to accuse the religious leaders of resisting the Holy Spirit and the prophets and of crucifying the Righteous One, the Messiah.

Why this long historical speech?

When God made a covenant with His people in the Old Testament, there was a historical prologue which showed how gracious God had been to His people. This served to motivate them to give Him loving obedience.

When the Old Testament prophets brought God's messages to the people, they commonly started right where the original covenant did—with a historical prologue, showing how gracious God had been to His people and how ungrateful they had been to God. There is a technical term for this kind of prophetic speech—a "covenant lawsuit" in which the prophet serves as the prosecuting attorney from the heavenly court. A good example of this kind of speech can be found in Micah 6. Stephen was giving an inspired "covenant lawsuit" speech before the religious leaders of the nation in the Sanhedrin.

But they did not like it. As a result they dragged him outside of the city and stoned him (verse 58). Just before this happened, however, Stephen, "full of the Holy Spirit, looked up to heaven and saw the glory of God, and Jesus standing at the right hand of God" (verse 55). And he witnessed to what he saw before the assembled group.

When a person looks into heaven and sees God sitting on His throne and Jesus standing at His right hand, that person is having a vision. People who have visions are, by definition, prophets. At that moment, technically speaking, Stephen was a prophet. But his audience would not hear or accept his vision; they rejected him and stoned him, sealing his lips in death. When Stephen died, *the last prophetic voice had spoken to Israel as the elect people of God.*

Of course, there are other prophets in the New Testament after Stephen—Paul and John, along with others. But the prophets who followed Stephen were prophets *to the Christian church,* not to the nation of Israel. A profound shift had taken place from prophecy directed to national Israel to prophecy directed to the Christian church. "Vision and prophet" had been sealed up to "your people and your holy city" (Daniel 9:24).

The second half of the final pair of events in verse 24 is the matter of anointing "the most holy." From the time of the early church, there have been two main opinions about this action. One school of thought has seen this as a reference to the anointing of the Messiah. There is a problem with this interpretation, however, as the phrase is not normally applied to persons. It is normally used in connection with the sanctuary. It can be used for the Holy Place, the Most Holy Place, or the sanctuary as a whole. It can also be connected with the vessels in the sanctuary. In any case, it is a sanctuary phrase and should be seen as such in this verse. Besides, the anointing of the Messiah is referred to in the next verse (verse 25), so we lose nothing by applying the phrase in verse 24 to the sanctuary.

The question then is, to which sanctuary does this anointing refer?

The tabernacle in the wilderness had long since gone out of use, and the first temple lay in ruins in Daniel's time. The soon-to-be-rebuilt second temple is not a very good candidate either, because Daniel 9:26 says of it: "The people of the ruler who will come will destroy the city and the sanctuary." This very prophecy contains a prediction of the destruction of the second temple. So by a process of elimination, we are left with only one other biblical sanctuary to which verse 24 could be referring—the heavenly sanctuary.

In ancient times, sanctuaries were anointed as part of the ceremony that commenced their ministry. A good example of this is found in Exodus 40 where the tabernacle and everything in it was anointed with oil to initiate its ministry. Parallel with this action, the anointing of the heavenly sanctuary should have taken place when Christ was inaugurated there as our great High Priest. The earthly sign of this heavenly anointing was the falling of the Holy Spirit on the Day of Pentecost.

This final event of the six listed in verse 24 is the one place in the prophecy of chapter 9 where earth and heaven are connected. The rest of the prophecy concerns events on earth. This link is, therefore, very precious, for it shows us that heaven and earth are very close.

THE STARTING POINT FOR THE SEVENTY-WEEK PROPHECY

Verse 25 begins the detailed part of this prophecy. It marks off two significant points in the prophecy's time frame—the starting point and the time when the Messiah would come.

The prophecy identifies the starting point as beginning with the word or decree that would lead to the rebuilding of the city of Jerusalem. It specifically names Jerusalem, so rebuilding only the temple would not fulfill this specification. Usually, ancient history is filled with gaps because a large number of original documents have been lost. Here, however, the problem is not a lack of original documents, but just the reverse. Four different decrees in Ezra and Nehemiah relate in one way or another to the rebuilding of Jerusalem. The problem is to sort them out and see which one best fits the specification of the prophecy.

FOUR DECREES

The book of Ezra begins with a decree from Cyrus (1:2–4) issued in 538 B.C. and giving the Jews permission to return to their homeland of Judah. It authorized them to rebuild the temple and allowed them to take financial assistance with them. A temple is not a city, however, so this is not the desired decree.

The returnees erected the altar in the temple courtyard before opposition from the Samaritans prevented them from carrying out the rest of the planned reconstruction. Not until 520 B.C., when Darius I issued a second decree for the rebuilding of the temple (see Ezra 6:1–12), did work resume. The temple was finished and dedicated four years later in 516 B.C. (see verses 15–18). Neither of these decrees affected the ruined city of Jerusalem. Further decrees were necessary to accomplish its reconstruction.

The next decree was given to Ezra himself (see Ezra 7:12–26). It bestowed extensive authority upon him to install public officials, requisition funds from the royal treasuries, and even teach God's law to non-Jews. This decree did not specifically mention rebuilding Jerusalem, but it is obvious that Ezra felt authority was granted him to do so, for upon his return to Judah in the summer of 457 B.C. he promptly rallied the people and started work on the city.

Because the book of Ezra does not follow a strict chronological sequence in relating these events, the order in which all this happened can become somewhat confusing. The decree under which Ezra operated to begin the rebuilding of Jerusalem is given in chapter 7. But the story of his doing so is given in chapter 4! Ezra 4 contains what might be called a topical parenthesis. The first twenty-three verses depart from the chronological sequence in order to treat the various oppositions the Jews encountered in rebuilding the temple and the city. Verses 1–5 recount the opposition in the time of Cyrus. Verse 6 relates the opposition in the time of Xerxes, and verses 7–23 deal with the opposition Ezra himself experienced in the time of Artaxerxes. Then the narrative comes back to the time of Darius in verse 24 and takes up the story of the successes of the Jews. The NIV does a nice job here by separating verses 23 and 24 into different paragraphs, showing that they belong to different times.

In Ezra 4, the account of the opposition Ezra faced in his rebuilding project is given in the form of a letter. The heading of the letter reads, "To King Artaxerxes, From your servants, the men of Trans-Euphrates" (verse 11). The men of Trans-Euphrates were the western governors of the Persian Empire. We have here both the name of the addressee (King Artaxerxes) and the return address of the writers (the western governors) so there is no doubt about the identity of the recipient of the letter. In spite of the fact that Ezra does not relate the events in strict chronological order, the letter is definitely addressed to the same King Artaxerxes who had authorized Ezra to return to Jerusalem.

What did the western governors report? The king, the report indicates, should know that "the Jews who came up to us from you have gone to Jerusalem and are rebuilding that rebellious and wicked city. They are restoring the walls and repairing the foundations" (verses 11, 12). Two important facts emerge here. First, there was clearly another return of the Jews to Jerusalem in the time of Artaxerxes, after the main return in the time of Cyrus. Second, it was this second group of Jewish returnees, under the leadership of Ezra, which supplied the stimulus to start rebuilding the city. Ezra 7 recounts that Ezra led this new group of returnees to Judah after receiving a decree from Artaxerxes authorizing him to do so, and the list of those who went with him is given in chapter 8.

Unfortunately, the Jewish building project was stopped once again. This time it was not the Samaritans who opposed their efforts; it was the western governors. They threatened the king with the loss of tax revenues if he let the city of Jerusalem be built. That argument was persuasive enough to Artaxerxes so that he told the governors to stop the building until he gave further word. The governors were quite happy to do so (see Ezra 4:13–23).

This sad state of affairs continued for thirteen years. Nothing further was done on the construction of the city of Jerusalem until Nehemiah, King Artaxerxes's Jewish cupbearer, intervened with the king. The king relented and sent Nehemiah as the governor of Judah with permission and responsibility to rebuild the city (see Nehemiah 1; 2). Much of the rest of Nehemiah's book is taken up with the story of how he led out in the reconstruction of the walls of the city, the opposition he received, and the celebration when the construction of the walls was finished. Once the walls were in place, the buildings within the city could be built at a more leisurely pace and under better protection.

Thus the decree of Darius I led to the completion of the work on the temple started under the decree of Cyrus. Likewise, Nehemiah's completion of the walls of the city under Artaxerxes's decree completed the first phase of the work started by Ezra. The letter that Artaxerxes gave to Nehemiah helped to fulfill the work started under the decree that the same king had earlier given to Ezra. So if we are looking for the decree which authorized the reconstruction of the city of Jerusalem, we should look to the decree Artaxerxes gave to Ezra (see Ezra 7:12–26). Nehemiah's letter of authorization merely served to complement the decree given to Ezra, enabling the work to be carried out.

Thus Artaxerxes's decree to Ezra is the one that best fits the specification of the prophecy in Daniel 9:25. This was the initial decree that went forth leading to the reconstruction and rebuilding of the city of Jerusalem.

DATING THE DECREE

Two more questions remain about this decree. When was it given, and according to which calendar should it be figured?

Because the seventy-week prophecy of Daniel 9:24–27 begins with the issuing of Artaxerxes's decree as recorded in Ezra 7, the date of that decree becomes important. The key to the date of the decree is tied to Artaxerxes's seventh year. Ezra 7:8 tells us that "Ezra arrived in Jerusalem in the fifth month of the seventh year of the king." Under conditions of a forced march, the Babylonian army could cover the 400 miles from Babylon to Jerusalem in one month. Ezra had a large body of slow moving people with him, and it took them five months to cover the same distance.

Fortunately, the dates for Artaxerxes's reign are well known and historically secure. They are based on several sources. First, Greek historians such as Herodotus preserved some of these dates in terms of their own dating system of Olympiads. Second, the astronomer Ptolemy who lived in Alexandria, Egypt, in the second century A.D., provided a table correlating the regnal years of certain rulers of the ancient world (the years that they reigned) with astronomical eclipses. This list is called Ptolemy's Canon, and it goes all the way back to the eighth century B.C. Some of those eclipses occurred during the reign of Artaxerxes and help to fix his dates. More recent archaeological discoveries have helped to refine the system provided by the Greek historians and the astronomer Ptolemy.

Third, the highest regnal dates on business tablets from Babylonia have been compiled from cuneiform texts; these extend from the seventh century B.C. to the first century A.D. Dates for the reign of Artaxerxes can be located in these tables. Finally, a series of papyri have been found in Egypt which bear two sets of dates—one using the Egyptian calendar and the other the Persian-Babylonian calendar. These papyri are letters and business documents written in Aramaic by Jews serving in the Persian army on the island of Elephantine in the Nile where they manned a Persian fort on Egypt's southern border. Since the Egyptian and the Persian-Babylonian calendars operated in different ways, these double dates serve as a check on each other and help to fix the regnal years of the kings during whose reigns they were written. Some of these documents come from the time Artaxerxes reigned and are an aid to confirming his regnal dates.

Thus there are four main lines of evidence which guide us in establishing the dates for Artaxerxes's reign—(1) the Greek historians, (2)

Ptolemy's Canon, (3) the Babylonian business tablets, and (4) the Elephantine papyri from Egypt. All four lines of evidence point to the same chronological conclusion: Xerxes died in 465 B.C., and Artaxerxes came to the throne in the latter part of that same year. Under the Persian and Babylonian system of counting regnal years, the remainder of the year in which a king died was considered to be Year 0 of the new king who succeeded him. It was called his "accession year." The new king's first official year began with the next new year which commenced in the spring. According to this reckoning, Artaxerxes's seventh year began in the spring of 458 B.C. and ended in the spring of 457 B.C. Thus by the Persian calendar Ezra would have begun his journey from Babylon in the spring of 458 B.C. and arrived in Jerusalem in the summer of that same year.

The Jews, however, considered the new year to begin in the fall according to the civil calendar by which they kept track of the reigns of their kings and those of other nations. (The Jews also used a religious calendar which began the year at a different time, much like our modern fiscal year often begins in July while the regular calendar year begins in January.) Thus by the Jewish civil calendar, Artaxerxes's seventh year would have begun in the fall of 458 B.C. and ended in the fall of 457 B.C. By this reckoning, Ezra would have begun his journey to Jerusalem in the spring of 457 B.C., arriving there in the summer of the same year. Since Ezra used the Jewish civil calendar, not the Persian calendar, we should apply his date—457 B.C.—to the decree Artaxerxes made regarding the rebuilding of Jerusalem rather than 458 B.C. as the Persians would have considered it. This date, 457 B.C., gives us the starting point for the prophecy of the seventy weeks given in Daniel 9:24.

To recap, this is how we arrive at the starting date for Daniel's seventy weeks which was to begin with a decree to rebuild Jerusalem:

- Of the four decrees mentioned in the books of Ezra and Nehemiah regarding the return of the Jews to Jerusalem, the third one, the one Artaxerxes gave to Ezra, is the one that fulfills most closely the specification of the prophecy in Daniel.
- Ezra 7:8 ties this decree to Artaxerxes's seventh year.

- From a variety of ancient documents, we can date Artaxerxes's seventh year to the year that overlaps what we know as 458 and 457 B.C.
- We then apply the Jewish calendar to that date and see that Ezra's journey occurred in 457 B.C. This process gives us the date of 457 B.C. for the commencement of the seventy prophetic weeks of Daniel 9.

THE FIRST 69 WEEKS AND THE ANOINTING OF THE MESSIAH

Daniel's prophecy divides the seventy weeks into different portions. The first time period covers sixty-nine weeks (seven weeks + sixty-two weeks) at which time the Messiah, "the Anointed One" (Daniel 9:25), is to come. The noun *Messiah* comes from a verb which means "to anoint." Thus, literally, a "Messiah" was an Anointed One. Gabriel tells Daniel, "Know and understand this: From the issuing of the decree to restore and rebuild Jerusalem until the Anointed One, the ruler, comes, there will be seven 'sevens,' and sixty-two 'sevens' " (verse 25). Sixty-nine weeks is 483 days (7 x 69 = 483). According to the year-for-a-day principle discussed above, each of those days should be understood as a literal year of actual time. Beginning the 483 years in 457 B.C. with the commencement of the seventy weeks, brings us down to A.D. 27 for their ending point (there is no Year 0 in calculating dates from B.C. to A.D.). At this time "the Anointed One, the ruler" is to come.

What does it mean for the Messiah, the Anointed One, to come? What event are we to look for in A.D. 27? Messiah's birth? His death? Something else?

When did Jesus of Nazareth become the Messiah? Since *Messiah* means "the Anointed One," Jesus became the Messiah, technically speaking, when He was anointed. When was this? He did not have oil poured over His head like the Old Testament kings and priests in Jerusalem. But was there a specific occasion when He was anointed and formally began His public ministry? Yes. This occurred at His baptism by John in the Jordan River when He was anointed by the Holy Spirit (see Matthew 3:13–17). God the Father was present on that occasion and marked it by His own pronouncement, "This is my Son, whom I love; with him I am well pleased" (verse 17).

Luke tells us that John the Baptist began his ministry in the fifteenth year of Tiberius Caesar (see Luke 3:1). Augustus, Tiberius's adoptive father, died in A.D. 14. Adding fifteen years to this date, we arrive at A.D. 29, not A.D. 27—two years too late for Daniel's prophecy. But there is a further factor here. Two years before Augustus died, the Roman Senate voted Tiberius co-ruler of the provinces with his father Augustus. Such an arrangement is called a co-regency and is similar to the situation when King David put Solomon on the throne with him before his own death (see 1 Kings 1).

Judea was among the provinces that came under the joint rule of Tiberius with Augustus in A.D. 12. Thus the events involving Jesus of Nazareth as the Messiah, which occurred in the Roman province of Judea, can reasonably be dated according to this arrangement by which Tiberius began to rule with his father in A.D. 12. Adding Luke's fifteen years of Tiberius's reign to this date brings us to the year A.D. 27 for the Messiah's public inauguration as Daniel's prophecy predicted.

Thus the prophetic details as we have seen them so far (we will discuss the seven weeks, or forty-nine years, later in this chapter) can be illustrated by the following chart:

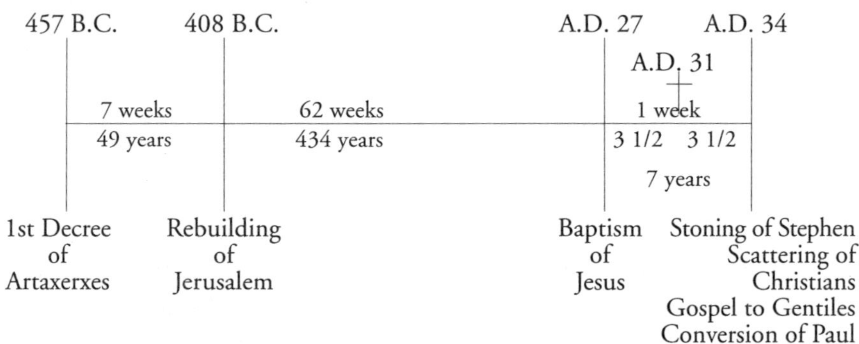

THE END OF THE SEVENTIETH WEEK

We have established 457 B.C. as the beginning date for Daniel's seventy weeks. We have seen that the sixty-nine weeks, or 483 years, ended in A.D. 27 with Jesus' baptism. The next questions become: When did the seventy weeks end, and what event marked its termination?

Seventy prophetic weeks equal 490 prophetic days or literal years. Simple addition tells us that if we add 490 years to 457 B.C. we reach A.D. 34. What happened in A.D. 34 to mark the conclusion of the seventy weeks? This date is too late for the crucifixion and resurrection of Jesus which took place three or four years earlier. Some other event must be considered.

The stoning of Stephen, described in Acts 7, is an event that has attracted considerable attention as marking the end of the seventy weeks—both for its theological significance as well as its timing. The narrative records no specific date for Stephen's death, but indirect evidence places it in A.D. 34. How do we arrive at this conclusion?

The estimated date for Stephen's martyrdom is based on the career of the apostle Paul. He was still unconverted at Stephen's death, since he stood by and held the coats of those who stoned him (see Acts 7:58). A short time later, Saul left for Damascus to persecute Christians there. On the way to Damascus he was converted from Saul the Pharisee to Paul the Christian apostle (see Acts 9:1–9). If Paul's conversion can be dated, the stoning of Stephen can also be placed within narrow limits.

In Galatians 1, Paul gives some biographical details about his career as an apostle, referring especially to his visits to Jerusalem. He made only brief and infrequent visits to Jerusalem, and he gives us some chronological information about them. He says the first visit came three years after his conversion (see verse 18); the second occurred fourteen years after the first (see Galatians 2:1). Then shortly after his second visit to Jerusalem, Paul left on his second missionary journey which took him to Corinth (see Acts 18). While at Corinth, Paul appeared before the proconsul Gallio (see verse 12). So Paul would have stood before Gallio seventeen years following his conversion (fourteen years between his second and first visit to Jerusalem added to the three years between his first Jerusalem visit and his conversion). From an inscription found in Corinth, we know that Gallio's one-year proconsulship in Corinth occurred in A.D. 51. If the seventeen years for Paul's two visits to Jerusalem are subtracted from the date of Paul's appearance before Gallio, then his conversion and Stephen's stoning should be dated to A.D. 34. This date, A.D. 34, is the one New Testament scholars commonly favor for Stephen's death and Paul's conversion. We can't be so precise as to determine the month or day, but it is a close estimate for the year itself.

Thus this book takes the position that Daniel's seventy weeks came to an end in A.D. 34 with the stoning of Stephen and the conversion of Paul. We have already discussed the theological significance of Stephen's death in the context of the last phrase of Daniel 9:24 (see above). There we said there were four areas of theological significance related to Stephen's martyrdom: (1) the group to whom Stephen gave his final speech—the Sanhedrin, the highest religious body in the land; (2) the form of his speech—a covenant lawsuit speech like those given by Old Testament prophets; (3) the prophetic nature of his experience at the time of his death when he looked up in vision into heaven itself; and (4) the fact that Paul's conversion has its roots in Stephen's death, so that Paul, the apostle to the Gentiles, takes the place of Stephen the powerful preacher to Israel. For these reasons, Stephen's death at the end of the seventy weeks can be seen as a highly significant point of transition from the era of Israel as the elect nation of God to the era of the church.

THE SEVEN WEEKS

Daniel 9:25 goes on to say, "It [Jerusalem] will be rebuilt with streets and a trench, but in times of trouble." We cannot date specifically from history the completion of this phase of Jerusalem's rebuilding, but it is clear from the books of Ezra and Nehemiah that this construction took place in a troubled time. When Ezra returned, he started rebuilding the city, but the western Persian governors soon intervened and got the work stopped (see Ezra 4:7–12). When Nehemiah took up the project anew, his opponents wanted to assassinate him. He resisted their efforts and refused to interrupt his work on the city (see Nehemiah 4). Thus the rebuilding of Jerusalem certainly took place in a troubled time.

The prophecy seems to point to some event marking a completion of this first phase of construction in 408 B.C. at the end of the first seven weeks, or forty-nine years (see verse 25). We are not able to determine specifically what event would correspond to this part of the prophecy. The reason we cannot date this event specifically is that we do not possess any historical documents which deal with that matter. The historical records of the Old Testament end about 420 B.C. so they don't reach to

408 B.C. Neither do Josephus, 1 and 2 Maccabees, inscriptions, nor papyri deal directly with the events of that time. Here we need to be careful not to abuse an argument from silence as either supporting or opposing the prophecy. The lack of documentation for a particular period is not negative evidence against a certain event happening. Neither is it positive evidence that some other event happened. It is simply neutral and presents us with a historical vacuum on that point. The prophecy should be judged and interpreted according to the points for which we do possess historical documentation—not upon those points where it is lacking. We have an abundance of evidence dealing with 457 B.C. and A.D. 27, and we have good indirect evidence dealing with A.D. 34. Our lack of direct evidence dealing with 408 B.C. does not negate these other points, and certainly this period was a troubled time—as the prophecy predicted. Future discoveries may fill in this vacuum, but for the present we must rest content with the evidence currently available.

THE CUTTING OFF OF THE ANOINTED ONE

Daniel 9:26 begins by saying, "After the sixty-two 'sevens,' the Anointed One will be cut off." These sixty-two weeks, first mentioned in verse 25, follow the first seven weeks and comprise the second interval of prophetic time within the seventy weeks. Thus the sixty-two weeks conclude with the end of the sixty-ninth week of the seventy-week prophecy.

But verse 26 says "*after* the sixty-two 'sevens' " (emphasis supplied), thus taking us slightly *beyond* the end of the sixty-ninth week. In other words, the Anointed One is not cut off right at the point at which the sixty-two weeks end, but slightly beyond that point. The specific use of the Hebrew word for "after" emphasizes this.

Where are we if we are just beyond the end of the sixty-ninth week? The answer is quite evident: We are in the seventieth week. Verse 26 does not specify exactly where in that week the Anointed One is to be cut off. That detail comes up in verse 27.

As we saw earlier, the sixty-nine weeks come to an end in A.D. 27 when the Messiah appeared to officially begin His public ministry. Sometime after the commencement of that ministry He was to be "cut off." The verb translated "cut off" is used here as a Hebrew idiom which means "to be killed." To be cut off is to be cut off from the land of the living, to die (see Genesis 9:11). But the verb here is in the passive form, meaning that the Anointed One is not going to die of His own volition; somebody is going to do this to Him. He is going to *be* cut off, *be* killed. This stipulation of the prophecy was fulfilled when the religious leaders of Judea conspired with the Roman governmental authorities to have Jesus of Nazareth crucified like a common criminal (see Matthew 27:1, 2).

In the Old Testament, we have two strands of messianic prophecies delineating Messiah's fate. One kind tells of His glorious reign (see Zechariah 9:9). The other describes a Messiah who will suffer and even die (see Isaiah 53:7–9). How are we to understand the relative sequence of these two types of prophecies?

Many Jews of Jesus' time expected the prophecy of a victorious, ruling Messiah to be fulfilled first and in their day. He would cast off the hated Roman yoke from Jewish shoulders. In the experience of Jesus of Nazareth, however, these prophecies developed in a different sequence. First the cross, then the crown. First His suffering, death, and resurrection, then the establishment of the glorious future kingdom at His second advent. One we look back to, one we still anticipate. Daniel 9, with its precise chronological sequence, is a major link that helps establish the true biblical order of the Messiah's works.

THE MESSIAH REJECTED

The next phrase of this prophecy in verse 26 is a short—but difficult—one. The NIV translates it: "The Anointed One . . . will have nothing." This a good translation because the phrase in the original language has to do with possession. Literally the Hebrew words mean "There shall not be [X] to/for him." Notice that the direct object is missing from this phrase, as has been indicated by the X in the translation above. The indirect object, *him,* is present and refers clearly to the Messiah, the Anointed One. But what is it that will not be to or for Him? The NIV, the RSV, and other versions supply the word, *thing,* making the phrase mean, "There shall be no*thing* for him." That would be a prophetic picture of the Messiah's poverty. Certainly Jesus of Nazareth had few, if any, material possessions beyond the clothes He wore. He Himself said, "Foxes have holes and birds of the air have nests, but the Son of Man has no place to lay his head" (Matthew 8:20).

It may be suggested, however, that there is something more important to God, and His Messiah, than mere material possessions. People are of greater importance to God, than their possessions. In fact, the next phrase of the prophecy in Daniel 9:26 places its stress on people: "The people of the ruler who will come. . . ." Thus it seems that missing word is better supplied by the word, *people,* than the word, *thing*. Thus we can translate this phrase: "There shall not be people for him," or more freely, "No one shall be for him."

This is a picture of rejection, not poverty. And this rejection takes place at a particular time, at the time when He was to be cut off. This is not a general rejection floating freely in time; it is a specific rejection occurring at the time of His death. This rejection was fulfilled in the experience of Jesus of Nazareth. When He went to the cross, He did so because the religious leaders and the tide of public opinion had turned against Him. The fickle crowd turned away from the popular enthusiasm they had displayed in favor of Jesus earlier during the final week of His ministry (see Matthew 21:1–11). Now, with equal enthusiasm, they shouted in favor of the death sentence against Him (see Matthew 27:20–26). His own disciples who stood about the foot of the cross did not understand what this was all about. Even after the cross they murmured, "We had hoped that he was the one who was going to redeem Israel" (Luke 24:21). At the time of Jesus' death, "no one was for him."

MORE DESTRUCTION

The next phrase of the prophecy in Daniel 9:26 shifts the focus from the Messiah to the Jewish people and what will happen to them. "The people of the ruler who will come will destroy the city and the sanctuary." Verse 26 begins with a prophecy of Jerusalem's reconstruction and ends with a prophecy of its re-destruction! Enclosed within these two historical poles and their extension in prophetic time lies the career of the Messiah. After that career was over, at some later point not specified, the city was to revert to ruins like those which Nebuchadnezzar had left behind when he conquered Jerusalem in 586 B.C.

The Romans accomplished this re-destruction of the city when they conquered and destroyed Jerusalem in A.D. 70. Visitors to the city today can still see the results of the Babylonian destruction of 586 B.C. in the archaeological garden on the eastern slope of Mount Ophel. Those same tourists can see the effects of the Roman destruction in A.D. 70 in the archaeological excavations around the southern retaining wall of the temple complex and in the archaeological museum nearby known as the Burnt House. These remains give vivid evidence of the destruction prophesied by Daniel. It can also be seen on the Arch of Titus in Rome where the booty taken from Judea, including the lampstand, or Menorah, from the sanctuary is depicted in sculpted stone relief.

Who are the "people of the ruler [or "prince," Hebrew: *nagid*]" who carried out this destruction? The Romans clearly destroyed Jerusalem in A.D. 70, so it has been suggested that this verse refers to the Roman people, or army, and that the "ruler" must refer either to the Roman general who led the army against Jerusalem or to the Caesar who ordered the attack. This generalization, however, fails to take into account some of the specific language used here.

The word used here for "prince" or "ruler," is *nagid,* the same word used in verse 25 for "the Anointed One, the ruler," also known as Messiah, the Prince. Note the following pattern of word use in this prophecy:

verse 25	Messiah	*nagid*
verse 26a	Messiah	—
verse 26b	—	*nagid*

In verse 25, the designation, "Messiah *nagid,*" forms a word pair—"the Anointed One, the ruler"—so that the two words are linked in a technical way. Verse 26a breaks the word pair apart and uses the first word of the pair. Then verse 26b uses the second word of the pair. This pattern suggests that all three references are to the same Messiah Prince designated by the first occurrence of this word pair in verse 25. If so, then "the people of the ruler who will come" refers to the people of the Messiah. It is they who are going to destroy Jerusalem and the sanctuary. The Messiah was a Jewish figure, and thus His people must be the Jewish people of that time. This same point is emphasized here by the use of the word "people" instead of the more correct military term "host" or "army."

If this interpretation is correct, in what sense did the people of the Jewish Messiah Prince destroy the city and the sanctuary in A.D. 70?

The Roman army was indeed the physical agent which brought about the literal destruction of Jerusalem. But why did they destroy it? They did so because Judea had rebelled against Rome. If Judea had not rebelled, the Roman army would never have come there and Jerusalem would have been spared. We are dealing here with causes and resulting events. The cause of Jerusalem's destruction was the Jewish rebellion; the event which resulted from that rebellion was the destruction of the city and its temple. In that sense, it can be said that the people of the Jewish Messiah Prince caused or brought about the destruction of Jerusalem in A.D. 70.

The final phrase of verse 26 amplifies the picture of that war and its consequences. "The end will come like a flood: War will continue until the end, and desolations have been decreed." The figurative language of a flood is a very apt description for the way the Roman army finally flowed into Jerusalem to conquer it. Isaiah described the assault of the Assyrian army in similar language: "Therefore the Lord is about to bring against them the mighty flood waters of the River—the king of Assyria with all his pomp. It will overflow all its channels, run over all its banks and sweep on into Judah, swirling over it, passing through it and reaching up to the neck. Its outspread wings will cover the breadth of your land, O Immanuel!" (Isaiah 8:7, 8). In the same way, Daniel prophesies, the Roman army will overflow Jerusalem and its temple like a flood. Jerusalem's northern wall was always the weakest of its defenses because there were valleys on the other three sides of the city. It was at this northern wall that the Roman troops finally penetrated the defenses bringing desolation that is still well revealed today by the archaeologist's spade.

CONFIRMING THE COVENANT

In some ways, the last verse of Daniel 9 is the most difficult of the chapter. It begins with two more statements about the work of the Messiah and then shifts back again to the work of Rome, the desolater.

Verse 27 makes two predictions concerning the Messiah. The first states, "He will confirm a covenant with many for one 'seven.' " This does not refer to the inception of a new covenant; it refers instead to an attempt to strengthen or renew a covenant already in existence. When

Hebrew writers wanted to refer to the inception of a new covenant, they used the verb "to cut" to express that action. "To cut" a covenant was to make a new covenant. But that is not the verb used here in verse 27. It says, instead, that the covenant would be "confirmed," meaning "made strong," or "strengthened." The verb used here is related to the Hebrew word for "a strong man," a "warrior."

This strengthening or reconfirming of an already-existing covenant refers to the covenant that was currently in force between God and Israel. It is not the offer of the New Covenant to the church. This strengthening, or confirming, of the covenant was God's final offer and call to the people of Israel as His elect people. This offer was made to them through Jesus, the Messiah. Jesus described to them what they could have had. His Sermon on the Mount at the beginning of His ministry was based upon an amplification of the Old Covenant. Taking several of the commandments of the Old Covenant and amplifying them, Jesus showed that they penetrate to the motives of the heart (see Matthew 5:17–48). Jesus was the true messenger of the covenant. Unfortunately, His hearers did not fully accept this great view of what Israel might have been under the Messiah's covenant leadership. It was this failure to grasp all that God was holding out to them that caused Jesus to weep bitterly over Jerusalem during the last week of His earthly ministry (Matthew 23:37–39).

THE END OF THE SACRIFICIAL SYSTEM

The second prediction of Daniel 9:27 foretold the end of the sacrificial system. Physically, the temple and its offerings came to an end when the Romans destroyed Jerusalem in A.D. 70. But that is not what this phrase of the prophecy is talking about because it gives a time frame for the end of the sacrifices and offerings that does not extend to A.D. 70.

Verse 27 begins by saying that Messiah would confirm the offer of the Old Covenant for one week. As we have seen from the dates worked out above, that week extended from the beginning of Jesus' public ministry in A.D. 27 to the stoning of Stephen in A.D. 34. The interesting thing about the duration of this seventieth week is that it extends beyond the Cross, thus showing the gracious mercy of God whose voice of invitation went out to His elect people even after His Son was crucified. Not until the deacon-prophet Stephen brought God's covenant lawsuit before the Sanhedrin did Israel's day as God's elect people pass. Individual Jews are still accepted by God on the basis of the life, death, and work of Jesus the Messiah, but national Israel is no longer God's elect nation. That time has passed. The church, spiritual Israel, gathered from all nations of the earth, now occupies that position (see Galatians 3:28, 29; Romans 9:6–8).

The second phrase of verse 27 says "in the middle of the 'seven' he will put an end to sacrifice and offering." The week referred to here is the seventieth week mentioned earlier in the same verse. We have seen that the seventieth week extended from A.D. 27 to A.D. 34. Thus the ending of the sacrifice and offering in the middle of that week should be located in A.D. 31.

Who is the one putting an end to these sacrifices and offerings? The antecedent to "He" is the Messiah Prince, not a Roman ruler. True, the Romans caused the direct physical cessation of the temple and its sacrifices by their destruction of the temple in A.D. 70. But even more important was the spiritual end of the sacrifices in the theological sense that they were no longer necessary after the death of Jesus. He Himself was the Passover lamb (see 1 Corinthians 5:7). With His death, the type of all of the Old Testament sacrifices met their antitype. They were no longer necessary. God signified this by rending the veil in the temple at the time that Jesus died (see Matthew 27:51). Thus, in the sense of Daniel 9:27, the sacrifices came to an end in A.D. 31 when Jesus died on the cross.

One question that arises here is: When did Jesus die? He died in the midst of the final week which we have dated to A.D. 27–34. Thus the mid-point of that week is A.D. 31. Can we prove beyond a shadow of doubt that Jesus died in A.D. 31?

Not yet. The problem is the precision that is required to establish such a date. At first glance, it appears to be a simple problem: just find a year within the range of A.D. 25–35 on which the Passover date of Nisan 14 fell on a Friday, which is the day on which the Gospels place the crucifixion and death of Jesus (see Luke 23:54–56). To work on this problem, two sets of tables are necessary: (1) a table of new moon dates, and (2) a table with the Julian day number equivalent of these new moon dates. In other words, one must first work out the date for the Passover according to the Jewish lunar calendar in effect in Jesus' time, and then one must consult the appropriate tables to determine what day of the week that was.

The problem lies in attaining the precision necessary to pin down this date to a single year to the exclusion of all others. This requires astronomical, observational, and historical accuracy to within less than one twenty-four-hour period. Historically, the Gospels themselves still leave questions. The Synoptic Gospels appear to date the Passover meal Jesus ate with His disciples to Thursday night of the Passion Week (see Matthew 26:2–19; Mark 14:1–16; Luke 22:1–15). John, on the other hand, appears to imply that on that year Passover fell on Friday (John 18:28; 19:14). How do we reconcile these accounts?

One suggestion is that John was calculating his date using the Roman reckoning in which the new day began at midnight, while the Synoptic writers were calculating the date using the Jewish method of beginning the day at sunset. But there may be more to it than that.

To determine the day of Passover, it is astronomically necessary to determine when the first crescent of the new moon could have been seen in Judea. Computer programs designed to make these types of calculations have been getting better and better. With these new programs, it is now possible to determine that Nisan 14 could easily have fallen on a Thursday night in A.D. 31. It is more doubtful that the date could be stretched to a Friday night that year.

Observationally, we also need to know what atmospheric conditions were like to observe the sky on those nights. Just because a new moon mathematically *should* have been visible does not mean that conditions were optimal to observe it visually. If they were not, the official beginning of the lunar month was delayed by a day. In Jesus' time, the lunar calendar of the Jews was also complicated by the fact that it was necessary to insert an extra, or thirteenth, month every third year or so to keep the lunar year in line with the solar year.

The variability of all these factors demonstrate why it is difficult to date the Passover of Jesus' death with precision. Without going into further detail, we can fairly say that all these factors narrow the historical choice down to either A.D. 30 or 31. Since the latter choice correlates best with the dates for the other historical points for the prophecy of Daniel 9, we have utilized A.D. 31 as the year in the spring of which Jesus was crucified.

THE FALL OF ROME

The final statement of this entire prophecy of Daniel 9:24–27 comes in the last half of verse 27. Following the literal word order, the original Hebrew of this prediction states: "Upon the wing of abomination [shall come] the desolater, until the end that is decreed is poured out on him." The first part of this translation is my own; the last part comes directly from the NIV. In the NIV, the first part of the sentence contains some additional words which the translators have added in an attempt to make sense out of the verse. But by doing so, they have obscured the meaning further.

"Upon the wing of" should be seen as an idiom which means to follow closely. In other words, the abominations come first, followed quickly by the desolation. The desolation was caused by the Roman army after its conquest of Jerusalem. The abominations were those things going on in Jerusalem preceding its destruction and desolation. As the Roman troops broke through the northern defenses of the city, one contingent of Judean troops retreated into the very temple building itself. It was a strong, substantial structure and therefore made a good final fortress. This required the Roman soldiers to attack the temple building even though their general wished to spare it. In the ensuing fight, the temple caught fire and burned. It was never God's purpose that His temple would be turned into a fortress for fighting in war, and to do so introduced the ultimate in secular abominations into that holy space. After that abominable course of action came the destruction and desolation, exactly as the prophecy described.

But the Romans themselves were not to go unpunished either. God permitted these events to occur because the people of Judea forsook His divine protection by their rejection of the Messiah. The Roman troops were, therefore, instruments of God's judgment at the time. The same type of thing occurred in the Old Testament when Assyria was permitted to conquer Samaria, but then received its own just judgment (see Nahum). In the same way, Babylon was permitted to conquer Jerusalem, but was later to receive its own just judgment (see Jeremiah 50; 51). Now the Romans were permitted to carry out the same kind of judgment upon Jerusalem, but Rome, too, was to be judged. That was also the message of some of the other prophecies of Daniel—that Rome would have its day upon the stage of history, but like the other powers that preceded it, Rome would also fall (see Daniel 2:40–44; 7:7, 8, 23, 24; 8:25). Thus the title of Gibbon's famous work of history, *The Decline and Fall of the Roman Empire,* actually illustrates the fulfillment of the final prophetic statement in Daniel 9.

SUMMARY

In summarizing the contents of this prophecy, we should focus our attention on the various aspects of the work of the Messiah that it outlines. These may be seen as follows:

1. Daniel 9:24c—He would make the great atonement.
2. Daniel 9:24d—That atonement would bring in everlasting righteousness.
3. Daniel 9:24f—The heavenly sanctuary would be anointed for the commencement of His high priestly work.
4. Daniel 9:25—The date for the coming of the Messiah.
5. Daniel 6:26a—The Messiah killed.
6. Daniel 9:26b—The Messiah rejected at His death.
7. Daniel 9:27a—The Messiah makes the final great offer of the Old Covenant to Israel.
8. Daniel 9:27b—The Messiah brings the sacrificial system to an end.

If we take all eight of these points and boil them down into one image, a central picture results. That picture is one of the Messiah as *sacrifice.* His death, His rejection at His death, the date for His death, and the manifold results of His death are featured prominently in this prophecy. Those results include atonement and righteousness, an end of the sacrificial system, and a beginning of a new priesthood in the heavenly sanctuary. This picture of the Messiah as sacrifice is a prelude and vital introduction to the prophecies of Daniel 8 and 7 that flow in reverse order from chapter 9. Daniel 9 forms a presupposition for the later events contained in those prophecies.

CHAPTER EIGHT

CHRIST AS PRIEST

Daniel 8 presents the prophetic preview, from Daniel's point in time, of two great conflicts to come. The first of these pitted Persia against Greece. In the vision, the prophet saw each of these two powers represented by an animal. A ram symbolized Persia (8:3, 20) and a goat symbolized Greece (vss. 5, 21). The clash between these two powers was represented by head-to-head combat between the two animals. Greece won, and the Persian ram was cast down to the ground and trampled upon by the goat (vss. 6, 7).

The second great conflict present in Daniel 8 pitted Rome against the forces of heaven. Rome was represented by the symbol of a little horn (vs. 9). Historically speaking, Rome existed in two major phases. There was the classical or Imperial phase—the Rome of the Caesars. Later came the religious or spiritual phase—the Rome of the popes. While the prophecy symbolizes both phases of Rome, the emphasis is upon the second phase.

According to the vision, a special target of contention between these two powers was to be the sanctuary or temple in heaven (vs. 11). Obviously, there is no physical way for an earthly power to attack a heavenly structure. The attack is spiritual, or theological, and that is what the symbols in the second half of this vision point toward. The challenge to the heavenly sanctuary is created by turning the attention of men and women to an earthly substitute, by turning their attention to religious rites in an earthly context which take the place of the true heavenly rites.

This struggle over the sanctuary was to go on for a prolonged period of time according to the time element connected with this prophecy—2,300 evenings-mornings, or days (vs. 14), which equal 2,300 historical years (see chapter 6 above). We are not shown the complete end of this phase of the conflict; that awaits the fuller picture of these events in Daniel 7. Chapter 8, however, does give us assurance that this conflict will be resolved in God's own prophetic time and in God's way.

THE PERSIAN RAM

In his introduction to this vision, Daniel says God gave it to him in the "third year of King Belshazzar" (8:1). In terms of our calendar, Belshazzar's third year equals approximately 548 B.C. Major changes were developing in the Near East at that time. Babylon was on the decline, and Persia was on the rise. In this vision, God showed Daniel just how far Persia would go. But even more, He also showed him the powers that would follow Persia.

The visions recorded earlier in Daniel came as dreams in the night. This was true of Nebuchadnezzar (2:1; 4:5), and it was true of Daniel (7:1). But the vision of chapter 8 comes to Daniel during the daytime. He seems to be in Susa, or Shushan, in the eastern province of Elam (vs. 2). This was the same place where the action of the book of Esther took place (Esther 1:2).

Elam was a border state between Babylonia and Persia. Sometimes it was under the control of Babylon; sometimes it was under the control of Persia. And at other times it was able to stand free and independent of both those powers.

In vision, Daniel seemed transported eastward from Babylon until he came to stand on the west bank of the Ulai river near Susa. He looked eastward across that river and saw a ram coming toward him from the east. It had two horns on its head, but they were uneven. The higher one came up later (vs. 3). Later, Gabriel, who was sent to Daniel to interpret the vision to him, explained this feature. "The two-horned ram that you saw represents the kings of Media and Persia" (vs. 20).

The Medes and the Persians were related peoples who occupied the Iranian plateau—the Medes in the north and the Persians in the south.

The Medes were the more powerful of the two, and they gave the Assyrians considerable difficulty on their eastern border from the ninth to the seventh centuries B.C. The royal houses of the Medes and Persians intermarried, and eventually, under Cyrus, the Persians became the stronger of the two. Cyrus conquered Media and incorporated it into his kingdom, hence the combined name of the Medo-Persian Empire (vss. 3, 20). This dual power is represented by the ram in this vision.

As Daniel watched, the ram charged off into three different directions. The accompanying statement makes it obvious that this represented conquests by this power: "No animal could stand against him, and none could rescue from his power" (vs. 4). The three directions of conquest were toward the north, the west, and the south. The major conquest of the Persians toward the north was the kingdom of Lydia in Anatolia or ancient Turkey. Cyrus conquered this area in 547 B.C. To the west, Persia, under Cyrus, conquered Babylon in 539 B.C. Daniel 5 and 6 refers to this event and its immediate consequences. To the south, Cyrus's son Cambyses conquered Egypt in 525 B.C. In this way the Medo-Persian Empire was extended in these three directions.

THE GREEK GOAT

Flushed with success, the Persian emperors tried to extend their conquests one step further in the north. They invaded Greece. Two different Persian kings, Darius I in 490 B.C. and Xerxes in 480 B.C., tried to subdue Greece. But after some initial successes, both were eventually turned back and had to return home. Thus ended the Persian attempts to conquer Greece.

But the Greek goat (vss. 5, 21) did not forget this national humiliation of a Persian invasion and the destruction they had wrought. Thus when the prophecy speaks about the eventual clash between these two powers it says that the goat ran at the ram "furiously" (vs. 6). Greece was out to even the score, and it did so—and then some. Alexander the Great defeated the Persians, and his victorious army marched all the way to the valley of the Indus River in northwestern India before returning.

All of this was symbolized by the actions of the goat in Daniel 8. In verse 21, Gabriel identifies the goat as Greece, adding, "The large horn between his eyes is the first king"—an obvious reference to Alexander. The rapidity of the Greek conquest is referred to by the symbolism of the goat flying across the earth (vs. 5). The defeat of the Persians and their last king, Darius III, is indicated by the way in which the goat treated the ram, "striking the ram and shattering his two horns. The ram was powerless to stand against him; the goat knocked him to the ground and trampled on him; and none could rescue the ram from his power" (vs. 7).

But Alexander did not live to enjoy the fruits of his conquests. At the young age of thirty-three, he died in Babylon after his return from India. His fate has been immortalized in a poem which contrasts his achievements with those of Jesus:

> Jesus and Alexander died at thirty-three.
> One lived and died for self,
> The other died for you and me.

The prophecy of Daniel 8 predicted Alexander's death. "The goat became very great, but at the height of his power his large horn was broken off" (v. 8). At the height of his powers and conquest, Alexander died in 323 B.C. He had a son, but this son did not inherit the kingdom (Dan. 11:4). Instead, Alexander's kingdom was divided among his generals. There was fighting among them for a period of about twenty years. But by 301 B.C., four kingdoms had emerged from the political chaos that ensued after the death of Alexander (8:8, 22). These were: (1) Macedonia under Cassander; (2) Thrace and northwestern Asia Minor under Lysimachus; (3) Syria and Babylonia under Seleucus; and (4) Egypt under Ptolemy. (These developments are depicted in a series of maps found in F. D. Nichol, ed., *The Seventh-day Adventist Bible Commentary,* vol. 4, pp. 824, 825.) These factions continued to battle back and forth, but the later prophecies of Daniel (chapter 11) came to concentrate on the struggles between the king of the north (Syria) and the king of the south (Egypt).

THE LITTLE HORN OF ROME—PHASE I

The four Hellenistic (Greek) kingdoms of the eastern Mediterranean region were represented in this prophecy by the four horns that came up in the place of Alexander's horn which was broken off (Daniel 8:8, 22). After they had been established, a new power came on the scene of action. This power was represented by a "small" horn" (vs. 9). Up to this point in the prophecy, the commentators have been relatively uniform in their interpretations of the symbols. For the most part, they follow the historical outline presented above. At this point in the vision, however, they diverge in a marked way.

One school of interpreters holds that the little horn represents an individual king, Antiochus IV Epiphanes, a Greek king of the Syrian kingdom. A second school of thought holds that this new horn represents Rome. The position taken in this volume follows the latter view. I have elaborated upon that view in chapter two of my book, *Selected Studies in Prophetic Interpretation*. Those who would like more details on this point can consult that work. (See also chapter 6.) Here, we can only note a few points in passing. There are seven reasons why Antiochus cannot be the small horn of Daniel 8. We will note three of the major ones.

First, the vision presents a progression in terms of the power utilized by the kingdoms involved. The Persian ram "magnified himself" (vs. 4, RSV). The Greek goat "magnified himself exceedingly" (vs. 8, RSV). The little horn then "magnified itself, even to the host of heaven . . . , even up to the prince of the host" (vss. 10, 11, RSV). This progression from the comparative to the superlative would be true in terms of the Roman Empire, but it would not be true in terms of an individual ruler such as Antiochus Epiphanes.

Second, Antiochus Epiphanes (175–163 B.C.) ruled in Syria about the *middle* of the Seleucid dynasty which lasted from 301 B.C until 64 B.C. He was the seventh king out of twenty-seven in the Seleucid dynasty. The little-horn power, however, appears on the scene of action "in the latter part of their reign" (vs. 23), that is, at the *latter* end of the rule of the four Greek kingdoms. In contrast, Rome did appear on the scene at the latter part of the rule of these four kingdoms, conquering each in turn—Greece in 168 B.C., Asia Minor in 133

B.C. (by inheritance), Syria in 64 B.C., and Egypt in 31 B.C. Thus Rome fulfills this characteristic of the vision, but Antiochus Epiphanes does not.

Third, we should note the direction of conquest specified by the vision. The little horn was to conquer to the east, the south, and the beautiful land (vs. 9). Antiochus IV had some success toward the south. In 169 B.C. he conquered the eastern half of the Egyptian delta. In 168 B.C. he came back to finish the job, but he was not able to do so. Instead he was turned back by a Roman ambassador and never returned to Egypt again. On his eastern campaign, Antiochus had some initial success, but he later died on this campaign. His record was even worse with regard to the "beautiful land," or Judea. When he came to the throne, this province belonged to his kingdom. But because of his persecution of the Jews, they rose up in revolt and threw off the Syrian yoke. In contrast to the vision, Antiochus Epiphanes did not conquer the "beautiful land," rather, he was the one responsible for losing it. Rome, on the other hand, made major conquests in all three of the directions specified by the vision. Here again, Rome fits the characteristics of the vision, but Antiochus does not.

Based on these reasons, we will take the position in this volume that the small horn in the vision of Daniel 8 represents Rome.

The first thing the small horn did after its appearance was to make conquests toward the east, the south, and the "beautiful land." These, as we have seen, correspond to the territorial conquests of Imperial Rome. In terms of conquering the four Greek horns, Rome conquered to the east in 168 and 133 B.C.; it conquered the "beautiful land" of Judea at the same time it conquered Syria in 63 B.C.; and it conquered Egypt to the south in 31 B.C.

THE LITTLE HORN OF ROME—PHASE II

The territorial conquests to the east, south, and the beautiful land in Daniel 8:9 represent territorial conquests by *Imperial* Rome. With verse 10, however, a transition takes place. The small horn of Rome has a new target, but it is not on earth. It is in heaven. The next three verses identify the targets of the small horn as the "starry host" of heaven (vs. 10), the "Prince" who leads that host (vs. 11), and the sanctuary in heaven along with the service carried on there (vss. 11, 12). This transition from horizontal earthly conquests to a vertical assault on heaven is referred to as the vertical dimension of apocalyptic.

This vertical dimension of apocalyptic also heralds a new phase of the work of the little horn. Conquest of territory in the east, south, and beautiful land is a military-political type of activity. An attack upon heaven, even if it is described in symbolic terms, is a distinctively religious activity. Thus with this phase of the work of the little horn the prophecy has entered upon its religious phase.

The vertical dimension of apocalyptic is demonstrated in this passage both by the verbs of motion used and also by the targets of the little horn's activity. "It grew until it reached the host of the heavens, and it threw some of the starry host down to the earth and trampled on them" (vs. 10). The symbolic actions depicted here operate in two opposite directions. The little horn reaches *up* to heaven, which is the vertical dimension, and then he throws *down* the stars to the earth in the other direction. But he is not content with merely throwing the stars down to the earth; he goes on to trample upon them, crushing them.

In this vision, the stars are not symbols for angels as they are in some other Bible symbolism. This does not refer to the casting down of Satan and a third of the angels at the time of his original rebellion. That occurred long before the historical action portrayed here was carried out by this religious power. Revelation 12:7–9 places the casting down of Satan and his angels back at the beginning of his great controversy with God. Nor did Satan trample on his angels, for he needed them to carry out his purposes. The casting down of the stars, spoken of here in Daniel 8:10, is explained in vs. 24, "He will destroy the mighty men and the holy people." The saints of the Most High are the targets of the little horn, and that tells us that the little horn was to be a persecuting power. The saints are compared to stars elsewhere in Daniel; when they finally emerge victorious, "they will shine like the brightness of the heavens" (Daniel 12:3).

Of course Imperial Rome *did* persecute Christians from time to time—first on a local basis and later on an empire-wide basis. But persecution was carried out for a longer time and to a greater extent by religious Rome under the papacy. The list of these persecutions is extensive.

The Crusades of the eleventh through the thirteenth centuries against "infidels" in the Middle East were holy wars directed by the papacy. From these, the idea of crusades against Christian "heretics" was developed, leading to attacks on the Albigenses in southern France and the Waldenses in northern Italy in the thirteenth century.

A later form of the inquisition was developed in Spain. And since Spain controlled a considerable portion of the New World, the inquisition was exported to Latin America where it was carried on until the early nineteenth century. Testimony to this fact is the Museum of the Inquisition in Lima, Peru, housed in the actual building in which this type of persecution was carried out. From Spain, this type of activity was also exported to Holland where the Duke of Alva led the Spanish troops in suppressing and killing Dutch Protestants in 1568.

France also saw aggressive action against Protestants. Thousands of Huguenots fell on St. Bartholomew's Day in 1572. Again, when the French king revoked the Edict of Toleration in 1685, many of the Huguenots had to flee to other countries. All this activity correlates well with the type of persecution which the little horn is said to carry out by casting down to the ground the stars, or the saints of the Most High, and trampling upon them (vs. 10).

The vision next brings to view a chief opponent of the little horn; he is known as the "Prince of the host" (vs. 11). The little horn "set itself up to be as great as the Prince of the host" (vs 11), but was not able to do any harm to him personally, although it was able to harm His followers. The word translated, *Prince,* is a political title, but in this chapter it is used in a priestly way. To Him belongs the sanctuary and the *tamid,* or daily service that went on there. This is indicated by the personal pronouns used with those objects. "The place of *his* [the Prince's] sanctuary was brought low" (vs. 11, emphasis supplied). The Hebrew verb used here means "to throw or cast down."

The word used for "Prince" is also a messianic term. We found the Messiah Prince mentioned in Daniel 9:25, 26 in the prophecy about the Messiah in relation to His people in the Promised Land. The word used here for "Prince" (*sar*) is a different Hebrew word than that used in

Daniel 9 (*nagid*). This usage in Daniel 8 reflects the Prince's heavenly position. The name or title for God is not used in this chapter. In this chapter, the Prince is the chief protagonist on God's side. Thus this Prince can be compared to the heavenly Michael who elsewhere in Daniel (10:13, 21; 12:1) is mentioned as a prince (_*ar*).

As the religious phase of Rome, the little horn has attacked the saints and has been able to harm some of them. He has challenged the Messiah Prince, Jesus Christ, in His heavenly setting, but he has not been able to do any harm to Him. He does, however, attack His sanctuary. It is cast down to the earth and is trampled upon (vs. 13). The Hebrew verb used for this casting down is *shalak*. The NIV translation, "brought low," does not capture the strength of this verb. It is commonly used for throwing a stone or a similar action. In this case, the translation, "cast down" (KJV and the NKJV), is to be preferred.

What does it mean for the heavenly sanctuary to be cast down to earth and trampled upon? Clearly, this is not a literal, physical casting down. There is no elevator between heaven and earth upon which the sanctuary building can go up and down. This is symbolic action. What would it mean to bring a heavenly sanctuary down to earth? It means that what was correctly represented as being located in heaven has now, in the eyes of human beings, been brought down here where we are by the activities of the little horn. The small horn now represents the heavenly ministry of Jesus Christ as requiring human or priestly activities on earth to mediate its grace to humanity. Human intermediaries have been interjected between God and the people. One of the central issues of the Reformation was a rejection of this very point. Martin Luther claimed that every Christian has immediate access to Christ's ministry in heaven. Each individual may have personal access to Jesus Christ and God; human, priestly intermediaries are not necessary for such access. "For there is one God and one mediator between God and men, the man Christ Jesus" (1 Timothy 2:5). This leaves no room for the mediation of priests, saints, angels, or Mary—as in the Roman system.

The final act carried out by the little horn against the sanctuary was to attempt to control the "daily" or "continual" ministry that goes on there. The NIV says the little horn "took away the daily sacrifice from him [the Prince]" (vs. 11). In actuality, the verb is in the passive: It "was taken away from him" (RSV). The clear implication, of course, is that it was the little horn that did this. More importantly, many versions, including the NIV, have supplied the word *sacrifice* here in connection with the word *daily*. Elsewhere in the Old Testament, this Hebrew word *tamid* (daily) is used as a modifier, referring to something that goes on daily, continually, or constantly. Here, however, the word is used as a noun; no word follows it for it to modify. Many Bible versions have supplied the word *sacrifice* because *tamid,* "daily," is sometimes used to modify the offering or sacrifice that was burnt daily on the altar in the courtyard of the earthly sanctuary (Exodus 29:38, 42). But *tamid* was also used to modify a number of other activities carried on in the sanctuary. It was used for the burning of the lamps of the seven-branched lampstand (Exodus 27:20–21), for the burning of incense on the altar of incense (Exodus 30:8), and for the bread of the Presence on the table of shewbread (Exodus 25:30). It was also used for other activities connected with the sanctuary (Exodus 28:29, 38; 1 Chronicles 16:6).

It is necessary then to translate *tamid* with a word that comprehends all of these activities connected with the sanctuary, not just the one idea of sacrifice. A word that is more broad and inclusive, encompassing all of these activities, is "ministry." All these activities which *tamid* is used to describe are activities carried out by the priest in the courtyard and the holy place of the sanctuary. They were part of his daily ministry there. It is this type of ministry that Jesus carries out in the heavenly sanctuary (see Hebrews 8:1) and which the little horn power attempted to counterfeit. It attempted to turn the eyes of mankind from Jesus' true, original ministry in heaven to an earthly, human substitute. That is the *tamid* which the little horn power attempted to take over and control.

It ultimately failed in this attempt, however, for the true heavenly ministry of Jesus continued. Eventually, by means of the Reformation and subsequent events, the eyes of people were again directed to Jesus' ministry in the heavenly sanctuary as the source of salvation.

The struggle and conflict envisioned here in Daniel 8:10–12 was of a distinctly religious nature. It involved persecution. It involved an attack upon the person of Christ. It attempted to point the attention of people away from His heavenly sanctuary to an earthly substitute. And it attempted to point the attention of people away from His heavenly ministry to an earthly human priesthood and their actions. All this was the work of the medieval papacy, the religious phase of Rome.

Why was this conflict so important? Because it dealt with the source of the plan of salvation. It was a struggle between two different plans of salvation—the original heavenly one and a later earthly substitute. Why do Seventh-day Adventists make so much out of the eighth chapter of Daniel? Because it involves the very plan of salvation. What could be more important?

It is also important to note that Daniel 8 does not paint a picture of the final resolution of this problem. When the vision faded from the prophet's eyes, the little horn still "prospered in everything it did" (vs. 12). However, verses 13 and 14 provide an assurance that this problem would eventually be resolved, but chapter 8 does not explain that resolution in detail. The full significance of what was involved in resolving this problem is depicted in Daniel 7 which we will study in the next chapter.

THE TWO ANGELS SPEAK

The visual portion of the prophecy of Daniel 8 ends with verse 12. As the screen of the prophet's view went blank, a new phenomenon occurred. Two angels came within range of his hearing, and he listened in on their conversation. In verse 13, the first angel asked a question. The second angel gave the answer in verse 14.

The NIV correctly translates the first part of the first angel's question as: "*How long* will it take for the vision to be fulfilled"? (vs. 13, emphasis supplied). The rest of the question goes on to identify the vision in question—"the vision concerning the daily sacrifice, the rebellion that causes desolation, and the surrender of the sanctuary and of the host that will be trampled underfoot?" The second angel's answer is found in verse 14: "It will take 2,300 evenings and mornings; then the sanctuary will be reconsecrated." Each element in this important verse needs to be examined in detail.

ESTABLISHING DATES FOR THE 2,300 DAYS

It is important to note that the question is about the length of *the vision,* not about the length of the activities of the little horn. The activities of the little horn are included within this vision, indeed they mark its climax, but they are not all that there is to the vision. The vision also includes the Persian ram, the Greek goat, and the four horns that precede the little horn of Rome's two phases. So when the angel asks, "How long is the vision?" the word, "vision," includes the whole of what Daniel saw in chapter 8—from the Persian ram to the little horn. This fact gives us an approximate starting point for the 2,300-day time-period mentioned in verse 14.

The vision starts with the Persian ram. Therefore the 2300 evening-mornings should begin with the Persian period. The prophecy does not give us a precise starting point within that period; we must obtain that point from Daniel 9. In the preceding chapter on the prophecy of Daniel 9, we paid considerable attention to the starting point for the prophecy of the seventy weeks (see pp. 154–159). From a study of the decrees of Ezra –5and Nehemiah and the chronology related to them, we established 5the date of 457 B.C. as the starting point of the seventy weeks. It remains now to connect these prophecies—that of chapter 9 and the vision of chapter 8—on a more specific basis. There are several lines of evidence for this linkage.

The first point is that Daniel 9:24 says the seventy weeks were "cut off" for Daniel's people and the holy city of Jerusalem. The NIV, along with a number of modern versions, prefers to translate this verb as "decreed." Unfortunately, this verb, *hatak,* occurs only this one time in the Old Testament, so in terms of the Bible itself, there is no comparative material with which we can evaluate it for possible alternate meanings. In such a case, we must go to the next most helpful source of such information—post-biblical Hebrew. This word, *hatak,* is used about a dozen times in post-biblical Jewish sources. In all but one instance it means "to cut." In only one case does it have the meaning, "to decree" or "to determine." Clearly, its dominant meaning in post-biblical Hebrew sources is "to cut," and thus that is the most likely meaning here in Daniel 9.

Another argument pointing to the same conclusion is the fact that the meaning of the roots of Hebrew words generally developed from the concrete to the abstract. In this case, the idea of "cutting" is the concrete, and the idea of "decreeing" is the more abstract idea. It isn't clear whether by Daniel's time the word, *hatak,* had developed from the concrete meaning "to cut" to the more abstract idea of "to decree" or "to determine." But certainly the earlier concrete idea of "to cut" was present in the word in Daniel's time. Thus the linguistic evidence—both the root meaning and the dominant usage—favors the meaning of "to cut" here in Daniel 9:24. Daniel 9:24 says that seventy weeks are to be "cut off" for the Jewish people. If a time period is "cut off," it must be cut off from another time period. From what longer time period could the seventy weeks be cut off? The most readily available time period is the 2,300 days of the preceding chapter, Daniel 8.

The second point linking chapters 9 and 8 of Daniel is the fact that Daniel obviously doesn't understand the second angel's climactic answer (8:14) to the question of the first angel (vs. 13). Verse 16 specifically commissions Gabriel to explain the vision to Daniel, including this exchange between the two angels. However, when we examine Gabriel's explanation as given in the remainder of chapter 8, we see that he explains virtually all the elements of the symbolic vision except the angel's statement about time in verse 14. In verse 26, Gabriel simply assures Daniel that the time element is "true." It was that particular element over which Daniel was especially confused (vs. 27). Thus when the same angel comes much later (in Daniel 9) to further explain matters to Daniel, we would certainly expect his explanation to be related especially to what Daniel did not understand about the preceding vision of chapter 8.

The specific words used by the angel, as recorded in the Hebrew text, make that connection even more direct. This constitutes the third argument for connecting these two time periods in chapters 8 and 9. When Gabriel came to give Daniel the prophecy of chapter 9 he pointed Daniel back to the preceding prophecy in a specific way: "Therefore, consider the message [which I Gabriel bring to you] and understand the vision [*mareh*]" (Dan. 9:23). There are two Hebrew words used for "vision" in the book of Daniel. One is *mareh*, and it refers to the appearance of a personal being in vision. An example is found in Daniel 10:5–7 where Daniel encounters the person of God. Of this he says, "I, Daniel, was the only one who saw the vision [*mareh*]" (vs. 7). The other word for "vision" in Daniel is *hazon*. This refers to a symbolic vision such as those containing beasts and their actions. An example of this is found in Daniel 8:1, 2 where this word is used three times to refer to the symbolic vision of the ram, goat, and horns.

In Daniel 8, both types of vision are present. From verse 1 to verse 12 there was a *hazon,* a symbolic vision. By verses 13 and 14, however, the *hazon* vision was over, and two angels, two personal beings, appeared. This appearance was a *mareh*. The Hebrew wording of Daniel 8:26 makes it clear that chapter 8 contains both types of visions: "The vision [*mareh*] of the evenings and mornings that has been given you is true, but seal up the vision [*hazon*], for it concerns the distant future."

When Gabriel came to Daniel in 9:23 and told Daniel that he had come to help him understand the "vision," he used the word *mareh*. What *mareh* is Gabriel referring to? Obviously this had to be a vision that Daniel had already received. Thus when Gabriel pointed Daniel back to a preceding *mareh* vision, he was pointing him right back to Daniel 8:26, which in turn refers to Daniel 8:14. Thus there is a direct link between Daniel 9:23 and Daniel 8:14 through Daniel 8:26. Gabriel did not give Daniel the prophecy of chapter 9 in order to explain the whole vision of Daniel 8; he gave it to him in order to explain the first part of the time element of that vision. The seventy weeks of Daniel 9 were to be cut off of the 2,300 days of Daniel 8 as the Hebrew wording of Gabriel's statement makes plain.

The language of Daniel 9, and its connection with Daniel 8, thus give a more specific date to the time period of Daniel 8. Daniel 8 indicates that it was to begin in general during the Persian period, and Daniel 9 pins down the beginning date as 457 B.C. (see the discussion of this date in the preceding chapter dealing with Daniel 9). If one adds 2,300 evenings-mornings, or days, to 457 B.C. on the basis of the year-for-a-day principle, (Ezekiel 4:6; Numbers 14:34), those 2,300 years extend to the year A.D. 1844. In this way we have established dates for both the beginning and the end of the time period in Daniel 8:14.

WHAT HAPPENED AT THE END OF THE 2,300 DAYS?

With the dates established for this time period, we may ask: What was to happen at the end of this time period? What was to happen in 1844?

Daniel 8:14 says, "Then the sanctuary will be reconsecrated." The sanctuary referred to in this verse is the sanctuary referred to previously in verses 11 and 12—the heavenly sanctuary. It was the same heavenly sanctuary that the little-horn power figuratively attempted to cast down to earth in the eyes of humanity. In so doing, it attempted to take over the prerogatives of that heavenly sanctuary, to usurp them for itself. Thus there have been two rival plans of sanctuary ministry and salvation—the heavenly original and the earthly substitute. There have been two rival sanctuaries and two rival priesthoods. There have been two rival high priests who have officiated over these plans. At some point in the history of this struggle there must come a time for a decision between these two plans and their results. There has to come a time of judgment that will decide between them. This judgment is what is brought to view in the time period of Daniel 8:14, the 2,300 days. The "cleansing" (KJV) or "reconsecration" (NIV) of the sanctuary thus has to do with righting the wrongs that the little horn has created in its attempt to establish an earthly substitute for the work of the heavenly sanctuary. Through this judgment it will become evident that all during this struggle the true sanctuary was the one in heaven (cf. Hebrews 8:2). It will become evident that the true priesthood was the priesthood in which Jesus is involved in heaven (cf. Hebrews 8:1). It will become evident that the true services of the true sanctuary were those located in heaven with Christ, the priestly Prince.

The verb which the Hebrew text uses to express this manifold restoration is *sadaq,* meaning "to be right or righteous." In Hebrew this is a very rich, broad word with various shades of meaning. In its broader aspects it takes in the various words—"cleansed," "reconsecrated," "vindicated," "restored," "victorious"—with which it has been translated. It is an umbrella word which includes all these other shades of meaning. The sanctuary has been defiled symbolically by the little horn; it will be cleansed by this judgment. It has been cast down in terms of symbolic action; it will be restored to heaven again, figuratively. The earthly judgments against the saints have been going against the judgments of the heavenly sanctuary; now it will be seen that the heavenly decisions were right and that those of earthly courts were wrong. Now the wrong decisions of earthly courts will be overturned, and the clear judgments of heaven will be made manifest. In all these ways, the sanctuary will be set right. It will be right; it will emerge victorious; it will be vindicated; it will be cleansed of the earthly contamination from which it has suffered. Thus "to be right" or "righteous" is the broad, rich theological meaning which encompasses all of these other shades of meaning. That whole rich and variegated picture will be brought about by a heavenly judgment in which all these aspects will be made manifest.

That heavenly judgment occurs at the end of the 2,300 days as is affirmed by various lines of evidence.

First, the situation or problem of Daniel 8:11–13 requires such a judgment to resolve it. Second, the heavenly judgment was shown Daniel in vision in chapter 7:9–14, which is in a parallel position in that vision with what is found here in Daniel 8:13, 14. An angel announces the coming of the judgment in Daniel 8:14, but it is not shown to the prophet at that point; it is shown to him in vision in Daniel 7:9–14. That is one reason these prophecies need to be studied in reverse order—because the announcement of the judgment in Daniel 8 leads logically to the picture of that judgment in Daniel 7. The other line of evidence for this judgment comes from typology found in the book of Leviticus.

LINKS AND PARALLELS BETWEEN DANIEL 8 AND LEVITICUS

It may seem strange, at first, to call attention to the book of Leviticus in the middle of discussing a prophetic book such as Daniel. Leviticus is a book of law, not prophecy. But when one considers the nature of the content of this prophecy, it can be seen more clearly how these two sources connect. They connect through the sanctuary. Daniel 8 is ultimately a prophecy about the sanctuary. Leviticus is a book of laws and regulations about what happened in the earthly sanctuary. Thus there is a natural, logical connection between these two books, and that link is reinforced by the nature of the symbols used in Daniel 8. A careful consideration of those symbols shows just how much Daniel 8 is a sanctuary prophecy.

First, there is the very word "sanctuary" itself which is used three times in Daniel 8 (vss. 11, 13, and 14).

Second, there is the word *tamid*, meaning "daily" or "continual." Although this word could be used as an ordinary adverb to modify other actions outside of the sanctuary, it was commonly used for various priestly activities that took place within the temple.

Third, there is the symbol of a ram that was used to represent Persia. The ram was a domesticated animal, in contrast to the wild beasts of the field that are found as symbols in Daniel 7. The ram was also an animal which was used for sacrifice in the sanctuary service.

Fourth, there is the symbol of a goat used to represent Greece. It, too, was a domesticated animal which was used for sacrifice.

Fifth, there is the "evening-morning" time unit that is employed in Daniel 8. The prophecy does not simply say "days"; it uses a compound unit of "evenings-mornings." What is an evening-morning? Genesis 1 indicates that the days of the Creation week consisted of an evening and a morning, so chronologically an evening-morning is equivalent to one whole twenty-four-hour day.

Beyond that, however, there may be a theological reason for selecting this time unit for the prophecy. Numbers 9:14–23 tells the story of the Israelites setting out on their travels in the Sinai peninsula. With them went the very presence of God, represented by the cloud over the sanctuary. When that cloud turned into a pillar of fire in the evening, the high priest knew that it was time to offer the evening sacrifice. When it turned back into a pillar of cloud in the morning, he knew that it was time to offer the morning sacrifice. Thus an evening-morning was also a sanctuary day, delineated by God Himself to indicate the times in that day when He wanted the various aspects of His service conducted.

From these five reasons we can see that Daniel 8 is a prophecy which draws heavily from the sanctuary services for its symbolism. So to understand that symbolism, we should turn to the book in the Bible which tells us the most about the sanctuary. The last portion of Exodus (chapters 25–40) tells us about how the sanctuary was built; the book of Leviticus tells about how the sanctuary was put into use and about the services that went on there.

There were basically two types of services in the sanctuary—the daily and the yearly. The daily services were those that were carried out every day. They are known by the word that we encounter in

Daniel—*tamid*. The other kind of services were those which came around only once a year. These were generally festivals of celebration and thanksgiving such as Passover and the Feast of Tabernacles (see Leviticus 23).

There was one of these annual festivals, however, which more than any of the others, brought an end to the yearly round of daily sacrifices and services. That was the Day of Atonement, *yom kippur*. All of the daily services met their final conclusion in that yearly service. With the blood of the Lord's goat, the sanctuary was cleansed of its record of sin for the past year and was made new and fresh all over again to begin another round of sacrifices for the next calendar year (see Leviticus 16). Thus in Leviticus we meet these two great aspects of the sanctuary service—the daily and the yearly.

We meet them also in Daniel 8. The daily is referred to as the *tamid* and we see it as an object of contention between the small horn and the Prince (8:11). This daily ministry in the heavenly sanctuary actually belonged to the Prince, but the little horn contended with him for it. In attempting to take over control of the services of the sanctuary in the eyes of men, this small horn power introduced false elements into that service (8:12). A false priesthood ministered for the people in a way that was not prescribed by God. When that happened in the earthly sanctuary in Old Testament times, the sanctuary was defiled. Defilement took place, for example, when its holiness was corrupted by idols (Leviticus 20:1–3; Jeremiah 7:30, 31) or by a priesthood that was not fit to serve there (Leviticus 21:6–8; Ezekiel 22:26). This type of defilement had to be cared for in a certain way, and that was through the services of the Day of Atonement.

But there was another element—the record of forgiven sins—which was introduced into the sanctuary. In Leviticus 4, we find instructions for the sin offering. In Leviticus 5 and 6, we find instructions for the guilt offering. When these types of sins were treated by these sacrifices, the blood or the flesh of the sacrifices was handled in a certain way. Either the blood was taken into the sanctuary or the priest was to eat a portion of the sacrifice in a holy place. Both procedures transferred the forgiven sin from the sinner to the sanctuary. This is made clear in the conclusions to these actions as described in Leviticus 4:20, 26, 31, 35.

When the priest had completed his manipulation of the blood from the slain sacrifice, he had made atonement for the sinner and he was forgiven. An Israelite did not have to wait until the Day of Atonement to find out if he was forgiven; he was forgiven from the moment the sacrifice was made and the priest handled the elements from the sacrifice in the appropriate way.

There is a very instructive case in relation to this point in Leviticus 10:16–20. The services of the sanctuary had just begun, and the priests were not yet very familiar with them. When Moses found out that the priests had taken neither the blood nor the flesh of the sacrifice into the sanctuary, he was very upset. He sternly reprimanded them. The importance of taking the blood or the flesh into the sanctuary lay in the fact that the sacrifice for sin was thus registered or transferred in one way or another. All of this was also part of the daily service.

When the daily service of the sanctuary shifted to the yearly service on the Day of Atonement, all of the sacrifices of the year were incorporated into the blood of the Lord's goat which was taken into the Most Holy Place only this once and applied to the mercy seat of the ark of the covenant. Thus the entire year's accumulation of sins which had been transferred from the sinner to the sanctuary through the daily sacrifices were "gathered up" as it were in the single sacrifice of the yearly service. That is why there was no confessing of sin over the head of the Lord's goat on the Day of Atonement (Leviticus 16:8, 9). The sins had already been confessed over the heads of the individual sin offerings throughout the year (Leviticus 4:29). With the blood of the Lord's goat on the Day of Atonement, the priest made atonement for the Most Holy Place, the Holy Place, and the altar in the courtyard of the sanctuary (Leviticus 16:16–18).

Now the sanctuary was cleansed. It was restored to its former state of purity and was ready to begin another round of sacrificial services for the next year (Leviticus 16:22–25). A final disposition of sin was made when all the sins, which had been forgiven and recorded in the sanctuary throughout the year, were brought out of the sanctuary, placed upon the head of the goat for Azazel, and sent into the wilderness, never to be seen by the people of Israel again (Leviticus 16:20–22).

Daniel 8 contains these same two elements—the daily and the yearly—now set in a prophetic relationship of type and antitype. Leviticus is the type, and Daniel is the antitype. The comparison can be seen as follows:

Daily Service	**Yearly Service**
a. Leviticus 1–15	a. Leviticus 16
b. During the 2,300 days	b. At the end of the 2,300 days

Just as there was a cleansing and restoration of the sanctuary on the Day of Atonement, just so would there also be a full restoration of the heavenly sanctuary when the judgment—the antitypical day of atonement—began at the end of the 2,300 days in A.D. 1844 (Daniel 8:14).

But the question comes up: What is it from which the heavenly sanctuary has to be cleansed or restored?

First, there is the matter of what the little horn has attempted to do to it. In symbol, the little horn has reached into heaven itself and defiled the purity of that sanctuary with its machinations. In Old Testament times, this was done *literally* by conquerors (Ezekiel 4:6–8; 7:20–24; 24:21), false priests (Leviticus 22:15; 2 Chronicles 36:13; Zephaniah 3:1–4), and idolaters. This reached its final culmination under the last king of Judah, Zedekiah. Of his times we read: "Furthermore, all the leaders of the priests and the people became more and more unfaithful, following all the detestable practices of the nations and defiling the temple of the Lord, which he had consecrated in Jerusalem" (2 Chronicles 36:14).

What befell the temple in literal terms can be projected into the realm of the heavenly sanctuary in symbolic terms. When the judgment convenes in the heavenly sanctuary, however, all of the long-standing questions about the plan of salvation will be made clear. That which has been impugned or made obscure will now stand pure and clear in the mercy and justice of God that shines forth from the heavenly sanctuary. The truth from that heavenly sanctuary about what has really been going on there will be made clear. Thus the sanctuary is said to be "cleansed" (8:14, KJV), "reconsecrated" (NIV), or "returned to its rightful state" (RSV).

But the judgment of the Day of Atonement in the Old Testament took care of more than just the impurities that had been introduced by foreigners or false priests. It also took care of, in a final way, the record of the forgiven sins of the saints, the righteous Israelites (Leviticus 16:16, 22). Thus the Day of Atonement accomplished two major events, (1) the cleansing or restoration of the sanctuary from the record of the sins of the righteous, and (2) its cleansing from any impurity that had been introduced by false conduct in relation to the sanctuary itself. Leviticus 16:16 says, "In this way he will make atonement for the Most Holy Place because of the uncleanness and rebellion [sins] of the Israelites, whatever their sins have been."

The uncleanness referred to is the state of uncleanness that defiles the sanctuary (Leviticus 11–15). The rebellion is the personal and corporate sins of Israel (Leviticus 1–7). In terms of the typological parallels in the book of Daniel, the sins of the righteous that are dealt with in the final heavenly judgment correspond to the forgiven sins of the Israelites that were recorded daily in the sanctuary; the uncleanness that the little horn has symbolically introduced into the sanctuary by defiling the knowledge of the work of the true sanctuary for humanity corresponds to the state of impurity or uncleanness from which the Old Testament sanctuary was cleansed. The pattern is this:

Leviticus 1–7	**Leviticus 11–15**	**Leviticus 16**
Sins of the righteous forgiven and recorded in the sanctuary	States of impurity and uncleanness that defile the sanctuary	Cleansing and restoration of the sanctuary by final judgment upon both
Daniel 8:14a	**Daniel 8:10–12**	**Daniel 8:14b**
Activities of the Prince as the heavenly High Priest. True application of the "daily" service during the 2,300 days	Activities of the little horn. False application of the "daily" service	Judgment at the end of the 2,300 evenings-mornings, at the climax of the "daily" services

Thus a fuller knowledge of the function of the sanctuary in the book of Leviticus can indeed illuminate the references to the sanctuary in the prophecy of Daniel 8. But the book of Daniel has more to say on this subject with the vision of Daniel 7. That will be the focus of our attention in the next chapter.

SUMMARY

The amount of discussion that has been devoted to this prophecy might imply that this is a complicated topic. In actuality, it is not. The prophecy begins with the story of the Persian ram—its origin, its successes, and its final demise. Then it goes on to the Greek goat and its initial successes and final dissolution. That dissolution led to the division of the Greek empire into four smaller kingdoms distributed around the eastern Mediterranean basin. Into this region came a new power represented by a little horn that grew greater and greater. Its greatness was first revealed by its conquest in the regions of the former Greek kingdoms. It successfully conquered and absorbed all four of those kingdoms.

In its later phase of existence, this power in Rome took on a more religious character. In this phase, it represents the church that has its seat in Rome, the church that had such a powerful influence in Europe throughout the Middle Ages. During those centuries, it exercised its power as a persecuting force, and this is clearly revealed by the Roman church's history. Its theology reveals something else: an approach to the plan of salvation which has been carried out through channels which are not approved of by the Bible. In this way, it has actually come to be something of a rival to the plan of salvation which it claimed to minister. This organization, which started out so well, actually came to find itself in opposition to the purposes of God through its desire to exercise control.

In this way a rivalry developed. On the one hand was the true heavenly sanctuary from which the true plan of salvation was ministered by the true High Priest, Jesus Christ. On the other hand was an earthly power attempting to divert attention away from that heavenly sanctuary and its Priest and its services and focus, instead, on an earthly substitute.

How long would this rivalry last? How would it be brought to an end? What are the results of the two alternate plans of salvation? The answers to these questions will all be made manifest in the judgment. This judgment at the end of time is what the prophecy is talking about when it refers to the (heavenly) sanctuary being cleansed, restored, and justified at the end of the 2,300 evenings-mornings. We can learn more about this "yearly" service, coming at the end of the "daily" services, by considering parallels from the book of Leviticus. Leviticus chapters 1–15 represent the daily, and chapter 16 describes the yearly. That yearly service, or Day of Atonement, was a day of judgment for ancient Israel. Likewise, the antitypical Day of Atonement brings to view a judgment in the heavenly sanctuary which will determine all who truly belong to the camp of the saints of the Most High.

It is not our part to judge who those saints will be; that is God's part in His judgment. Only He knows how much light and truth any individual has received. Our task is to apply ourselves to His Word so that we may truly come to know Him as our Lord and Savior. Our task is to receive His Spirit so that we may live for Him. All other aspects of judgment we may safely leave with Him, our God of mercy and justice.

CHAPTER NINE

CHRIST AS KING

Daniel 7 is the most detailed and complete of the symbolic visions in the book of Daniel. It begins with the contemporary kingdom of Babylon under which Daniel lived at the time the vision was given. It continues all the way down through human history and ends with the kingdom of God that will ultimately be set up. Thus it covers the whole time from Daniel's day to ours—and beyond into eternity. Daniel 2 covers a similar time span, but it does so in less detail. There we simply find the kingdoms involved represented by different metals, whereas in Daniel 7 they are symbolized by different beasts which can convey more detailed characteristics. Those characteristics represent the activities of the kingdoms. The other main prophecies in the book of Daniel cover shorter time periods in their prophetic content than does Daniel 7. Daniel 8 starts with Persia, not Babylon, and it does not extend to the final kingdom of God. Daniel 9 is even shorter, covering only the period from Persian to Roman times. Daniel 11 does extend to the final kingdom of God, but it starts with Persia, not Babylon. Thus it can be said that Daniel 7 is the most complete and detailed symbolic vision in the book.

Chapter 7 spells out the fourfold kingdoms of this earth that would dominate the Mediterranean world for many centuries. However, unlike the prophecy in chapter 8, the angel's explanation of the vision to Daniel does not name any of these kingdoms. How, then, are we to identify these beast-kingdoms? The answer is that they must be identified by cross-correlating them with other prophecies in Daniel which do name these successive kingdoms or identify them in some other way.

Basically there are four of these great "outline" prophecies in Daniel—chapters 2, 7, 8, and 11. (Daniel 9, the other major prophecy in the book, is of a different nature. It does not outline the nations that were to rise and fall. As a matter of fact, it does not even mention them, except indirectly. Rather, Daniel 9 concentrates upon the prophetic history of the Jewish people and thus lies outside the realm of the outline prophecies that describe the fourfold rise and fall of kingdoms.) In terms of symbols, Daniel 7 gives the most complete representation of the sequence of world kingdoms.

But the climax of the vision in chapter 7 does not come with the final beast. The climax comes, rather, in what happens after the final beast when God takes charge of human history and brings it to an end (7:13, 14, 26–28). How does God do that? Daniel 7 provides an interesting answer. When God takes over, one final phase to world history remains before He sets up His eternal kingdom. Daniel 7 assures us that God's kingdom will be set up, but just how does He go about it? The answer comes in verses 9–14. We will study that passage in detail.

As we study Daniel 7, we will concentrate upon key words. How do we identify key words? One way is to see what words occur most frequently in a given passage. If a biblical author uses a word over and over again, that word and the thought it represents must have been very much uppermost in his mind. Daniel 7 contains several words that are used with considerable frequency. One of those is "dominion," used seven times in chapter 7. (Note that the NIV is not consistent in translating the word as "dominion." Synonyms are used.)

As we consider this key word, we should ask: Who has dominion? We will see that chapter 7 indicates that the first beast was to have dominion for a time, but then it was to lose it to the second beast. Then the second beast was to lose dominion to the third beast, and so on until the sequence is finished. A practical question comes up at this point: Are human beings always to suffer under these constantly changing kingdoms and their governments? Many of these governments were oppressive and unjust—especially to God's righteous people. Is this to be the common lot of humanity forever? The prophecy assures us that it will not ever be so. God will step in and put an end to these earthly kingdoms and their injustice. He will set up a kingdom of His own making, "wherein dwelleth righteousness" (2 Peter 3:13, KJV). In God's eternal kingdom we will enjoy peace, prosperity, and the eternal vigor of youth and immortality (see Revelation 21:1–4). God's dominion will be radically different from any kind of dominion that human beings have enjoyed previously. That is what Daniel 7 assures us.

From that conclusion we need to go back and look at the details to see how we will arrive at that point in the course of history.

THE SETTING

Daniel 7:1 tells us that Daniel received the vision of this chapter as a dream or night vision while he was asleep. In that sense, it was similar to the two night dreams Nebuchadnezzar received as recorded in chapters 2 and 4. In these previous cases, Daniel had functioned as an inspired wise man who could go in to the king and explain his dreams to him. In this case, however, the dream was given directly to God's servant without the intermediary of the pagan king.

All of this happened in the first year of Belshazzar or about 550 B.C. We have already referred several times previously to the unusual circumstances under which Belshazzar came to the throne. His father Nabonidus left Babylon to live in Tema in Arabia for a period of ten years from about 550 B.C. to about 540 B.C. He returned just in time to try to defend Babylon from the Persians. But he came back too late, and that defense was unsuccessful. The vision of Daniel 7 was given at the beginning of that unusual ten-year period at a time when Nabonidus had just left for the desert of Arabia and Belshazzar had just been put in charge of affairs in Babylon as co-king with his father. Why would God have given this particular vision at that special time? There may have been at least one good reason.

By 550 B.C. it was already evident that the kingdom of Babylon was weakening and on its way to being overthrown by some other power. Thus one function of this vision was to spell out the events that would take place when this happened. These developments were not to take the people of God by surprise. Ten years later when the Persian bear took over from the Babylonian lion, the people of God would find assurance that they were indeed being led by God—that He had given evidence through His prophet that He was still in charge of human affairs and that He knew what would happen. Thus one explanation for the giving of this vision at this particular time was to strengthen the faith of the people of Judah during their captivity.

THE FIRST THREE BEASTS

Daniel saw a series of beasts coming up out of the water of the great sea (7:3). Revelation 17:15 tells us that in apocalyptic prophecies such as those of Daniel and Revelation, waters represent multitudes of people. So we can see these kingdoms arising out of great populations. But those multitudes of people were located in and around what is known as the great sea (7:2). Thus this symbol of water was not just a general representation of all kinds of people everywhere. It specifically referred to the peoples in one particular place. For biblical people, the great sea meant the Mediterranean Sea. This means then that these powers were Mediterranean kingdoms. As their identifications are developed below, we will see that this sequence begins with Babylon and continues on through Medo-Persia, Greece, and Rome.

Where were these four powers located? They were all situated around, or even *in*, the Mediterranean Sea. That is self-evident for Greece and Rome, but what about Babylon and Media-Persia? How could they be classified as Mediterranean powers? One needs to look at their conquests.

Nebuchadnezzar led the Babylonian army into Syria and Palestine on many occasions. We have the records of these campaigns preserved on Babylonian tablets in the annals for the first thirteen years of his reign. Thus Babylon was a Mediterranean power by virtue of conquest. This was even more true of Persia which inherited Syria and Palestine when it conquered Babylon. It went beyond the Babylonian limits, however, and conquered Egypt and twice invaded Greece, although it did not hold it as a part of its kingdom. Thus we have four Mediterranean powers represented here: Rome and Greece by right of geographical location and Babylon and Persia which became Mediterranean powers by conquest.

It is significant to point out the Mediterranean focus of this prophecy since the question sometimes arises why India and China are not represented in this prophecy of world empires. It was not the purpose of the prophecy to cover all of the history of all the world. It focused upon one major and very influential segment of that history—that which took place around the Mediterranean basin, the location of God's special covenant people, Israel.

It is also of interest to note here that although the prophecy does depict certain details regarding these beasts, they are basically inactive. After they popped up out of the sea, they didn't go anywhere. They did not charge off in one direction or another to complete their conquests. They were animate, but inactive. In contrast, the ram in Daniel 8 charges westward, and the goat charges east. We do not have such directional elements here in Daniel 7. The vision is more pictorial in nature. It shows us the beasts and their characteristics and lets us decode them with the interpreting angel's help (see vss. 15–27). Conquests are indicated—for example by means of the ribs in the bear's mouth—but they are shown statically as events having already taken place, rather than being represented by actions depicted as taking place in the prophecy itself.

THE FIRST BEAST

The first beast is a lion (7:4). The interpreting angel does not tell us what kingdom the lion represents. We must make that identification by connecting this prophecy with Daniel 2. There, in the metallic image, we see the head of gold in first place (2:32). In that prophecy, the prophet himself identifies the head of gold for us. He said to Nebuchadnezzar, "You are that head of gold" (vs. 38). As if to clarify that he was talking about kingdoms and not just Nebuchadnezzar, Daniel went on to say, "After you, another kingdom will rise, inferior to yours" (vs. 39).

This connection is clarified by the use of numbers. The prophecies in both chapters (2 and 7) use some elements from the sequence of first, second, third, and fourth. It isn't just that we can count four metals in the image of Daniel 2 and four beasts in the vision of chapter 7; the prophet himself has counted them for us before. Clearly, therefore, the sequence is the same in both chapters. Since Daniel 2 begins with the golden head and identifies it for us as Babylon, that cross-connection points directly to the lion, the first beast in Daniel 7, as also representing Babylon.

The lion was a particularly appropriate representation of Babylon. In the city of Babylon, lions were depicted in detail by means of colored bricks on the great processional way and the Ishtar gate to which it led. This was the main entrance to Babylon from the north. Lions made of colored bricks appeared also on the outer wall of the throne room in the palace. In addition, the great lion of Babylon, a huge statue carved from black basalt stone, stood in the courtyard of the palace. Lions were also kept in the royal zoo, as the story of Daniel 6 tells us. Daniel undoubtedly walked many, many times past these representations of lions. The lion is, therefore, a singularly appropriate representation of the kingdom of Babylon.

What detailed characteristics of this lion does the vision provide? This lion started out with the wings of an eagle, but then those wings were torn off, and the lion was given the heart of a man. Elsewhere in Daniel wings represent speed of conquest, as is seen by comparing the leopard representing Greece in Daniel 7:6 with the goat representing Greece in Daniel 8:5. So tearing off the eagle's wings from the lion would represent the decline of its voracious and conquering nature. When did this happen?

The history of the Neo-Babylonian kingdom can be divided into two main segments: the reign of Nebuchadnezzar (605–562 B.C.) and those kings who followed after him (562–539 B.C.). Nebuchadnezzar ruled Babylon about twice as long as did the five kings who followed him (including Belshazzar) combined. In addition, these five kings were much more ineffective than Nebuchadnezzar was. He built up the kingdom of Babylon, and they frittered it away, as shown, for example, by the prolonged absence of Nabonidus from Babylon. So this succession of weak-hearted rulers could well be represented by the "the heart of a man" that was given, symbolically, to the now wingless lion (vs. 4).

The other possibility is that this is a representation of Nebuchadnezzar's own experience as described especially in Daniel 4. When the sentence of God's judgment fell upon him, he went out and lived among the animals of the field. He was in this mental state for a period of seven years. During this time he was, of course, incapacitated from carrying out any affairs of state such as leading military campaigns that would be represented by the wings of an eagle. At the end of this period of insanity, Nebuchadnezzar's mental faculties returned, and he was restored to his kingdom. His mind—or heart—came back to him as he joined mankind again. The vision could be referring to either of these scenarios; however, the former seems slightly more in keeping with the viewpoint of the prophecy.

THE SECOND BEAST

The second beast in the vision of chapter 7 was a bear (7:5). The bear is a mountain dweller, making it an apt symbol for a mountainous country such as Media which was later joined to the country of Persia on the elevated plateau of Iran. To reach Media-Persia, the forces of Assyria or Babylon had to march up through the Zagros mountains. Nebuchadnezzar built the famous hanging gardens of Babylon for his Median wife because she was lonesome for her native mountains and bored by the flat plain of Mesopotamia.

This bear had an unusual feature—he was lopsided. One side was raised up higher than the other side. The ram in Daniel 8:3 has the same characteristic in that one horn was raised up over the other horn. The interpretation given in 8:20 is that the two horns represent the dual kingdoms of Media and Persia. Combined they make up the Media-Persian Empire. The lopsided bear in Daniel 7 should logically represent the same combination. The Median power was stronger at first, but then the Persian part arose and eventually became more prominent than the Medes (8:3). Thus the bear in Daniel 7 and the ram in Daniel 8 represent the same power—Media-Persia.

The other feature of the bear in Daniel 7 is that he has three ribs in his mouth. In the natural world this would represent animals that he had eaten. In the prophetic symbol, therefore, this should represent the kingdoms the bear power had absorbed or conquered. Daniel 8:4 depicts the same characteristic when it notes that the ram charged off in three directions, to the north, the west, and the south. Thus the three directions of conquest in Daniel 8 and the three ribs of conquest in Daniel 7 both represent the same thing—three major conquests of the Media-Persians. In the commentary on Daniel 8, we identified these conquests as Lydia in Asia Minor to the north of Persia, Babylon to the west, and Egypt to the south. Cyrus conquered Lydia and Babylon, and Cambyses, his son, conquered Egypt.

THE THIRD BEAST

The third beast of Daniel 7 is the leopard (7:6). This is clearly not a natural leopard, but a symbolic figure. This leopard has a fourfold nature; he has four heads and four wings. This fourfold nature matches well with the four horns that came out of the head of the Greek goat in Daniel 8:8. The angel identifies that goat by name as Greece in 8:21. So we can apply that same identification to the leopard in chapter 7. In Daniel 8, the goat flew over the ground without touching it; in chapter 7, the leopard is given wings to accomplish the same purpose. Once again the common characteristics between the beasts in these two chapters establish a correlation that allows us to identify the leopard in chapter 7 and the goat in chapter 8 as one and the same—the kingdom of Greece. The fourfold nature of these two beasts refers to the divisions into which the Greek kingdom split after the death of Alexander.

Thus far we have been able to identify the first three beasts of Daniel 7 by cross correlations with the symbols in other chapters in the book where they are specifically named. The cross-correlation with Daniel 2 identifies the lion in chapter 7 as Babylon. Cross-correlations with Daniel 8 identify the next two beasts in Daniel 7, the bear and the leopard, as Media-Persia and Greece. This is also the order in which these powers appeared historically. Persia conquered Babylon under Cyrus, and that conquest is recorded for us right in the book of Daniel itself (chapter 5). Alexander the Great then led the armies of Macedonian Greece to defeat and conquer Persia. Thus the identifications made in the book of Daniel have proved to be correct by historical comparisons from outside that book.

THE FOURTH BEAST

The fourth beast of Dan. 7:7 is not identified for us by name anywhere in the book of Daniel—not in chapter 2, nor in chapter 8, nor in chapter 11. That leaves us with a historical question: What power succeeded Greece?

Historically the answer is quite simple. It was Rome. This was seen in our discussion of the four horns of the goat in Daniel 8:8. These four horns represented the four main divisions of Alexander's empire—mainland Greece, Asia Minor, Syria (including Babylon), and Egypt. Who was eventually responsible for the overthrow of all four of these kingdoms? The answer is Rome. Rome first conquered Greece. Then it had Asia Minor willed to it by the king of Pergamum who had no male offspring. Next, Syria, along with Judea, fell to Pompey and his legions. Finally, Egypt, the last of the four, fell to Rome. In this way Rome made its conquest of the eastern Mediterranean basin complete. The fourth beast that followed the four heads of the leopard can readily be identified as Rome.

Daniel does not describe the appearance of the fourth beast as completely as he does the third; for that reason it is sometimes called the "non-descript" beast. Whatever it may have looked like, the fourth beast shocked Daniel by its appearance. It was, he said, "terrifying and frightening and very powerful" (Daniel 7:7). This power went on and "crushed and devoured its victims and trampled underfoot whatever was left" (vs. 7). The picture is one of very, very thorough conquests. Archaeology has shown how thorough Roman engineers were in destroying previously existent cities in order to make way for the new Roman occupation. Jerusalem itself was an example. When Rome conquered and destroyed Jerusalem in A.D. 70, the debris from that destruction was scraped into a valley on the west side of the city. Today, that valley, the Tyropoean, no longer even exists because it has been completely filled with the Roman debris from the destruction of the city. Roman destruction of the Herodian, or Second, Temple was so thorough that even today archaeologists still do not know for sure where it stood on the temple platform. Jesus prophesied of this when He predicted that not "one stone" of the temple would "be left on another; every one will be thrown down" (Matthew 24:2).

The prophecy gives an interesting detail about this fourth beast; it says it had teeth of iron (Daniel 7:7). These iron teeth further represent the conquering and destructive nature of this kingdom, but it also forms a direct link with the fourth kingdom in Daniel 2 where the fourth kingdom was represented by the iron legs of the image (2:33, 40). Iron was connected with the fourth kingdom in each prophecy, indicating that the powers represented were one and the same. In both cases, Rome is the kingdom brought to view.

The other major characteristic of this fourth beast given in Daniel 7 is that it had ten horns. In the second half of the chapter, the angel interpreter gives us the explanation: "The ten horns are ten kings who will come from this kingdom" (vs. 24). One might at first take this literally and look for ten caesars to come out of Rome. However, it should be noted that there is a precedent in Daniel for using the word, "king," to mean "kingdom." As we have already noted in Daniel 2, the prophet told Nebuchadnezzar, "You, O king, . . . are that head of gold" (vss. 36, 38). He immediately went on to say, "After you, another kingdom will arise" (vs. 39). This same parallel usage is found in Daniel 7. In his first and more simple explanation the angel said to Daniel, "the four great beasts are four kingdoms [literally, 'kings'] that will rise from the earth" (vs. 17, NIV). Then later in the chapter the angel tells Daniel, "The fourth beast is a fourth kingdom that will appear on earth" (vs. 23). Thus in the original Aramaic text of Daniel 7 there is an example of "king" and "kingdom" being used with parallel meanings just as in Daniel 2.

With this usage in mind, we can see that the ten horns represent not individual kings, but kingdoms that arose out of the political and military turmoil occurring when Imperial Rome broke up under the assaults of the barbarian tribes from the east and the north. This historical process took a couple of centuries to accomplish, beginning in the fifth century A.D. or even before. Gradually the barbarian tribes that had filled the vacuum left by the fall of Imperial Rome settled down to occupy their respective territories, and eventually they evolved into what we now view as the modern nations of Europe. The list of these as commonly given includes the Ostrogoths, Visigoths, Franks, Vandals, Suevi, Alamanni, Anglo-Saxons, Heruli, Lombards, and Burgundians.

It is not necessary to be adamant about precisely what tribes were involved. There was a flux in the number of tribes migrating through Europe, and so likewise, there has also been a flux in the number of modern nations derivative from them. We can take the number, ten, as a representative number for the corporate whole of such tribes and nations. A historic debate over this point occurred during the pre-session for the 1888 Seventh-day Adventist General Conference session. The particular point at issue was whether the Alamanni or the Huns belonged in the list. The debate was sharp and pointed and became very partisan—so much so that participants went around asking, "Are you a Hun or an Alamanni?" There is no need to try to split hairs that fine. It is clear historically that when Imperial Rome crumbled, the tribes that took over its territories evolved into approximately ten kingdoms. No other single empire succeeded Imperial Rome after its fall and division. Daniel 2:43 suggests that after Rome's fall, its former territory—represented by the toes and feet (2:43, 42)—would remain divided until the setting up of God's eternal kingdom (vss. 44, 45).

THE LITTLE HORN

The division of Imperial Rome made way for the rise of yet another power. This power is represented by another horn, an eleventh one (7:8). There is something about this power, however, that set it apart from other ten. It was distinctly a religious power, while the others were political in nature. Just as there was a distinctly religious phase to the work of the little horn in Daniel 8 (see vss. 9, 10), so the little horn here in Daniel 7 also swings into operation as a distinctly religious power. That religious character is demonstrated by the great words that it speaks against the Most High God and by its persecution of God's saints (7:8, 25). This religious characteristic stands in contrast to the purely political actions of the four powers that have appeared previously in the prophecy. In the discussion of the little horn in Daniel 8, we concluded that this religious phase of its work represented the Roman Church headed up by the papacy, since this was the religious phase of Rome that succeeded the imperial phase. The same identification fits well here in Daniel 7 for a number of reasons.

First, we should note where this little horn comes from. It originated from the fourth or Roman beast (7:8), not any of the previous three. Thus this power must be Roman in character. But it is not Imperial Rome itself for that power was represented by the beast from which this horn grew.

Second, the time this horn arose should be noted. It came up *after* the other ten horns were already in place. That means that it arose on the ruins of the broken empire of Imperial Rome. That is exactly when the papacy really came to the fore. The capital of the Roman Empire had been moved to Constantinople by Justinian in the sixth century A.D. That left a power vacuum in the city of Rome itself, when it was not under the control of the barbarian tribes. With the aid of Justinian, that vacuum was soon filled by the bishop of Rome. Justinian decreed that the bishop of Rome was the head of all the churches (A.D. 533). He also sent his army to liberate Rome from the Gothic siege (A.D. 537–538). He even gave the Roman bishop certain civil powers. In the words of Revelation 13:2, "the dragon gave the beast his power and his throne and great authority."

Third, three horns were plucked up before the little horn. An interesting phenomenon occurred in the sixth century A.D. During that century, there were a series of wars that were both political and religious in nature. They were political because some of the barbarian tribes suffered defeats during the course of these wars. But those defeated tribes were Christian! Here we have the spectacle of one Christian power—the Roman empire led by the emperor and the bishop of Rome—opposing other Christian powers such as the Ostrogoths, the Vandals, and perhaps the Visigoths. These tribes were Christians, but they embraced a particular kind of Christianity. They were Arians. The Arians believed that Christ was a created being and thus of lesser stature than God the Father. This doctrine was not acceptable to the bishop in Rome, and he fought it with the arm of the state. From the point of view of the state, the defeat of these powers accomplished certain desirable political ends. From the point of the view of the church, the defeat of these Arian powers accomplished the plucking up of heresy. The military arm of the state was employed for the theological aims of the church. Thus were these three tribal horns, or powers, plucked up before this new horn of papal Rome.

Fourth, this power was a persecuting power. This is explicitly stated in Dan. 7:15, 21. We discussed this feature of the little horn's work in chapter 5 and also in the preceding chapter in our treatment of 8:10. The same recital of persecution listed there can be applied here also.

Fifth, this power attempted to do something with God's law. The prediction was that he will "try to change the set times and the laws" (vs. 25). There are two words for time in this verse. One is *iddan,* used to describe the duration of the little horn's persecution of the saints; it would last three and a half times ("a time, [two] times and half a time"). The word *iddan* means a span of time. The other word for time used in this verse is *zeman* (plural, *zimmin*). "He will . . . try to change the set times and the laws." This Aramaic word has more of a function of a point in time, but it is in the plural form indicating repeated points of time. These are connected with God's law (the word for "law" is singular in the original language). The feature of God's law which best fits this description is the fourth commandment where the recurring seventh day is featured as a point of time, or as regularly occurring points of time.

The New Testament indicates that the early Christian church observed the Sabbath (see Acts 13:14, 44, 16:13; 17:2; 18:4), but gradually the practice of worshiping on the first day of the week was introduced. The process was a gradual, complex one, and anti-semitism played a considerable part in the church's desire to distance itself from the biblical Sabbath. According to some early church historians, this movement to abandon the seventh-day Sabbath developed most rapidly in Rome and Alexandria, but eventually it became widespread. The Church of Rome considers its sponsorship of this shift in worship practice from the seventh day of the week to the first to be a result of its *magisterium,* or teaching authority from God. (For more on this change, see chapter 5.)

Sixth, this power was to speak great words against the Most High, or commit blasphemy. A number of the claims made for this power fall into this category including some of its titles and its functions such as forgiveness of sins by a priest, excommunication, and the interdict (the exclusion of individuals and whole populations from participation in spiritual things). The sixth century A.D., in which the bishop of Rome rose to special prominence, was also a time for the production of what have come to be called pseudo-decretals, or false documents, making wide-ranging claims for the powers of the papacy. (See chapter 5 for a more detailed examination of these claims.)

Seventh, there is the link between the little horn of Daniel 7:8 and the little horn of Daniel 8:9. Both horns are modified with the same adjective—"little" (or "small") when starting out, but both grew to be great. This word "little" or "small" is of interest in itself. The Hebrew word translated "little" in Daniel 8 is not the usual Hebrew word for "little." Daniel had a much more common word readily available to him, but he chose this relatively rare word in order to match it with the Aramaic word for "little" used in chapter 7 to describe the horn depicted there. The distinct linguistic connection between these two prophetic symbols shows that they are the same entity. All of the characteristics we have examined earlier in connection with the little horn in Daniel 8—persecution, rivalry with Christ's heavenly ministry, and directing mankind to an earthly substitute for the heavenly sanctuary—can also be applied to those given to the little horn described here in Daniel 7.

Eighth, there are the dates for the duration of the persecution and dominion carried out by this power. This time period is identified as three and a half "times" in Daniel 7:25. These "times" (vs. 25) can be identified as years on the basis of parallels with Dan. 4:16, 23, and 25 where seven "times," or years, were to pass over Nebuchadnezzar until he regained his sanity. The Greek Old Testament even translates "times" as "years" in Daniel 4. The "times" of Daniel 4 were literal Babylonian calendar years, but here in chapter 7 we are dealing with symbolic years in an apocalyptic prophecy. Revelation 12 makes this same equation of "times" with "years." Verse 6 allots 1,260 days for this same persecuting of the church, and verse 14 re-states that same time period as three and a half "times," a phrase quoted from Daniel 7:25. Each of the 1,260 symbolic days in these three and a half years needs to be interpreted according to the rule of a day-for-a-year (see chapter 6 of this book for further discussion of this principle of prophetic interpretation). In Revelation 11:2 and 13:5 this same time period is identified as forty-two months. Thus the mathematics of this equation can be worked out to show that 1,260 days equals forty-two months equals three and a half years or "times." A prophetic month thus equals 30 days uniformly. It has been rounded off from other calendars for ease of calculation.

All these prophecies indicate that the period of domination by the little horn power was to last 1,260 years. The beginning of this period can be dated to A.D. 538. Justinian's decree making the bishop of Rome the head of all the churches took place in A.D. 533. That decree could not go into effect, however, until the city of Rome itself was liberated from the control of the Ostrogoths. That took place in A.D. 538 when the Ostrogoths' siege of Rome was broken by the general Belisarius who led the emperor's troops in pursuit of the Goths all the way to their capital of Ravenna. The Ostrogoths were not completely eliminated until A.D. 555, but in 538 the bishop of Rome stood free and clear to exercise the authority with which he had been invested by the emperor. This was the first time in sixty years (A.D. 476–538) that the bishop of Rome had been out from under the influence of barbarian tribes.

The end of this 1,260 year prophetic period is even easier to document. It came with the fall of papacy and the exile of the pope in 1798 by the troops of France. Napoleon crossed the Alps into northern Italy in 1796. At Campo Formio he defeated the Austrians in 1797. The French Directory, which was atheistic in its orientation, ordered Napoleon to conquer Rome and abolish the papacy. Napoleon, however, was called away to other duties, leaving the Italian campaign of the French army under the direction of General Berthier. Berthier seized the city of Rome on February 10, 1798 and deposed Pope Pius VI on February 15. The pope was taken captive and died the next year. In addition to the church's massive losses of land and priests in France during the French Revolution, the head of the church was now dethroned.

But it was not ever to remain so. Beginning with the Concordat in 1801 between Napoleon and the papacy, the restoration of the Roman Church started with the new pope, Pius VII. Since then, the influence of the papacy has continued to expand up through the present. In the terms of Revelation 13:3, "One of the heads of the beast seemed to have had a fatal wound [in 1798], but the fatal wound had been healed [beginning in 1801]." Thus the year 1798 marks a fitting end to the great prophetic period outlined in Daniel 7:25.

From these eight points about the activities of the little horn, we can draw up a summary that will help us in identifying it. The fourth beast of this prophecy represented Imperial Rome. That empire was to be broken up, and as predicted, it happened with the barbarian invasions of the midfirst millennium A.D. After the rise of those divisions, a new power came to prominence, represented by the little horn in this prophecy. It had its origin from the Roman beast and was therefore Roman in character. In contrast to the previous political powers depicted in this prophecy, however, the little horn was distinctly religious in character. This religious nature was demonstrated by its persecution of the saints, its blasphemy, and its attack—through the forces of the state—upon those Christian powers which disagreed with its theology. These Arian wars of the sixth century added to the prestige of the bishop of Rome and his church. The power of the little horn was not to last forever; the prophecy limited it to a prophetic time period of 1,260 day-years. These began with the liberation of Rome in A.D. 538 and came to an end with the conquest of Rome and the deposing of the pope in A.D. 1798. Thus the Roman Church and its leadership fit the characteristics of this power as outlined above.

It should be recalled, however, that God alone can read the conscience. When we identify the work of this religious power by means of the characteristics present in this prophecy, we are not speaking about the individual consciences of believers. Rather we are dealing here with a political and theological system which went astray from its spiritual origins. That drift has led to unbiblical beliefs and practices, but individuals may have participated in that communion with a complete sincerity which God recognizes and will honor.

THE HEAVENLY COURT SCENE

One would naturally think that the way to solve the problems introduced by the different nations outlined in this prophecy would be for God to set up His kingdom, a kingdom of a radically different nature. And that *is* the ultimate answer this prophecy provides to the problems under which human beings suffer (7:14, 27). The prophecy describes an intermediate state which leads to that final result. The prophecy presents that intermediate stage in terms of a judgment. In other words, when human history concludes, God will sit in judgment upon it and upon the people involved in it (7:9, 10, 26). This judgment is distinct from the executive phase of judgment, which takes place when Christ comes the second time and passes out His rewards (see, for example, Revelation 22:12). The judgment described here takes place in heaven before Christ comes to earth. For that reason, it is sometimes referred to as the preadvent judgment., which also locates it in terms of time.

THE SETTING OF THE JUDGMENT

A large number of prophecies in the Old Testament speak about God's judgment from His sanctuary—either the earthly temple or the heavenly temple. Examples can be found in Isaiah 6, Ezekiel 1, Micah 1, Amos 1, and 1 Kings 22. These were limited, local judgments, either upon the people of Israel or upon their enemies. These judgments were a microcosm of what Daniel 7:9–14 indicates will happen at the end of time on cosmic scale. This great final cosmic judgment will conclude the plan of salvation. When this judgment in heaven is finished, Christ can come for His people—those who have been clearly identified by that judgment as the saints of the Most High. Then those saints will be taken home to their eternal reward.

As evidence for the fact that a new work of judgment takes place at this time, the scene set in heaven begins with the preparations for that work. This involves bringing the fiery, glorious throne of God into the heavenly courtroom, His audience chamber. Archaeology provides some interesting examples of this very type of thing. The kings of the ancient world commonly had a large, separate chamber in which to hold court and audiences. There citizens or ambassadors appeared before the king to present their cases or describe their negotiations. Audience chambers commonly had a raised dias or platform at one end of the room. The king's throne was portable, and his servants would bring it out of the palace to place it upon that platform. Then when the royal audience was over, the throne would be taken back into the palace until the next time the king was to hold court.

The heavenly throne scene of Daniel 7 portrays a similar setting. Daniel saw the flaming fiery chariot of God, His portable throne, coming into the heavenly audience chamber. "Thrones were set in place" (vs. 9). The fire is Daniel's description of the glory that surrounds the personal being of God; it is not literal fire. Three times in verses 9 and 10 God's glory is described as "fire." Fire is not only descriptive of the glory Daniel saw, but it is appropriate as one of the results of the judgment. God's enemies are to be destroyed by fire—a fire that comes from Him who conducts this judgment (vss. 11, 26). The movement involved here shows action, and it reveals that action to be a new activity. Our God is not a static God; He is dynamically active. There is movement to judgment. This judgment takes place when that movement brings God into this scene. In other words, this is a judgment that takes place at a certain point in time.

The outline of the prophecy can give us an idea of when that judgment was to begin. First the prophecy describes four beast-kingdoms that were to rise and fall—Babylon, Media-Persia, Greece, and Rome. But the judgment still has not convened. Then Rome was to be divided, and the little horn was to arise after those divisions. Following that, the little horn was to have its prolonged period of religio-political dominion, lasting, as we have described above, from A.D. 538 to 1798. After that, the judgment comes. So even before we turn to Daniel 8 for more precise dating, we have an implied date for this judgment here in chapter 7. It must begin sometime after 1798. The prophecy of chapter 7 does not say exactly how long after 1798 the judgment was to begin, but chapter 8 gives us the answer in the 2,300 day prophecy. That prophecy brought us, as we have seen in the previous chapter, to A.D. 1844. Daniel 8:14 refers to the event that was to occur in 1844 as the cleansing, or restoration, of the (heavenly) sanctuary. This cleansing of the sanctuary was a time of judgment, as we discovered by comparing Daniel 8 with Leviticus. Daniel 7:9–14, 26 talks about the same judgment scene—with one difference. In Daniel 8, the prophet was only *told* about the judgment; he listened in on the conversation of two angels who assured him that the judgment would come at the end of the 2,300 day period. Here in Daniel 7, however, the prophet was *shown* the heavenly court session as a scene of his vision. What he was told about in Daniel 8:14 he was shown in Dan. 7:9–14, 26. Daniel 7 gives an approximate date for the judgment (sometime after 1798) while Daniel 8 gives its exact date as beginning in 1844 at the end of the 2,300 days. These two points occur in parallel positions in their respective visions, and they explain each other in various ways.

The prophecy of Daniel 7 next goes on to describe the person of God who comes in to begin this judgment (vs. 9). He is surrounded by the glorious appearance of fire. The hair of His head is described as white like wool, giving, in human appearance, the look of great age. The same thing is emphasized by the title He is given here—"the Ancient of Days" (vs. 9). This title is used for God nowhere else in the entire Bible. What is its significance here?

When God takes up the work of judgment, He judges human beings who have lived in every age of earth's history. But none of them have outlived God or lived at a time before Him. God could say to all of the people judged in the judgment, "I knew you; I was contemporary with you. You did nothing that lay outside the realm of my knowledge." He is also a pure and righteous judge. Human courts may, or may not, give just judgments, but God's judgment is always just and righteous (see Revelation 15:3, 4; 16:4–7; 19:2). This is represented by the white color of His garments.

Daniel next sees the angels come into this heavenly court (vs. 10). The judgment cannot start without the angels being there as well as God. What function do the angels serve in the judgment?

Chapter 7 poetically describes the angels in the judgment scene in these words: "Thousands upon thousands attended him; ten thousand times ten thousand stood before him" (vs. 10). This poetic progression is not given to express a literal number of angels; it is given to express totality. All of God's faithful angels will be there. Every human being who has ever lived has had a guardian angel, and all of those guardian angels will be there in the judgment to testify for their charges. Believers will not be unrepresented in that judgment. With Christ, our High Priest and Advocate, and our guardian angel present, we will be well represented.

The concluding statement of this opening passage from the judgment section states, "The court was seated, and the books were opened" (vs. 10; see also vs. 26). The scene here is typical of what we know of human courts. The judge comes in and takes his seat. Those in attendance in the court sit down, and then they get to work. They have to examine the materials of the case. The records are opened. So it is in the heavenly judgment. There are record "books" of some sort that are examined (vs. 10). For that reason this judgment has been called an "investigative judgment." The records obviously are the records of the lives of those being judged. Did they accept Christ as their Saviour and receive forgiveness for their repentance? Or did they turn away from the great salvation offered in Christ? Did they accept God as Lord of their lives and live for Him, or not? All of this is recorded in these books. The ultimate question in the judgment is this: What was your relationship to Christ? The decision is ours; God does not change it. He merely reviews the decisions that have been made to see who will enter the eternal kingdom with the saints of the Most High and who will not. This naturally leads to the consequence that when Christ comes, He comes ready to distribute His rewards (Matthew 16:27). These rewards have been decided upon in this preadvent, investigative judgment. This judgment is the necessary intermediate stage between the last phase of human history and the beginning of heaven's history.

AN INTERLUDE

At this point in the prophecy, there is an interlude or parenthesis. It is found in verses 11 and 12. In verses 9 and 10, the prophet saw events from the viewpoint of heaven; he was shown the beginning of the preadvent judgment taking place in heaven. But in verses 11 and 12, Daniel's viewpoint is brought back down to earth temporarily, and he is shown earthly events. These deal mainly with the destruction of the fourth beast and the little horn. It is true that Imperial Rome came to an end in the latter part of the fifth century A.D. How, then, does Daniel view its destruction along with the little horn at the close of world history?

Imperial Rome does not live on in exactly the same way that it did during the early centuries of this era, but the ten horns which represent its divisions do live on in the modern nations of Europe which are descendants of the tribal divisions of that empire. To carry these horns through to the end, the fourth beast continues in the prophecy, although in modified form. The same point is made in Revelation 13:1–3; 17:3, 9–12. The fourth beast carrying its various horns, along with what started out as the little horn, will remain until the end and be destroyed by fire (Daniel 7:11). The NIV has done well to put verse 12 in parenthesis for that is where it belongs. Verse 12 reflects back upon the fate of the first three beast-kingdoms: "The other beasts had been stripped of their authority, but were allowed to live for a period of time." Babylon was conquered by Persia in 539 B.C., but it lasted as a city until A.D. 75. Greece still exists today, but not with the power of Alexander's empire. Until recent years Iran (Persia) was ruled by Shahs who considered themselves direct descendants of the Persian kings (the Achaemenids) of the sixth through the fourth centuries B.C. In this way, each of these powers lived on after its dominion was taken away.

THE SON OF MAN AND THE CONCLUSION OF THE JUDGMENT

With Daniel 7:13, the prophet's view returns to the heavenly court scene. Verses 13 and 14 depict the conclusion of the judgment when Christ receives full authority from the Father just prior to returning to earth at the second advent. Some have seen verses 13 and 14 as referring to the second advent itself. But that interpretation does not correlate well with the explanation of verses 13 and 14 given in verses 26 and 27. The Millerites made the mistake of identifying verses 13 and 14 with the second advent. Only after their disappointment on October 22, 1844 did they come to understand that what was predicted here was an event that was to transpire in heaven. It is not the coming of Christ to earth, but the coming of Christ to God the Father in heaven—an event that takes place in heaven before Jesus comes to earth.

Christ is described here in Daniel 7 as the "son of man" (vs. 13). Jesus used this title for Himself many times according to the Gospels (for just a few instances, see Matthew 9:6; 11:19; 12:8; 13:41; 16:13; 16:28, etc.). This was a well-understood messianic title in His time. Some scholars think that Jesus' use of this title goes directly back to Daniel 7:13. In any event, He surely was identifying Himself with that figure. In Daniel, however, the title serves a slightly different purpose. It is descriptive. It is preceded by the comparative preposition, "like." Daniel saw someone in heaven who looked "like a son of man," that is, He looked like a human being. From the point of view of Daniel's time, such a title is quite remarkable. Daniel saw God and the angels in heaven (vss. 9, 10). There is nothing remarkable about that; that is their normal dwelling place. But then Daniel sees someone who looks like a human being up in heaven!

Even more remarkable, this human being is receiving universal rulership. "He was given, authority, glory and sovereign power; all peoples, nations and men of every language worshiped him. His dominion is an everlasting dominion that will not pass away, and his kingdom is one that will never be destroyed" (vs. 14). There are two dimensions here. The first is time. In contrast to the temporary kingdoms of earth, the kingdom and dominion that this "son of man" receives will go on for ever; it will never be interrupted or given to another. The other dimension includes the earth, the horizontal dimension. Everybody who lives on the surface of the earth in those days will worship and serve Him. The whole earth will be full of His glory.

Who is this Son of man? Jesus has identified this figure for us by His use of it in the Gospels to apply to Himself. But what about the time perspective of Daniel? What identity would this figure have in terms of this vision in the sixth century B.C.?

We have already referred to the fact that the son of man looked like a human being. But there was another aspect to His appearance—He is accompanied by clouds (vs. 13). A word study of "clouds" in a concordance yields references (after those to atmospheric clouds are excluded) that suggest clouds are an attribute of divinity. Psalm 97:2 is an example. "Clouds and thick darkness surround him; righteousness and justice are the foundation of his throne." Thus we find an interesting combination here in Daniel 7. The title "son of man" refers to His humanity, while the description of clouds accompanying Him refers to His divinity. Thus the language of the vision gives evidence that the "son of man" is a divine-human being. How can this be? There is only one being in all the history of the universe that combined those elements in Himself, and that was Jesus Christ. By virtue of the Incarnation, He combined both divinity and humanity in His one person. As Daniel was shown a view of the judgment that was to take place well into the Christian era, long after his own time, he was also shown a view of the resurrected God-man ministering in that judgment, and ultimately receiving the benefit of that judgment by reaffirming his kingship over the saved of the human race.

The combination of the Father and Son here in this vision—the Ancient of Days and the Son of man—brings together some prophetic time symbols from Daniel 8. The great time prophecy which extended to the beginning of this judgment was measured in the unusual time units of "evening-mornings" (8:14). In the preceding chapter, we identified these "evening-mornings" from Genesis 1 as a twenty-four-hour day; we also identified them as a sanctuary day using Numbers 9:15ff. The Lord marked off the sanctuary day by a pillar of fire over the sanctuary during the night and a pillar of cloud over it during the day. These same two elements are brought together again in Daniel 8:14 and Daniel 7:9, 13. The fire which surrounds the Ancient of Days reminds us of the pillar of fire over the sanctuary, and the Son of man comes with clouds, like those that were seen over the sanctuary during the day. Thus Daniel 8:14 gives us sanctuary days marked off by fire in the evening and by a cloud in the day; Daniel 7:9, 13 gives us those same two elements coming together at the end of the 2,300 sanctuary days. When the judgment was to start these two heavenly elements came together.

Basically, three events result from this judgment: (1) the wicked are destroyed (Daniel 7:11, 26); (2) the kingship of the Son of man is reaffirmed (vss. 13, 14); and (3) the saints of the Most High inherit the kingdom (vs. 27). The last verse of the angel's explanation is very important for it gives the final solution to the problems the saints have suffered on earth. In God's great eternal kingdom they will "worship and obey him [the Son of man]" (vs. 27). Verses 14 and 27 are reciprocals. Both describe the people of God who will be in the eternal kingdom. Verse 14 tells who will rule over them—the Son of man. Verse 27 tells what they will do in relationship to Him—they will serve Him in worship, and they will obey Him. Some of these people will be those who have suffered unjustly from human courts. The divine court in heaven will redress these wrongs. That is what verse 22 means when it refers to the time when "the Ancient of Days came and pronounced judgment in favor of the saints of the Most High, and the time came when they possessed the kingdom." In many cases in human courts there are two sides to an issue. For example, both sides may claim a piece of property. When the court makes its decision, it will decide in favor of one party and against the other. So it is with the divine court. It will decide *against* the wicked and *in favor* of the righteous. To decide in favor of the righteous, God must know the righteous and know that they are—through Christ—righteous. Then they will be vindicated by God in judgment; "vindicated" is one of the meanings of the verb that is employed in Daniel 8:14 and translated as "cleansed" in the KJV and "reconsecrated" in the NIV.

SUMMARY

In this symbolic vision, God gave Daniel a mighty overview of history from his own day to the end of time. This depiction began with four beast nations—a lion representing Babylon, a bear standing for Media-Persia, a leopard symbolizing Greece, and a final beast representing Rome. These kingdoms have already covered 1,000 years from Daniel's time. The prophecy does not foresee any further world empires like these. Instead, the fourth kingdom was to break up into divisions represented by ten horns. After those divisions were in place, an eleventh horn came up. It started out little and then became great. It was distinct in nature from the other powers depicted. Its nature was religious, in contrast to the political powers that had gone before. This religious power came to exercise political powers, however, through a union of purpose between church and state.

This was the form of the church that developed during the Middle Ages when the church reached the zenith of its power. The prophecy identifies eight major characteristics of this medieval Roman Church. These all occurred as predicted by the prophecy. Prominent among these was persecution which was carried out by the Roman Church as amply demonstrated by historical sources (see chapter 5). What had started out as a persecuted body under the caesars, now turned around under the popes to do the persecuting. The prophecy further states that this power would attempt to change God's law, especially those aspects connected with time. This points to the fourth or Sabbath commandment. This power has claimed special authority over the Sabbath enabling it to transfer that sacred institution to another day, Sunday, the first day of the week. The historical sources quoted toward the end of chapter 5 demonstrate just how this course of action has worked out.

DANIEL

The conditions caused by these beast nations and the little horn were not to last forever. Dominion was to pass from one to another, and thus these powers rose and fell on the scene of action. But God had a more final answer ready. That final answer has been introduced by the judgment that is taking place in heaven now according to the description of Daniel 7:9–14. When that great final judgment in heaven comes to an end, the kingship of God's eternal kingdom will be reaffirmed to the Son of man, Jesus Christ. Then He will return to earth and gather up all of His saints, living and dead, and take them to His kingdom. And so shall we ever be with the Lord. "Even so, Come, Lord Jesus" (Revelation 22:20, KJV). God is ultimately in control of the direction of human history as it moves inexorably toward His goal, and that goal will come about soon.

SUMMARY OF PARALLEL PROPHECIES			
Identification	**Daniel 2**	**Daniel 7**	**Daniel 8**
Babylon	Gold	Lion	not represented
Persia	Silver	Bear	Ram
Greece	Bronze	Leopard	Goat
divisions	not represented	4 heads and wings	4 horns
Rome, Imperial	Iron	4th beast	little horn, phase I
divisions	iron and clay	10 horns	not represented
Rome, papal	not represented	little horn	little horn, phase II
Preadvent judgment	not represented	heavenly court scene, Ancient of Days	Cleansing of the sanctuary at end of 2,300 days
Kingdom of God	Stone kingdom	Saints of Most High ruled by Son of man	not represented

CHAPTER TEN

SUMMARY OF DANIEL 7–9

Some obvious connections exist between the three prophecies listed above. They describe some of the same events and cover some of the same historical periods. But other connections between these prophecies are not as readily apparent. One such connection, which the Adventist pioneers (and the Millerites before them) emphasized, is the connection between the time prophecies of Daniel 8 and 9. As described in detail in the preceding chapters, the seventy weeks of Daniel 9 have been cut off from the longer time period in chapter 8—the 2,300 days. As a matter of fact, the original language makes that link even more specific.

But there is yet another kind of link between these prophecies which we have not emphasized. That link lies in the fact that as one progresses through these prophecies, successive steps in the ministry of Christ are brought to view. We may have failed to readily recognize this progression due to the fact that these prophecies are presented in Semitic thought order, that is, in an order that reasons from effect back to cause. In modern western European thought processes, we reason from cause to effect. The ancients could do that too, but they commonly thought and wrote in the reverse of this order. This feature explains much about the connections between these prophecies and why they appear in the order that they do. When we understand this feature of these prophecies, the logical progression in the work of Christ the Messiah becomes clear. In this way an even stronger link is forged between these three prophecies. This summary chapter will focus on these connections.

SUMMARY OF DANIEL 9—CHRIST AS SACRIFICE

From our study of Daniel 9 (see chapter 7 above), we may summarize as follows the main emphases in that prophecy regarding the work of the Messiah. The prophecy of Daniel 9 foretold:

1. The time for the appearing of the Messiah (vs. 25).
2. That He would be "cut off," that is, killed (vs. 26a).
3. That He would bring the sacrificial system to an end (vs. 27a).
4. That He would make a strong offer of the covenant to many people in His teaching and ministry (vs. 27a).
5. That He would make the great atonement for iniquity (vs. 24c).
6. That by making this atonement He would bring in everlasting righteousness (vs. 24d).
7. That a new sanctuary in heaven would be anointed or dedicated for His work as our high priest (vss. 24, 25).

All the specifications of this prophecy with regard to the Messiah were fulfilled in the life, death, resurrection, and ascension of Jesus of Nazareth. He becomes its center and focus; all else in it revolves around Him. The list given above can be condensed into one central teaching about Jesus Christ as the Messiah: He was the great suffering Servant of God who came to give His life as a sacrifice for sin. The picture that lies at the heart of the prophecy of Daniel 9 is the picture of *Jesus as Sacrifice.*

SUMMARY OF DANIEL 8—CHRIST AS PRIEST

Moving to Daniel 8, we come to a prophecy of a different character. The prophecy in this chapter is a symbolic prophecy involving beast-nations and horns along with symbolic actions characterizing their future course. The outline of the first half of the prophecy is relatively straightforward, and the details are agreed upon by most commentators. The action begins with the ascendancy of the Medo-Persian ram (vss. 3, 20), followed by the Greek goat (vss. 5, 21). The Greek goat's great horn is Alexander, whose reign is followed by the breakup of his empire into four kingdoms symbolized by the four horns (vss. 8, 21, 22).

PAGAN ROME

At this point a new "little" horn comes upon the scene. Historicist commentators see this little horn as Rome whose conquests to the east, south, and the glorious land of Judea are described in Daniel 8:9. Most interpreters in other prophetic schools identify this little horn with Antiochus IV Epiphanes. This interpretation has been dealt with in detail earlier in this book and need not be discussed further here. This volume takes the position that we are dealing with Rome under this symbol.

PAPAL ROME

A new phase of Rome begins in verse 11. This new phase is symbolized by actions that introduce the horn's vertical dimension beyond the stellar heaven in contrast with the horizontal conquests it has carried out previously. The symbolic nature of these actions should be stressed. We are not dealing with a literal horn, nor did it literally reach up to heaven. This is a symbol for a human organization that makes a fourfold attack against God: (1) it persecutes the saints of the Most High or the holy people; (2) it casts down the sanctuary in heaven (thus implying, in contrast, its elevation of an earthly temple in which it dwells and functions, compare 2 Thessalonians 2:3, 4); (3) it attacks the "daily" or "continual" (not a single sacrifice as some translators would have it, but a "ministration" that covers all types of activity going on in the heavenly sanctuary on a daily basis); and (4) it attacks the Prince to whom the sanctuary belongs (8:11, 12, 24, 25).

In other words, the climax of this prophecy describes a great conflict pitting the heavenly Prince against the little horn, a conflict involving nothing less than the plan of salvation. On one hand is the true plan of salvation, ministered by the true heavenly High Priest. On the other hand is a substitute, an earthly priesthood functioning in earthly temples designed to take the eyes of mankind off the true High Priest in His true sanctuary (compare Hebrews 8:1, 2). Who is this great heavenly High Priest, and who is this priestly Prince? None other than Jesus Christ. His priesthood is identified especially in Hebrews 7–9. And the anointing of His sanctuary in heaven is referred to in the prophecies of Daniel (Daniel 9:24, 25). The prophecy of Daniel 8 presents *Jesus as Priest.*

DANIEL

SUMMARY OF DANIEL 7—CHRIST AS KING

In the great prophecy of Daniel 7, we also have a succession of kingdoms symbolized by a series of beasts. These can be readily identified as Babylon, Media-Persia, Greece, and Rome (7:3–7, 17). The kingdom or empire of Rome was then to be broken up, as symbolized by the ten horns upon the head of the Roman beast. Among these ten horns would sprout another "little" horn. The prophecy gives a number of characteristics by which we can determine that it does the same type of work as does the little horn of Daniel 8. Thus we can identify this little horn as a Roman horn—the religious phase of that power (7:7, 8, 20, 21, 23–25; see also the discussion in the previous chapter).

A particular period of time was allotted to this little horn for it to exercise power and dominion. Verse 25 specifies this time period as three and a half "times" or years. Applying the year-day principle to this time prophecy, we identify its 1,260 years with the Middle or Dark Ages, from A.D. 538 to A.D. 1798.

God has an answer to all of the beast-kingdoms and horns found in this prophecy. The answer is His judgment. That judgment is described in Daniel 7:9, 10, 13, 14. Here the prophet looks into the heavenly sanctuary and sees the great heavenly tribunal begin (vss. 9, 10). The Ancient of Days comes to sit upon His throne, placed upon a dais at the commencement of this court session. All the angels gather, the court sits in judgment, and the books of record out of which the judgment is to be conducted are opened.

Three important decisions stem from this judgment: (1) The saints of the Most High will go into the heavenly kingdom (vs. 22); (2) the little horn, the beasts, and those allied with them will be destroyed (vss. 11, 22, 26); and (3) the kingship of the eternal kingdom of God is reaffirmed to the Son of man (vss. 13, 14). The Son of man is brought before the Ancient of Days by a retinue of angels and with the clouds of heaven. He is awarded direct and physical rule over God's eternal kingdom. Emphatically we are told that His kingdom will include all who will dwell on earth in the future and that this kingdom, in contrast with those that have gone before it, will last for ever and ever. It will never be interrupted or brought to an end.

Who, then, is this Son of man who receives the eternal kingdom? Jesus took this very title Himself when He made such statements as, "The Son of man is come to seek and to save that which was lost" (Luke 19:10, KJV). Revelation 14:14 makes this connection explicit using the same title, phrased in the same way, in the same context (the clouds of heaven) in a reference to the second coming of Jesus. From a New Testament perspective, therefore, there can be no question that this title, Son of man, refers to King Jesus. At the heart of the prophecy of Daniel 7, therefore, is the picture of *Jesus as King.*

INTERRELATIONS OF DANIEL 7; 8; 9

We have identified three pictures of Jesus at the heart of three prophecies in the heart of the book of Daniel. In chapter 9, the picture is one of *Jesus as Sacrifice.* In chapter 8, the picture that emerges is that of *Jesus as Priest.* And in chapter 7 the picture is of *Jesus as King.*

At this point a question may arise about the order in which these features have been presented. Why are the portrayals not presented in the sequence of their actual occurrence—sacrifice, priest, and king? Why are they presented in the reverse sequence—king (chapter 7); priest (chapter 8); and sacrifice (chapter 9)?

As we noted above, one reason for the literary order has to do with Semitic thought processes. Modern western European thinking reasons from cause to effect; ancient Semitic people commonly reasoned from effect back to cause. Instead of saying, "You are a sinful, wicked, and rebellious people, therefore your land will be destroyed," the biblical prophets could also put the matter the other way around: "Your land will be destroyed." Why? "Because you are a sinful, wicked, and rebellious people." A good biblical example of this kind of thought order can be found in Micah 1:10–15 where the cities that mourn for the exiles are listed first, followed by a list of the cities from which the exiles came. We would put the matter the other way around.

Seventh-day Adventists emphasize that the seventy weeks of Daniel 9 is connected with, or "cut off" from, the 2,300 days of Daniel 8. This is working backwards, if you please. The three pictures of Jesus in these prophecies follow the same kind of pattern, although we are dealing in this case with thematic relations, not time.

We can see the effect of these thematic relations as we read Daniel's book from the beginning. By the time we reach chapter 7 and encounter the picture of the messianic king, the natural questions are: Who is this Being? Where does He come from? Daniel 8 answers by saying, "The King becomes king, in part, because previously He has been the priest. He is the one who has ministered on behalf of the saints of the Most High; now He can accept them into His kingdom."

But that response simply raises another question: How did He qualify as priest? In order to become a priest one has to have something to offer, a sacrifice (see Hebrews 8:3). Where do we find the answer to that question? In Daniel 9. The sacrifice of Daniel 9 enabled the priest of Daniel 8 to become priest, and the priesthood of the Prince enabled the Prince of chapter 8 to become the king of chapter 7. There is a logical, consistent, and interrelated sequence here that is quite direct and reasonable when we understand that the sequence begins at the end and works backward as far as the literary order of the book is concerned.

TEMPORAL RELATIONSHIPS

Another way to look at this sequence is to relate the pictures of Jesus to the time elements found in these prophecies. It is evident that Daniel 9 is the shortest of the three prophecies because its time span extends only for seventy prophetic weeks or 490 years (9:24). The time period of this prophecy, understood historically, takes us from 457 B.C. to first century A.D. Roman times when Jesus walked this earth and was crucified under that power.

The prophecy in Daniel 8, on the other hand, is longer in length, simply by virtue of the fact that its time period extends for 2,300 "evenings-mornings" or days (8:14), which is the symbolic equivalent of 2,300 historical years. This takes us from 457 B.C. into the Christian Era, through the Middle Ages and beyond, down to relatively recent times—the nineteenth century A.D. This means that the priest of that prophecy has been functioning through a part of that time period (beginning at the ascension in A.D. 31).

At the same time His counterfeit has been active too. But the prophecy of Daniel 8 tells about a time when this activity will come to an end. It tells about it verbally; its end is not shown to the prophet in vision.

When the visual portion of the prophecy concludes in Daniel 8:12, the little horn is still practicing and prospering.

Likewise, Daniel 8 does not take the saints of the Most High into the final eternal kingdom. It speaks to the fact that there will be a judgment to bring the bad things of that chapter to an end, but it does not refer directly to the reward of the saints at all. That is reserved for the final prophecy in this backward sequence.

In Daniel 7 we see the final culmination when the King receives His kingdom (vss. 13, 14) and the saints are ushered into that eternal realm (vs. 27). This is the longest in length of these three prophecies at the heart of the book of Daniel. Daniel 9 is the short-length prophecy in terms of time; Daniel 8 is the intermediate-length prophecy; and Daniel 7 is the longest-length prophecy in terms of the events that it describes. These relationships can be summarized by the following diagram:

THREE PICTURES OF JESUS IN THE PROPHECIES AT THE HEART OF DANIEL

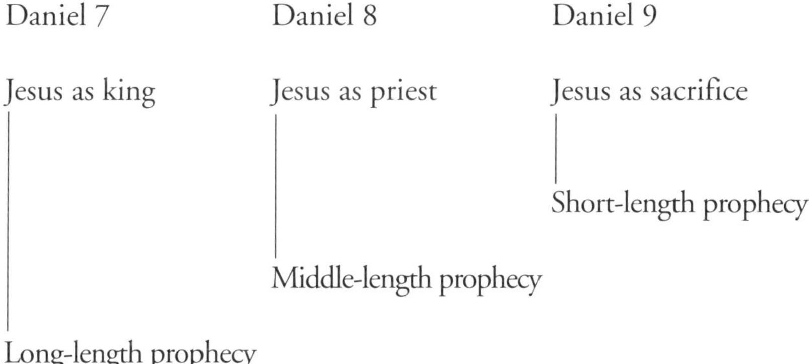

SPIRITUAL RELATIONSHIPS

We are not interested in just the mega-picture of what Daniel's prophecies tell us; we are interested also in what they have to say to us personally and how they apply to our own lives. In this case, we can look at these same three prophecies through our own individual spiritual experience with them. They are not just academic or philosophical exercises to prove the foreknowledge of God. They bring to us personal spiritual experiences with the God of these prophecies and with His Son. That Son we have seen in three phases of His work. As we reflect upon these, we see that these three phases of His work take place in our own lives too. As we look back to the cross, through the eyes of Daniel 9, we see Christ as our sacrifice upon the cross. From Him we receive forgiveness in response to our repentance—not through our own merits, but through His atonement that was worked out on the cross as He died for us (Matthew 26:28). The suffering Messiah of Daniel 9 is *our* sacrifice for sin (1 Peter 2:24). The everlasting righteousness that He thus obtained is for *us*. As we look back in history to the cross and see Him dying there as our Saviour, we claim Him as our Lord. That is the past tense of salvation in these prophecies. We may call that experience justification.

But our salvation does not end there. There is also salvation in the present tense. That is what Daniel 8 is talking about in terms of our personal spiritual experience. As we look up to the heavenly sanctuary today, we can know and have confidence that we have a great High Priest there and that it is the same person as the One who died on the cross, Jesus Christ the Righteous (Hebrews 8:1–3). He is Himself both the sacrifice and the priest who ministers the sacrifice (Hebrews 9:26–28). He is there at the throne of God today interceding for us (1 John 2:1, 2; Romans 8:34). Our prayers go up to Him with the incense of the Holy Spirit (Revelation 8:4). He is our great Mediator, and He is carrying out that role today so that we may receive the Holy Spirit in our lives. He sends forth the promised Comforter to minister to us and live in our hearts, giving us the spiritual strength that we need to live for Christ. This is salvation in the present tense. It is sometimes called sanctification.

But our spiritual experience with these prophecies does not end with justification and sanctification. There is something more awaiting us. That is described for us in the prophecy of Daniel 7. There we see the line of history leading into the future where it will culminate in God's kingdom. There King Jesus will lead and govern His people. There the saints of the Most High will find their long-awaited rest. There they will be glorified with their new immortal bodies and eternal life (1 Corinthians 15:51–53). This eternal life will be lived out as King Jesus leads His people in the kingdom that will occupy the earth made new. The capital of that new world will be the New Jerusalem (Revelation 21; 22). That will be the kingdom of glory. Just as the saints have lived here and now in the kingdom of grace, so one day they will come home to the kingdom of glory. This phase of the plan of salvation is sometimes called glorification.

Thus the three interrelated prophecies of Daniel 9, 8, and 7 bring into view three phases of our spiritual experience. We have a spiritual experience with the Messiah of Daniel 9 because He was our sacrifice in the past and from that sacrifice we received atonement and justification. In the present tense, we have a spiritual experience with Him because He has been pictured in Daniel 8 as our Great High Priest, the heavenly Prince, our Intercessor and Mediator. We receive from Him today the sanctification of our lives. Finally one day, according to the promise of the prophecy of Daniel 7, those lives will be transformed into the glorified lives of the saints in the new earth. There they will be led by the glorious King Jesus in a kingdom that will be all over glorious. No longer will the dim shadows of sin darken the glory of this earth. In those future days of promise it will stand forth with all the radiance of God's re-creation.

The prophetic tenses of these prophecies—past, present, and future—may be added into a chart along with the corresponding spiritual experiences—justification, sanctification, and glorification. All of this can be added together to make up the complete picture of how these prophecies are interconnected. The remarkable picture looks something like this when it is fully realized:

Prophecy	**Daniel 9**	**Daniel 8**	**Daniel 7**
Length	Short	Medium	Long
Picture of Christ	Sacrifice	Priest	King
Spiritual Point of View	Past	Present	Future
Spiritual experience of salvation	Justification	Sanctification	Glorification

CHAPTER ELEVEN

The Final Message—Part 1

Daniel's final prophecy covers three chapters in the book—chapters 10, 11, and 12. Chapter 10 is the introduction or prologue, chapter 11 is the body of the prophecy, and chapter 12 is the conclusion or epilogue. All three belong together as shown by the fact that elements in chapter 10 reappear in chapter 12.

Chapter 11, the body of the prophecy, is the most detailed prophecy in Daniel's book. Previous prophecies have talked about kingdoms; chapter 11 now gets down to the details and talks about individual kings. No symbolic vision precedes this detailed explanation. It is an oral, didactic type of prophecy given directly from the angel Gabriel to the prophet Daniel. The truth of the prophecy is sealed by the appearance of God Himself in chapter 10 and by His oath recorded in chapter 12.

According to the content of chapter 10, a local issue—probably the rebuilding of the temple in Jerusalem—forms part of the situation that is being dealt with. Chapter 11 takes the prophecy from the Persian present (according to Daniel's viewpoint) into the remote future when God would conclude the plan of salvation and set up His eternal kingdom. That event is described in the first four verses of chapter 12.

Remember that the chapter divisions of the English Bible were not present in the scroll of this book as originally written by Daniel. They were added during the twelfth century A.D. This means that chapter 10 should read consecutively into Daniel 11, and Daniel 11 should read progressively into Daniel 12 unseparated by any major breaks.

The Final Message—Part 1

THE DATE

Daniel 10 begins with a date—the third year of Cyrus (vs. 1). The Persians, under Cyrus, took over in Babylon in October of 539 B.C., so Cyrus's first full official year of rulership in Babylon would have begun in the spring of 538 B.C. according to Babylonian and Persian reckoning. Adding three years to 538 B.C. means that this revelation was given to Daniel in the Babylonian-Persian year that began in the spring of 536 B.C. and ended in the spring of 535 B.C. Dates may appear at first to add very little to the story, but they do give us a setting for other events that were happening in the world at the same time.

THE PROBLEM

Daniel tells us that a problem was going on at this time, but he does not tell us the nature of the problem. The date, however, gives us a clue. By the third year of Cyrus, the Jews had returned to Judea. In his first year, Cyrus gave the decree permitting them to return, and they had arrived in Jerusalem by the second year. So the problem bothering Daniel was not whether the Jews were going to return to their own land; that had already been accomplished. The problem must have concerned some trouble which the Jewish people had gotten themselves into after arriving in Jerusalem. The book of Ezra tells us that they did indeed find themselves in trouble.

Ezra 1 tells of the decree of Cyrus permitting the Jews to return to their land. Ezra 2 gives the list of those who went back. Ezra 3 tells some of the first things that they did when they arrived at the site of the destroyed temple and began to work. They erected the altar and began the sacrifices, but when they came to address building the temple itself, they ran into difficulty. The Samaritans came and wanted to help with the temple construction. These were the mixed descendants of those Israelites who had been left in the land after the Assyrian and Babylonian deportations and non-Jewish people who had been moved in from the east to occupy some of the old Israelite territory. They were polytheists and idolaters. The Jewish returnees, remembering the reason for their captivity, were afraid that the Samaritans would introduce these practices into the new temple, so they refused their offer to help with its reconstruction. That is where the problem arose.

Having been rebuffed, the Samaritans turned to obstructionism. "If you won't let us help you," they said in effect, "we will do everything we can to see that the temple is never rebuilt." And they successfully brought the work to a halt. Ezra 4:5 says, "They [the Samaritans] hired counselors to work against them [the Jews] and frustrate their plans during the entire reign of Cyrus king of Persia and down to the reign of Darius king of Persia." Darius I did not come to the throne until 522 B.C., so this indicates a rather prolonged period of time. From 536 B.C. to 522 B.C. nothing much happened on the temple site in terms of rebuilding.

Ezra says that the Samaritans "hired counselors" to work against the Jews. Where would those counselors carry out their work? Not at Jerusalem, but rather at the centers of political power in the Persian empire. The most sensitive place for these counselors to try to obstruct the work would be at the court of the king. And since they appear to have had success in getting the work stopped, they must have gotten the ear of the king and his court.

Another person critical to this whole situation was the prince of Persia, and Daniel mentions him later (10:13, 20). Whoever they were talking to, these counselors had success and got the building program in the temple area in Jerusalem stopped. This occurred right about the time that Daniel was fasting about an unspecified problem in chapter 10. Since the major problem for the Jews right at that time was the work stoppage in regard to the rebuilding of the Jerusalem temple, it is logical to put these two pieces of the puzzle together to suggest that this was the problem Daniel was fasting about. The text of Daniel 10 does not say this directly, but this seems the most likely candidate from what we know of the history of that time.

THE APPEARANCE OF GOD

Daniel was out by the Tigris River with a few of his friends (10:4). They were concerned about this issue of the temple. Would the temple never be rebuilt? Would God never have His earthly sanctuary to come back to? In Exodus 25:8 God had directed, "Then have them make a sanctuary for me, and I will dwell among them." That directive led to the construction of the tabernacle in the wilderness, followed in turn by Solomon's temple in Jerusalem. But now that magnificent structure lay in ruins. If there was no temple in which God could dwell and manifest His presence, how could He meet with His people? God soon answered that concern directly by a manifestation of His person.

When God manifested His presence, this is what Daniel saw: "I looked up and there before me was a man dressed in linen, with a belt of finest gold around his waist. His body was like chrysolite, and his face like lightning, his eyes like flaming torches, his arms and legs like the gleam of burnished bronze, and his voice like the sound of a multitude" (Daniel 10:5, 6). This is no ordinary being, not even an angel. The angel Gabriel appears to Daniel later in this chapter, and two other angels appear standing on each side of the river according to chapter 12, but this majestic being outshone them all by far. The prophet tells us of the majesty and glory of the being he saw. He mentions the radiance of His clothes and His body. Then he speaks of His face, His eyes, and His extremities. All over, He was bright and glorious. This is the numinous resplendent effulgence of the personal being of God. We have a hard time finding words to describe this, and so did Daniel. That is why he compared these features to various bright features of nature.

Daniel called this a vision, but he used a particular Hebrew word that refers especially to the appearance of a personal being, in contrast to a symbolic vision such as in Daniel 7 and 8. This could also be called a theophany, a personal appearance of God. At the end of his earthly ministry as a prophet of God, Daniel meets personally the Lord whom he had been serving for all of this time. That personal presence of God brought assurance to the prophet. It assured him that his work for God had been accepted and that God was still working on behalf of His people.

Solomon had said at the dedication of the temple that regardless of how great and glorious any earthly temple might be, it was not adequate to contain the great God (see 2 Chronicles 6:18). So it was in Daniel's time. Whether the temple was rebuilt now or later, God was still with His people—and He was still with His prophet. In this vision of God's presence there was assurance for Daniel personally, and there was assurance for the people of God, that He would help them to overcome the obstacles in their way.

DANIEL

THE DAY OF THE WEEK

There are some clues in these verses that may make it possible for us to estimate rather precisely when this appearance of God came to Daniel. He says that he had been mourning and fasting for three "full" weeks and that then God appeared to him on the twenty-fourth day of the first month—Nisan (10:4). Given the close proximity of these statements, the implication is that the twenty-fourth day of the first month took place immediately at the end of the three weeks of fasting. The original language uses an idiom here to indicate that the weeks were "full." Full weeks come to an end after seven days; they end on Sabbath, the seventh day. Since this vision appeared to Daniel at the end of three full weeks, it must also have come to him on a Sabbath day. That means that this final prophecy of the book of Daniel was most likely given on a Sabbath. This is the only vision in the book that we can date with such precision.

In this regard, there is a rather direct parallel between Daniel and John who was the recipient of the visions of the book of Revelation. John says he received his vision on the "Lord's day" (Revelation 1:10). As we know from both the Old Testament and the New Testament, the day that the Lord has claimed as His special possession is the Sabbath (Isa. 58:13; Mark 2:28). Thus Daniel received his final prophecy on the Sabbath, and John received the visions of his book on that day too. Both of these men were elderly at the time. Daniel had been in Babylonian captivity for seventy years and was nearing ninety years of age at the time. John received his vision in A.D. 96 and had not seen Jesus personally for almost seventy years. We do not know John's precise age, but if he became a disciple of Jesus at about the same age as Daniel when he was carried into exile, then the two men would be approximately the same age at the time they received their visions.

Likewise, both were exiles at the time they received their visions. Daniel was in Babylon, and John was imprisoned on the island of Patmos "because of the word of God and the testimony of Jesus" (Revelation 1:9). Their visions were also of the same character. Both contain a special type of prophecy that is known as apocalyptic. These prophecies narrate history down to its end and the setting up of the kingdom of God.

A comparison can also be made between the form God's appearance took in both Daniel 10 and in Revelation 1. John saw Jesus Christ standing among the lampstands of the sanctuary, dressed like a priest, but also exhibiting the radiance and the glory of the person of God. When one looks elsewhere in the Bible for a further explanation of the appearance of God described in Daniel 10, two texts stand out: Revelation 1 and Ezekiel 1. Ezekiel, like John, saw a similar being with many of the same features. Of this view of God Ezekiel said, "This was the appearance of the likeness of the glory of the Lord" (Ezekiel 1:28).

To Ezekiel and Daniel, the experience was the same. Ezekiel wrote, "When I saw it [the vision of God], I fell facedown, and I heard the voice of one speaking" (vs. 28). Daniel too was overcome in a similar way. He fell into a deep sleep with his face to the ground (Daniel 10:9).

THE ANGEL

The angel Gabriel touched Daniel to restore his strength so that he could receive the prophecy the angel desired to give him. This gave him enough strength to get up on his hands and knees, and then slowly and laboriously he rose to a fully erect stance, even though he was still trembling from the experience (10:10). This should give us a sense of the might, majesty, and glory of God. There are two contrasting elements in religion that teach us how we should approach God and how we should view Him. These two elements are transcendence and immanence. The transcendence of God says that He is great and mighty and glorious and that He runs the universe from His throne. The immanence of God tells us that He is our friend who has come down to dwell beside us. How can both of these views be true? How can the great majestic God of the universe also stoop low to become our personal friend? That is the great tension of religion, a tension that was ultimately resolved in the Incarnation. Jesus came to live alongside of us with His divinity shielded from us by His humanity. Thus the great God of the universe becomes our personal friend in Jesus Christ, and in that capacity He has a tender, loving concern for us. That is part of what the vision of God/Jesus in Ezekiel 1, Daniel 10, and Revelation 1 tells us.

Gabriel we have seen before. He appeared to Daniel to give him the prophecy of Daniel 9:24–27. He also appeared to Daniel at the time of the vision of Daniel 8:1–12 in order to give to him the interpretation of that symbolic vision. Gabriel is mentioned there as the one whom Daniel had seen "in the earlier vision" (Daniel 9:21), thus connecting the two prophecies of Daniel 8 and 9. Likewise, chapters 10 and 11 are connected to chapters 8 and 9 by Daniel's statement that after receiving the explanation given in chapter 11, he had understanding of the previous vision (Daniel 10:1). Although Gabriel is not named in chapter 10 or 11, his position next to Michael makes him the logical candidate for the angel that brought this message to the prophet (Daniel 10:13, 20). Thus these three prophecies are tied together by their common presenter and interpreter, Gabriel. He appeared after the symbolic vision of chapter 8 to explain it to Daniel, and he appeared to present the prophecies of chapters 9 and 11 without any immediately preceding vision. One could almost refer to chapters 8–12 as the book of the Revelations of Gabriel, just as the Apocalypse is referred to as the book of the Revelation of Jesus Christ. We find Gabriel again in the New Testament. He not only gave the prophecy of chapter 9, he also came to announce the completion of one of its major segments when he announced the forthcoming birth of the forerunner of Jesus, John the Baptist (Luke 1:1, 19).

DIVINE INTERVENTION IN HUMAN AFFAIRS

We already know that there was a problem over which Daniel was mourning and fasting. It has been suggested that the problem concerning him was the rebuilding of the temple which had stopped due to the intervention of the Samaritans. Daniel had been fasting and mourning for three weeks. If God's earthly servant was so concerned about this turn of events, why wasn't God Himself doing something about it? He was, and Gabriel tells us so. During the same three-week period during which Daniel had been mourning and fasting, Gabriel and his superior, Michael the archangel, had been wrestling with the prince of Persia (10:12, 13). Thus the prince of Persia must have had something to do with causing the problem.

Most commentaries view the prince of Persia in Daniel 10 as the symbol of an evil angel who works as a national genius or supervising spirit for Persia. Thus the good angels, Michael and Gabriel, are pitted against him as they battle over the fate of God's people. But neither Satan nor any of his angels were princes in the kingdom of Persia.

Since the chapter names the *king* of Persia we can readily identify who the *prince* of Persia was at this time. The prince of Persia would be Cambyses, the son of king Cyrus. When Cyrus died, Cambyses succeeded to the throne. Before that, he was the crown prince. Logically, he should be the prince of Persia mentioned in Daniel 10.

Why would Cambyses be mentioned here in Daniel 10? For two main reasons: (1) because of his political influence and power as prince; and (2) because he was very much in opposition to all foreign religious cults. As crown prince, Cambyses was very much involved in the affairs of the province of Babylon. Cyrus even elevated him to the rank of co-king or co-regent, just as Nabonidus had done with Belshazzar. Cambyses was an ardent Zoroastrian who worshiped the god Ahura Mazda. He had no tolerance for the cults of other gods. Historians have told us that he even destroyed the temples of some of those foreign gods, especially in Egypt. It undoubtedly was no accident that the Jews accomplished nothing toward rebuilding the temple in Jerusalem throughout the reign of Cambyses (530-522 B.C.). The neglect shown to the temple during that period would certainly be consonant with the policy of Cambyses. Even before his sole reign, Cambyses was of great influence in the province of Babylon to which Syria and Judah belonged. These provinces were known as Babylon and Beyond the River, meaning the Trans-Euphrates region. Not until the reorganization of the political structure of the empire by Darius I were Syria and Judah split off from the province of Babylon.

Thus if some counselors hired by the Samaritans came to Babylon and encountered Cambyses, he probably would have been happy to oblige them in their request. The Jews were not able to rebuild the temple in Jerusalem through the remainder of Cyrus's reign and during all the reign of Cambyses. Not until a new king, Darius I, came on the scene of action with a new policy were the Jews able to get something done about rebuilding the temple (see Ezra 4:5).

Behind the scene of action, however, unseen forces were at work. The powers of heaven were being brought to bear upon the stubborn Persian prince as the angels of God worked to bring about His will. Despite heavenly efforts, however, the choice still resides with man, and as far as we can tell, Cambyses never did yield to these influences. It should also be noted that he came to a sad end, a probable suicide on his way back to Persia from Egypt. He fell upon his sword and died from the wound. Some said it was an accident while others said it was a suicide. In either event, Cambyses came to a sad end, and part of that sad picture includes his evident opposition to the true God of the Jews.

MICHAEL

Gabriel assures Daniel that the forces of heaven have not yet given up their struggle for the people of God. After leaving Daniel, he would return to continue his struggle with the prince of Persia. He would be supported in this effort by Michael (10:20, 21). Michael is called "one of the chief princes," "your prince," and "the great prince who protects your people" (10:13, 21; 12:1). He is the heavenly prince in contrast to the earthly prince Cambyses. The Old Testament does not tell us everything there is to know about Michael. In order to fill out the picture we need to go to Jude 9 in the New Testament where Michael is identified as the archangel with the power of the resurrection and to Revelation 12:7 where we find that he was leader of the heavenly host against Satan and his rebel forces in heaven before the creation of man. Clearly, these two New Testament texts can be referring only to Jesus Christ. Therefore, we can safely assume that the Old Testament references to Michael should be understood as referring to Christ also.

Michael is mentioned by name only in Daniel 10 and 12. In Daniel 10, He is involved in a local, limited problem. In Daniel 12, He is involved, as we will see, in a final and universal conflict, the conclusion of the battle between good and evil. Wherever found, all the Michael passages in the Bible have this characteristic: they involve conflict, and Michael is portrayed as the leader in the battle on the side of God. Thus the pictures of Michael in Daniel 10 and 12 make a kind of envelope around the prophecy of Daniel 11. Michael is introduced in Daniel 10 in connection with the controversy taking place in the prophet's own time (10:13, 21). The final picture of Michael appears at the end of time in the final controversy (12:1). In all of these cases, He protects the people of God. So He did in the sixth century B.C., and so He will do at the end of time.

From the controversy swirling around Michael versus Cambyses, Gabriel goes on to carry Daniel through the prophetic future down to the time when Michael will appear on the scene of action one final time as the plan of salvation draws to its close and Michael takes His people home. That prophetic future narrated by Gabriel is the subject of Daniel 11.

DANIEL 11

Daniel 11 has been a difficult chapter for interpreters to understand. There is a great amount of detail given, and it can become easy to miss the forest for the trees. In the following section we will be looking at "the king of the south" and "the king of the north." We will be examining the history of the Persian and Greek kings following the time of Daniel. Chapter 11 brings to view a great many historical details. But all these serve merely to set the stage for the prophecy's overall purpose, which is to carry the action down through the future until the time when Michael will appear on the scene one final time to bring the plan of salvation to a close and take His people home.

Despite its mass of historical detail for the centuries between Daniel's day and the coming of the Messiah, the prophecy of chapter 11, like that of chapters 8 and 9, is concerned with the outworking of the great plan of salvation and the eternal fate of God's people. As such, it is closely linked to the great outline prophecy of chapters 8 and 9, and amplifies that prophecy further as is shown by the following chart:

THE RELATIONSHIP OF DANIEL 11 TO DANIEL 8 AND 9			
	Daniel 11		**Daniel 8, 9**
11:2	The kingdom of Persia	8:20	the ram of Persia
11:2	The kingdom of Greece	8:21	the goat of Greece
11:3	A mighty king appears in Greece	8:21	the large horn as the first king of Greece = Alexander the Great
11:4	The four winds = the scattering of the empire of the great king	8:22	The four kingdoms that rise out of the large horn of Greece
11:16	The Beautiful Land is conquered	8:9	Pagan Rome conquers the Beautiful Land of Israel
11:22	Prince of the covenant will be destroyed	9:25	Pagan Rome cuts off the Anointed One at Calvary

DANIEL

PERSIA—DANIEL 11:2

Daniel 11:2 refers to three Persian kings who were to "appear," followed by a fourth king. Since Cyrus was on the throne when Gabriel gave Daniel this prophecy, we should begin counting with his son Cambyses as the first of the three. Before leaving for Egypt, Cambyses assassinated his brother Smerdis. But while Cambyses was away, Bardiyya, an imposter, took the throne claiming to be Smerdis. Cambyses was on his way back from Egypt to rectify this situation when he died. After a short time, Darius I Hystaspes took the throne following his military conquest of the rebels against the central government, including the false Smerdis. Darius was not in line for the throne, but he secured that position by means of his military conquests. Thus the three Persian kings who would "appear" (11:2) were Cambyses, the false Smerdis, and Darius I Hystaspes.

The fourth king who followed these three was especially significant; the prophecy says he "will be far richer than all the others. When he has gained power by his wealth, he will stir up everyone against the kingdom of Greece" (11:2). This wealthy king was Xerxes, the Persian king described in the book of Esther. Xerxes was the second of the Persian kings to stir up Greece by invading it; Darius had been the first. Xerxes invaded Greece in 480 B.C. Greece did not retaliate for more than a century, but the Greeks never forgot the humiliation that the Persians had visited upon their country. When finally they did come to redress those wrongs, it was in direct response to what the Persians had done to them so many years before. The Greek retaliation took place under Alexander the Great.

Some students of Daniel 11 have said that the author did not know his Persian history well because he did not go on to enumerate and characterize the Persian kings after Xerxes. This observation misses the point. The purpose of the prophecy was not to give a thorough survey of Persian history, but to trace it to the point at which the next power was introduced on the scene of action. Since Xerxes was the one who eventually brought the Greeks into the realm of Near Eastern politics, there was no need for the prophecy to recite more of Persian history after that point. The prophecy then shifted to the new power on the scene of action in order to trace the rise and fall of these kings and their kingdoms.

GREECE—DANIEL 11:3, 4

The first king to arise after Greece came on the scene of action is described as a mighty king "who will rule with great power and do as he pleases" (vs. 3). The text does not say so directly, but the clear implication is that this new and powerful king obtained his power and kingdom from his defeat of the Persian kings before him. This king obviously was Alexander the Great. There is a direct linguistic link between Daniel 8:8, 21 and Daniel 11:4 in terms of Alexander's fate; the same Hebrew verb is used in all three verses to express how he was to be "broken." Daniel 11 adds the detail that his kingdom would not go to his direct posterity. This was fulfilled in the life and death of Alexander the Great. He had one young son at the time of his death, but this son did not inherit any part of his father's empire.

Instead, his kingdom was to be divided, "to the four winds of heaven," or to the four directions of the compass. This is the same language used in Daniel 8:8, referring to the breakup of Alexander's empire into the four horns, or kingdoms, that his generals came to control. These divisions have already been discussed in the commentary on Daniel 7 and 8, where they were also represented by the four heads and wings on the leopard (7:6) and by the four horns on the head of the goat (8:8, 22). This is another marker point at which the prophecies of Daniel intersect, and this juncture serves as one of the landmarks as we progress through the complicated political succession of Daniel 11.

HISTORICAL KINGS OF NORTH AND SOUTH—DANIEL 11:5-15

From the standpoint of the Jews living in Judah, the most important divisions of the Greek Empire were Syria, including the province of Babylon, which lay immediately to their north, and Egypt which lay to their south. These dynasties were known as the Ptolemies in Egypt and the Seleucids in Syria based on the names of their first rulers, Ptolemy I and Seleucus I respectively. During this period, the Jews were first under the control of the Ptolemies and then came under the control of the Seleucids. Finally, as a result of a war of independence, the Jews had their own kings known as the Maccabean kings of the Hasmonean house. The history of this intertestamental period, as described down to Daniel 11:13, can be followed without great difficulty in history books which cover that period. It can be outlined briefly as follows. (At this point it would be well for the reader to review Daniel 11:5–15 carefully.)

Verse 5 begins with the first prominent king of the south, or Egypt, who may be identified as Ptolemy I Soter. His commander, who came into a kingdom greater than his, may be identified as Seleucus I Nicator. This commander had had to flee from Syria to Egypt, but eventually he was able to win these Syrian lands back from Antigonus, the ruler of Syria. "After some years" (vs. 6), by 250 B.C., the king of the south, Ptolemy II Philadelphus and the king of the north at that time, Antiochus II Theos, formed an alliance cemented by the diplomatic marriage of Bernice to Antiochus. When Ptolemy died, however, this arrangement fell apart, and Laodice, the former wife of Antiochus, was able to engineer the deaths of Antiochus, Bernice, and Bernice's son (vs. 6).

To avenge the death of Bernice and her son, "one from her family line" (vs. 7), Ptolemy III Euergetes, came against the north and even captured its capital (vs. 7). For a time he controlled much of the territory of the king of the north in Syria, but he later relinquished it and returned to Egypt, carrying away from there much booty and even some of the gods of the Syrians. This is simply an extension of human politics into the realm of the gods, for this indicated that the gods of Egypt had prevailed over the gods of Syria (vs. 8). Ptolemy III returned to Egypt and did not attack the king of the north again for some time (vs. 8b). Then Seleucus II attacked him in retaliation, but was not successful (vs. 9).

The sons of the king of the north referred to at the beginning of verse 10 were Seleucus III Ceraunus and Antiochus III Magnus. The former was a short-reigned king (226 B.C. to 223 B.C.) but the latter was a ruler of great importance, hence the significance of his name, Magnus, or "Great." He reigned from 223 B.C. to 187 B.C. The reign of Antiochus III may be divided into unequal thirds. The first third was demarcated by the disastrous battle of Raphia on the border between Egypt and Palestine where he was defeated by Ptolemy IV Philopater of Egypt (vs. 11). From that defeat Antiochus III turned his attention to the east where he attempted to win back possessions of the Seleucid kingdom that had been lost. In this he was largely successful. Following that success, he turned again to the problem of Egypt, and this time he had more success than he did in his first encounter (vs. 13). At the battle of Panaeus, in 198 B.C., and as a result of the follow-up from it, the province of Judea came into his hands. Thus the territory of the Jews changed hands, and they were transferred from being vassals of the king of the south to being vassals of the king of the north.

Up to this point, the time of Antiochus III (verse 13), almost all commentators agree upon the identifications of the various kings of the north and the south. The question is: What happened after the time of Antiochus III?

Futurist interpreters take everything from verse 13 to verse 35 as referring to Antiochus IV Epiphanes, whereas preterist interpreters apply everything from this point to the end of the chapter to Antiochus IV. The position of this volume is that only verses 14b, 15 refer to Antiochus IV. Since he was responsible for introducing Rome on to the scene of action in the Middle East, he makes an appropriate transition point to Rome, just as Xerxes made an appropriate transition point to Greece.

By applying only verses 14b and 15 to Antiochus IV Epiphanes, we whittle him down to his proper historical size. He was, after all, only a minor king who ruled a minor kingdom only a short time (175 B.C. to 163 B.C.). He did behave badly toward the Jews in Judea, but the major turning point in his reign was when he had to cave in to diplomatic pressure from Rome. Rome was already the major power on the horizon in the Middle East in the time of Antiochus Epiphanes, and he knew better than to try to thwart its designs. It required only a single Roman ambassador, not an army, to turn back Antiochus Epiphanes from his second invasion of Egypt in 168 B.C.

The first part of verse 14 refers to those who rise up against the king of the south. This could include quite a number of players. First there was Antiochus III and his Syrian troops. Then there were his confederates. Antiochus III entered into a secret alliance with Philip V of Macedonia to divide up the Ptolemaic possessions outside Egypt. Philip, unfortunately, fell afoul of the Romans and suffered a defeat at their hands in the Second Macedonian War (200 B.C. to 196 B.C.). In spite of his alliance with Philip, Antiochus III declined to oppose the Romans on this occasion. One can also see verse 14a as referring to those Egyptians who rebelled against Ptolomy V in Egypt. These events are recorded in Polybius' work (*The Histories* 5.107). Last, but not necessarily least, the "many" of verse 14a could include the Jews, previously under Ptolemaic control until delivered from it by Antiochus III. At the time, after having been under Ptolemaic control for more than a century, it must have seemed like a great deliverance. As a token of this promise of a new day, Antiochus III granted special rights to the Jewish religious state of Judea. But this promise soon failed, and the Jews became confirmed antagonists of Antiochus III. So there were indeed many who rose up against the king of the south at this time as Daniel 11:14a records.

What does the rest of this verse mean? This has been a difficult problem in interpretation for a long time. Literally the text reads, "and the sons of the breakers of your people shall be lifted up, bear, be carried. . . ." The first of these two verbs means "to break in" or "to break out" as in breaching a wall. The second verb normally means "to lift up," "to bear," or "carry away." Combining these meanings should result in a the sentence saying something like, "the sons of the breakers of your people were taken away." This meaning would be parallel to verse 12 which says "the army is carried off" and uses the same verb. But who is verse 14 referring to as being taken away? Who are "the sons of the breakers of your people"? It was the Egyptians. As a result of their defeat at the battle of Paneas (198 B.C.), the Egyptians were removed and taken out of the picture as far as Judea or southern Syria were concerned. Thus the phrase in verse 14 should be translated, rather literally, as "the sons of the breakers of your people were taken away [or, will be taken away, in the future prophetic sense]." It means that the Syrians took the Egyptians away by defeating them and thus the oppressors of God's people in Judea were removed.

The final phrase of verse 14 is an interesting one, for it refers to the fulfilling of a vision. Commentators have had considerable difficulty understanding what this phrase means, but if one considers the historical and political changes that took place in Judea at this time, a more direct answer can be determined. When the Syrians defeated the Egyptians at Paneas, the Egyptian horn of the four Greek horns (Daniel 8:7) had been taken out of the way as far as Judea was concerned. It was replaced by the Syrian horn. Unfortunately for the Jews, that Syrian horn power, soon to be led by Antiochus IV Epiphanes, made life difficult for them by persecuting them.

The persecution by Antiochus IV against the Jews has been seen by many interpreters as constituting the fulfillment of a major portion of the rest of Daniel 11. However, the prophetic statement in verse 14 should caution us against this interpretation; it implies these people—the Syrians under Antiochus IV—will be "without success." No, Antiochus is not the fulfillment of this prophecy. We will have to look for another fulfillment by a greater power on the horizon at that time. We will have to look to Rome.

Daniel 11:15 tells of a campaign against the king of the south conducted by the king of the north. The focus of this campaign centered around a well-fortified city. Various cities and various campaigns of the Seleucid kings have been suggested as the interpretation of these elements, but given the succession of events at this point in the prophecy, the campaign that fits best is Antiochus IV's campaign of 169 B.C. against Egypt. The focus of that campaign centered around the target city of Pelusium, the major city guarding the entrance into the eastern delta of Egypt. Pelusium fell to the troops of Antiochus IV during the campaign, and thus he conquered the eastern half of the delta. Then he returned to Syria for the winter of 169/168 B.C. That was a major error in strategy, and it led to the introduction of the next power in the prophecy.

IMPERIAL ROME—DANIEL 11:16–22

Daniel 11:16 introduces a new actor to the scene of action. He is not referred to either as the king of the south or the king of the north, but as "he who comes" (or "the invader" in the NIV). Since Antiochus IV was victorious at the end of verse 15, it seems logical that he should be the one against whom this new power fights. At this point we find the king of the north does not appear again in chapter 11 until verse 40. He disappears from the narrative when this new power is introduced. The king of the north, the Syrian Seleucid king, recedes, and this new power (Rome) takes over.

Emphasizing the fact that this is a new power appearing upon the scene of action, the text says that he "will do as he pleases" (vs. 16). This is a technical phrase used in introducing new powers to the attention of the prophecy. It was used for Greece in verse 3, and now it is used in verse 16 for Rome, the power which came to Antiochus IV Epiphanes and deterred him from his Egyptian conquests. The third important phrase in verse 16 in connection with this new power is the reference to the "Beautiful Land." This power will stand in it, and all of it will be in his hand. This has no conceivable application to Antiochus IV because Judea was already part of his kingdom when he inherited it from his father. It was not necessary for him to conquer it. Rome on the other hand, took Judea over by conquest. When Rome conquered Syria in 64 B.C., it included Judea in its conquests. As has already been pointed out, this is a cross link with the prophecy in Daniel 8, where in verse 9 the "Beautiful Land" (*sebi*), crops up in terms of the conquests of the little horn.

The other interesting linguistic aspect of verse 16 is the way in which the verse refers to the confrontation between Antiochus IV and Rome. When battles and war are referred to in Daniel 11, the preposition *'al*, "against," is commonly used. But not in this case. Thus the NIV translation "no one will be able to stand against him" is not entirely accurate. The preposition used in the original Hebrew of this verse is *'el,* "to," or "unto." In other words, when the Roman diplomat came to confront Antiochus IV upon his return to Egypt, he did not come with all of the forces of Rome to back him up. It was a diplomatic mission, one that was successful because of the implied threat of bringing down upon Antiochus IV all the power of Rome. But in terms of the meeting, Rome only came "unto" him, not "against" him.

It is open to question whether verse 16 refers to Rome in general or to a specific Roman general who accomplished these actions. Certainly Pompey and his forces were the ones who stood up with strength in the "Beautiful Land," subjugating it in 63 B.C. On the other hand, in Daniel 8, the little horn is not so much indicative of a specific ruler as it is of a political power including all its rulers. If verse 16 is taken as an introduction of the new power as a whole, then the following verses can be understood as elaborating the fates of individual rulers. That seems to be the course the text follows.

Dealing now with an individual ruler, Daniel 11:17 says "he will determine to come with the might of his entire kingdom." Here is a description of further movement beyond Judea, a campaign to another country. The coming of Rome in verse 17 is not to Judea; that is already described in verse 16. Rome had already conquered the northland; now it continued on to the south, to Egypt. Egypt was not formally incorporated into the Roman Empire until Octavian's success there in 30 B.C., but Julius Caesar entered Egypt and influenced its affairs earlier, in 48 B.C. It is interesting to note that he entered Egypt in pursuit of Pompey, who was killed there by an officer of Ptolemy. If verse 16 is referring to Pompey who had caused Rome to establish itself in the "Beautiful Land" (11:16) and who had led the action against Egypt, then the next figure on the scene of action is Julius Caesar.

Julius Caesar then, appears to fit best with the verses 17–19. If the first phrase of verse 17 really has to do with bringing terms of peace or arranging an alliance, then Julius was certainly responsible for that. It was through his political and military maneuvers that he propped up the rulership of Cleopatra and Ptolemy XIV. Literally, the next phrase of verse 17 reads, "and he shall give the daughter of women to him to spoil [ruin, corrupt] her, but she shall not stand and she shall not be[long] to him." This fits well with the notorious dalliance between Caesar and Cleopatra. She apparently bore him a child, Caesarian, and followed him to Rome as his consort. Since Caesar was assassinated shortly after that, however, Cleopatra had to flee back to Egypt to protect her throne. For a time she was partly successful, but when Octavian arrived on the scene of action in Egypt, she is supposed to have died by the bite of a poisonous asp. In this sense she did not stand, that is, continue to rule, nor did she belong to Caesar except for a brief time.

Just as "he" (the invader of verse 16) turned his face toward Egypt at the beginning of verse 17, so now at the beginning of verse 18 he turned his face to the *'iyyim*. This word can be translated as "islands" or "coastlands." Coastlands makes better sense here. Julius Caesar conducted three campaigns after he left Egypt, to the Bosporus, to North Africa, and to Spain. The first two, definitely, and the third, probably, can be considered as coastlands to which he turned his face, that is, his military attention. Then came his final denouement, at the hands of his trusted friends and aides. The text appears to refer to this as turning "his insolence back on him" (vs. 18). Caesar's downfall in his last year of rule came about through his increasingly monarchical and dictatorial style of government. He set himself up for his final fall, however, by pardoning, reinstating, and installing in office the very supposed friends who eventually assassinated him on the ides of March, 44 B.C. A word play is present here. The word for "abuse," "scorn," "insolence," *herpa*, parallels the word for "dagger" or "sword," *hereb,* the instrument which Caeser's friends turned upon him so viciously. His literal and figurative fall and death are described at the end of verse 19.

Verse 20 gives two characteristics the person who was to arise in Caesar's place. First he would send tax collectors throughout the kingdom, and second he would die in a time of peace, not in battle, even though he had fought many battles earlier in his career. Both of these facets of the career of this figure were fulfilled in the life of Caesar Augustus. He is noted for his census taking in Egypt and elsewhere throughout the kingdom, and these census rolls served as a tax base. The taxation system installed under his administration is well represented by the publicans in the New Testament. Jesus came to be born in Bethlehem as the result of an enrollment by Augustus (Luke 2:1). Augustus died of an illness on August 19, A.D. 14, thus fulfilling the latter specification of this portion of the prophecy.

The person who succeeded Augustus was Tiberius, and verse 21 of the prophecy pays attention to the way he gained access to rulership, placing a low evaluation upon him. Tiberius was not the natural born child of Augustus. The son of Livia by a priest also named Tiberius, he came into Augustus's household when Augustus took his mother as his wife by force. According to Roman historians, Tiberius became quite sadistic. Although we cannot completely trust the historians of Rome in his case, there obviously is considerable merit to the evaluation given of Tiberius here in this prophecy. Augustus did not like him or even want him as his successor, but lacking any other logical choice, he had to put up with the idea.

In terms of war, mentioned at the beginning of verse 22, Tiberius was charged especially with taking revenge upon Arminius in Germany, who had wiped out three legions of Roman soldiers. Tiberius was wholly successful in defeating him. He engaged in other occasional wars and acts of savage repression. Included in the latter was his putting down of a provincial rebellion with considerable bloodshed. The prophecy speaks of armies being swept away before him (vs. 22), and this fits Tiberius, but there were many other rulers of ancient times to whom this statement could apply with equal force. The next statement in verse 22, however, is specifically an act of Tiberius.

Daniel 11:22b says "a prince of the covenant" would also be broken before the ruler referred to in this verse. This phrase, "prince of the covenant," is quite specific in its links with Daniel 9:24–27. In other places in the book of Daniel, the word employed for "prince" is *sar*. Here in Daniel 11:22, however, the word used is *nagid*. This word is used only one other place in the book of Daniel—Daniel 9:24–27. On a linguistic basis, therefore, these two prophecies should be tied together at this point. In Daniel 9:24–27 it is also the Messiah Prince (*nagid*, "ruler" in NIV) who makes a strong covenant with many for one week. Hence the "prince" and the "covenant" are linked in both of these prophecies.

Both the historicist and futurist approaches to Daniel 9:24–27 see the Messiah Prince mentioned verse 25 as none other than Jesus Christ. Identifying Jesus as the Messiah Prince of Daniel 9:24–27 means that when we come to this time in the prophecy, we have come to the time of Jesus of Nazareth as the fulfillment of those aspects of that prophecy. This gives us a chronological linchpin upon which to hang verse 22 in the narrative of Daniel 11. By the time we reach this point in Daniel 11 we have reached the first century A.D., and the events described here should surround that point.

CHAPTER TWELVE

The Final Message—Part 2

Let's summarize what we learned in the preceding chapter as we examined Daniel 10:1–11:22. We said that chapter 10 comprises the introduction to that prophecy and involves the appearance of God and a conversation with an angel, probably Gabriel, to confirm the truth of this prophecy. In chapter 11, the angel messenger began to recite the prophetic history of kings and nations that were to follow after Daniel's time. That prophecy began with the kings of Persia (11:2) and then moved on to Alexander the Great of Greece (11:2). After Alexander died, his kingdom broke up into four main pieces (11:4). Daniel 8 refers to all four of these divisions of Alexander's kingdom through the symbol of four horns (8:8, 22). Daniel 11, however, concentrates especially upon only two of these four. Those two are "the king of the north," whose royal residence was at Antioch in Syria (11:6), and "the king of the south," who came from Egypt (11:5). Since Judea was sandwiched between these two powers, it was passed back and forth between them. Eventually this situation was brought to an end by Rome which defeated both Syria and Egypt, conquering Judea at the same time that it conquered Syria (11:16). Thus Rome came to be in power in Judea in the first century A.D. when Jesus of Nazareth, "prince of the covenant," was broken or executed on the cross by the Roman power (11:22).

At this point in the prophecy, verse 23 takes up with a new phase of the power of Rome. That is where our study in this chapter begins.

Verse 23 marks a transition in the prophecy of chapter 11. Verses 1–22 have carried the action down from the time of Daniel himself to the coming of the Messiah, the "prince of the covenant." Although these verses contain a vast amount of historical detail, the interpretation is often problematical. If anything, the detail and the interpretive difficulties increase in the second section of chapter 11, verses 23–45.

In spite of these problems, however, the underlying purpose and intent of the prophecy in verses 1–22 is evident. In the first section, the action between the king of the north and the king of the south has much to do with the affairs of God's people; the struggle is essentially a spiritual one which culminates with the appearance of the Messiah and His confirming the covenant with many by His death.

Likewise, the second section of the prophecy (vss. 23–45), although framed in terms of conflicting kingdoms, concerns the spiritual struggles between God's people and His truth on the one hand, and on the other, the persecuting power that seeks to obscure God's sanctuary in heaven and the salvation that is being ministered there for us by our faithful High Priest, Jesus Christ. As we look at the details, we need to also keep in mind the grand sweep of salvation history that lies behind them.

PAPAL ROME—DANIEL 11:23–39

By 11:22 the prophecy has reached the time of Jesus Christ under Imperial Rome in the first century A.D. The question is: Where does the prophecy go from there? It could continue with Imperial Rome for a further stretch of history. That is the way Uriah Smith treated the text in his Adventist classic, *Thoughts on Daniel.* For Smith, verses 23–30 repeated the history of the same three Caesars. Such a repetition is possibly in line with Hebrew parallelism of thought, but it is not very likely that such a repetition would occur in a consecutive, historically prophetic narrative text such as we have here in Daniel 11.

Or the text, beginning in verse 23, might skip down to the time of the Roman conquest of Jerusalem in A.D. 70, but there does not appear to be much reference to such a war and siege in these verses. The time of Constantine would make another major historical transition, with the conversion of the Roman Empire to Christianity, but Constantine does not appear to fit well in this passage either.

Having eliminated these important historical events as subjects of the prophecy in the rest of chapter 11, we are left with the time of papal Rome's rise in the sixth century A.D. If this is the subject of these verses, then the prophecy would bring us to the next segment of history that we have seen in other prophecies in Daniel—the rise of Rome's second phase, which is medieval, papal Rome as contrasted with Imperial Rome. In that case, Daniel 11 would parallel what we have found in Daniel 7 and 8. Based on this understanding, this volume takes the position that Daniel 11:23–30 is dealing with the activities of Rome's second phase, papal Rome, and that the "king of the north" in these verses refers to this power.

Secular and church historians have noted that this transition from Imperial to papal Rome took place in the sixth century A.D. That was a time of the decline of the glory of Imperial Rome, but it was also a time for the rise of the power of the church as it filled the vacuum left behind by that decline. The power base of the empire had shifted to Constantinople in the east, leaving the church largely in charge in the west.

Verses 23–39 do not necessarily present the activities of the papal power in chronologically consecutive order. Rather, in this case, they are apparently arranged in topical order. The elements present in verses 23–39 can be outlined in the following fashion.

1. Verses 23–30 actual military campaigning
2. Verse 30 subversion of the system of salvation
3. Verses 32–34 persecution
4. Verses 35–39 self-exaltation

The last three of these elements are also described in Daniel 8 in terms of the activities of the little horn. The comparison may be drawn in this way:

Event	Daniel 7	Daniel 8	Daniel 11
Taking away the Daily (chap. 8) Abolish the Daily (chap. 11)	—	Dan. 8:11	Dan. 11:31
persecution	Dan. 7:25	Dan. 8:10b	Dan. 11:32-34
self-exaltation	Dan. 7:8, 20, 25a	Dan. 8:10a	Dan. 35-39

All three chapters mention persecution and self-exaltation, but only chapters 8 and 11 mention taking away the daily. Daniel 11 also contains one element in this outline of activities—the actual military campaigning—that is not present in Daniel 8. Daniel 8:9 does mention military campaigns, but these refer to the conquests of *Imperial* Rome to the east, south, and the glorious land—not to military activity by the *papal* phase of Rome. The military campaigns found in Daniel 8:9 find their corresponding parallel in 11:16 which portrays the activity of the troops of the Roman general Pompey standing in the glorious land of Judea and its capital of Jerusalem.

THE CRUSADES

Daniel 11:23–30 deals with another type of military campaign. These campaigns are conducted by the papacy, which is represented in 11:23–30 as the king of the north or in chapter 8 as the second phase of the little horn. This activity by Rome in its papal phase resembles what imperial Rome did earlier under Pompey and Julius Caesar. But these campaigns do not take place in the sixth century A.D., the time when Rome was in the early phase of rising up from littleness. The campaigns pictured in 11:23–30 occurred considerably later when Rome had moved into its papal phase.

The classic example of this type of military activity as conducted by the papacy were the Crusades of the eleventh to the thirteenth centuries. At this time, more than at any other time in history, the papacy, the king of the north, became directly involved in warfare. This warfare was designed to win back the holy places for Christianity, but in doing so the crusaders brought down upon themselves the wrath of Egypt, the king of the south. The last battle of the first crusade involved forces from Egypt, and the last battle of the last crusade involved an unsuccessful invasion of Egypt.

This pattern fits what is described in 11:23–30. The forces of the king of the north make their conquests first, and then the forces of the king of the south come on the scene of action. That is exactly what happened during the first crusade in the eleventh century A.D. Then the last crusade involved an actual invasion of Egypt by sea, but the forces from the north were defeated. That is also just what chapter 11 says in verses 29, 30.

Daniel 11:40–45 is the most difficult passage to interpret *prophetically* because its events still lie in the future, but Daniel 11:23–30 is the most difficult passage to interpret *historically* in terms of events that now lie in the past. It is difficult to be definite about the interpretation of Daniel 11:23–30, and we should keep this difficulty in mind when studying this passage. There are at least five different possible interpretations for these verses. For the present, we will proceed with the working hypothesis that Daniel 11:23–30 describes the Crusades carried out at the behest of the papal power in the eleventh to the thirteenth centuries. As we do so, let's see how well the historical details of those events match what is described prophetically in these verses.

There is quite a gap between the death of Jesus Christ, described in 11:22 to the time of the Crusades 1,000 years later, described in verse 23. While this gap is large, we have already seen that gaps exist in the course of the prophecy of Daniel 11. From the time of Xerxes, the last Persian king mentioned in verse 2, until the time of Alexander, the first Greek king mentioned in verse 3, a century and a half elapsed, and the prophecy makes no attempt to fill in that gap by mentioning the other later Persian kings. It simply goes from one significant figure to the next which appears on the scene of action. The same is true in 11:22, 23. It was Jesus, brought to view in verse 22 as the "prince of the covenant," who created the church that came to be the papal power referred to in verse 23. It was that church's attempt to conquer back the holy places connected with Jesus that led to the crusades that are described beginning in verse 23.

This new section of chapter 11 (verses 23–30) begins with the making of an "agreement" or covenant (vs. 23). This is not the new covenant in Jesus' blood for this covenant was created in deceit, according to verse 23.

"With only a few people [literally, "a small people"] he will rise to power" (vs. 23). This could refer to the numbers of the crusaders in relation to the hordes of Islam that they faced in the Middle East. Or it could refer, even more classically, to the Children's Crusade of A.D. 1217–1221. "The richest provinces" (vs. 24) that are invaded by this military movement fits well as the glorious or "Beautiful Land" referred to in verse 16. Thus verse 24 would refer to the land of Judea. Verse 24 also says that this power "will achieve what neither his fathers nor his forefathers did." This does not fit very well with Imperial Rome, for each of the Caesars (Julius, Augustus, Tiberius) could only say that he was doing what his fathers had done before him. In the case of the papacy, however, the call for the Crusades was a call for something entirely new in the history of that institution. The world had never seen anything like it before.

The text of verse 24 talks about this power distributing plunder, loot, and wealth among his followers. While this could be said of many armies in many times, it was especially true of the Crusades. The motivation behind the Crusades was twofold: to obtain spiritual benefits and to obtain wealth. Knights who participated in the Crusades commonly were those who had not inherited land in Europe because they were not the eldest in their families. The Crusades were a route to riches in a way that was not an option open to them at home.

The last phrase of verse 24 requires a different translation from that given by the NIV—"he will plot the overthrow of fortresses." The phrase begins with preposition *'al* followed by the plural noun for "fortresses." Translators have commonly interpreted this phrase as referring to military attacks upon fortresses, but there is no verb here for such attacks. Instead, the verb which follows, in a dual emphatic form, is the verb which means "to think," "to consider," "to give attention to." In other words, these forces are going to give thought or attention to fortresses—their own fortresses! When one visits Israel and Jordan today, one can see the results of that thought. The crusader castles and fortresses that were constructed for defensive purposes during the twelfth and thirteenth centuries still dot the land. They are some of the most remarkable archaeological remains still present in the Holy Land. Some of them are in a good state of preservation. In the twentieth century, the British used the crusader fortress at Akko as a jail for political prisoners during the days of the Palestine mandate (1918 to 1948)! Verse 24 concludes by stating that this attention to and construction of fortresses would last only for a time. The crusaders' occupation of the Holy Land lasted less than two centuries, and now these fortresses stand as monuments to a long-gone era.

It is only after these initial successes that the king of the south mounts his forces and comes against the forces from the north (11:25b). The last battle of the first Crusade was fought against forces that came out of Egypt to meet the crusaders after they had conquered Jerusalem. That battle took place at Ascalon on the southwestern coast of Palestine (see 11:26). The situation is well described in the following quote from a history of the Crusades:

> On 12 August 1099 battle was joined on level ground near the Egyptian harbour-fortress of Ascalon. The Egyptians were taken by surprise while still in their camp and were completely defeated. Their commander, the vizier al-Afdal (1094-1121) fled back to Egypt. On 13 August the victorious army returned in triumph to Jerusalem. The success of the crusade was now assured. The regaining of the Holy Land was an astonishing achievement. The rejoicing in Christendom was fully justified (H. E. Mayer, 57).

Verse 27 says that two kings will sit at the same table and lie to each other, their hearts bent upon evil. In the light of this verse, it is interesting to note the political jockeying that took place after the fall of Jerusalem. The question was: Who would be king of the new Crusader state there? In both the secular and the sacred realm there was infighting. In the secular struggle there were two candidates for king—Raymond and Godfrey. Godfrey finally obtained the job of ruler (without the title of "king") by trickery. In the sacred realm there was also a dispute to decide who would be the patriarch of Jerusalem. Arnulf from Normandy was finally given the job even though he was not qualified for it because he was illegitimate and not even a subdeacon. He soon solidified his position as leader of the church, however, by finding a relic—the true cross! Then there was also the question of the relationship between these two "rulers" in their dual realms of church and state.

Daniel 11:28 says that the king of the north was to return to his own country with great wealth and take action against the holy covenant. Of the crusader leaders in the first Crusade, four left for their homes in Europe, and only two remained with the mini-kingdom of Jerusalem.

Three hundred knights and 3,000 foot soldiers remained in Jerusalem with Godfrey while the majority returned to Europe with their leaders and their spoils. Papal control of the church in Jerusalem was evident from the fact that on three occasions the pope either suspended or deposed the patriarch there.

This was also the period in history when the papacy reached some of its greatest heights of power. As an example, Innocent III (1198–1216), having learned from the Crusades in the Middle East, next launched a Crusade against the heretical Albigenses in southern France in 1208. The fighting lasted until 1227 when Raymond of Toulouse signed the Peace of Paris in which he swore allegiance to the king and the church. Although the Albigenses were not orthodox Christians, this episode illustrates how the church dealt with dissenters.

Daniel 11:29, 30 tells of another campaign against the south by this power. According to the geographical designations employed in chapter 11 thus far, the south represents Egypt, thus we should expect a campaign directly against Egypt. In the first Crusade, the Egyptians came out of Egypt to do battle with the crusaders in Palestine (11:25b), but in the last Crusade the invasion took place by sea directly against Egypt. That action fits the description of verses 29, 30 when correctly understood.

The first part of verse 30 is commonly translated as the "ships of Chittim" (KJV) going *against* the king of the north. But that is not the preposition used in the original Hebrew text. When the Hebrew wants to say that one army is going *against* another, it uses the preposition *'al.* However, the text here uses *be* or *beth,* which means, "by," "in," "at," "with." Thus the ships of the Chittim, or western coastlands, did not come *against* the king of the north; they came "with" him; they were *his* ships. This is precisely the way the final Crusade attempted to invade Egypt. This Crusade was led by the devout French king Louis IX. He wintered at the end of 1248 on the island of Cyprus, but in the spring of 1249 he set sail for Egypt, invading it by the Damietta branch of the Nile. The major battle of the campaign was fought at Mansourah in the delta of Egypt in February of 1250. It was a major defeat for the crusader forces, and they had to retreat to Damietta where they surrendered to the Egyptians in April. Louis IX himself was taken prisoner and held for ransom. When he finally did leave Egypt, only 1,400 troops were left to go with him. He traveled first to Palestine, but eventually returned to France where he still devoutly supported the papacy in spite of his defeat (Daniel 11:30b).

With this disaster, the last of the Crusades to the Middle East came to an end. The crusader states in Palestine lived on for a few more decades, but then they too were wiped out, and no more Crusades came to their aid. The French king felt that his defeat was a judgment from God. To attempt to make up for his failures Louis tried one more campaign, this time to North Africa, not the Middle East. He invaded Tunisia in 1270, but this was an even bigger disaster than the previous defeat in Egypt. A plague struck the camp of the crusaders, and even the king died as a result. It was not an army that returned to France, but a great funeral procession.

All of this crusader activity took place under the aegis of the papacy in Rome. Each Crusade was begun with a commission from the pope. Becoming a knight in the crusader army was known as "taking the cross." The ultimate aims of these Crusades were religious in nature and directed by the papacy. Soldiers could obtain indulgences by virtue of fighting in one of the Crusades. Daniel 11:23–28 gives a description of how this kind of activity began, and Daniel 11:29, 30 gives a description of how it ended. It was all under the direction of the second phase of the little horn of Daniel 8, known in this part of chapter 11 as "the king of the north."

Interestingly, this passage three times refers to time factors that seem to have been involved in these activities. These time references are not specific as in other prophecies of Daniel, rather they are general references to time. Verse 24 says that this power was to give attention to fortresses, but "only for a time." Verse 27 says that when the two kings plot at a table it will be fruitless, but later "an end will still come at the appointed time." That time finally does come, according to verse 29, when "at the appointed time" the king of the north invades the king of the south for the last time and is defeated. In addition to these three references to time, verse 23 implies a time element when it talks about the events that will come "after coming to an agreement [covenant] with him." That was the covenant, agreement, or decree which launched the first of these campaigns.

Basically the Crusades lasted for a century and a half. The crusader forces captured Jerusalem in the summer of A.D. 1099 at the conclusion of the first Crusade, and the defeat suffered by the last Crusade in the delta of Egypt occurred during the winter of A.D. 1249/1250. From 1099 to 1249 is 150 years, or five months of prophetic time. This military activity had a beginning, a duration, and an end, as the language of this passage of Daniel 11 describes. The parallel with the fifth trumpet of the book of Revelation (9:1–11) is worth noting in that the locusts (soldiers) of that prophecy were to torment men for five months. Reckoning each day for a year, according to the prophetic rule, makes the duration of the fifth trumpet 150 years. The events described in Revelation 9:1–11 are historically similar to what Daniel 11:23–30 describes.

DESECRATION OF GOD'S SANCTUARY

The next action of the king of the north/little horn is its activity in relation to the sanctuary. "His armed forces will rise up to desecrate the temple fortress and will abolish the daily sacrifice" (vs. 31). The text does not give the location of this temple. In fact, there is some evidence that it is talking about another temple than God's temple, for it is called "the temple fortress," a word construction that is never used in the book of Daniel for the earthly temple in Jerusalem. The words imply something greater, grander, and stronger than the earthly temple. What temple is verse 31 referring to?

According to the vertical dimension employed by the prophecy of Daniel 8:11, the temple that was attacked by this power was the temple located in heaven. The direct language parallels between Daniel 8:11 and Daniel 11:31 indicate that the "temple fortress" of 11:31 is the strong heavenly temple. This is the object of attack by the little horn/king of the north power.

The NIV uses the English verb "desecrate" in this verse to describe the action of the forces of the king of the north (papal Rome). A better translation is that they "profaned" it (Hebrew *halal*). Desecration, defilement, or uncleanness comes about in a temple when unclean and impure objects are introduced into its precincts. On the other hand, one can *profane* a temple, or God's name, from a distance. One need not be bodily present in a temple to profane it.

Daniel 8:11 says that as a result of the actions of this little horn power the heavenly temple was "cast down" (KJV) or "brought low" (NIV) to the earth (Hebrew *shalak*), meaning that the ministry of that temple was presented to the inhabitants of earth as under the control of an earthly power. But the heavenly temple did not come down to earth literally or physically; it was only made to appear cast down in the eyes of men. So too with the profanation of the temple carried out by this same power in 11:31. The papal power did not need to be literally and physically present in the heavenly temple in order to profane it. By the work that the papacy carried out here on earth, it brought about that profanation. The "daily" ministry, discussed earlier in our treatment of Daniel 8, was the property and activity of the Prince in the heavenly sanctuary. But now this earthly power claims to control that ministry and that its forces (a spiritual army known as a priesthood) can dispense the merits derived from it. This was how an earthly religious power substituted its activity for the work of Christ.

After obscuring the true "daily" ministry from the eyes of mankind, this power was to set something else up in its place. Something known as "the abomination of desolation" (11:31, KJV). What does this phrase mean?

In the Old Testament, an unauthorized intrusion into the literal temple area was considered to be an abomination which had to be cleansed by ritual. Likewise, the power of the state, either local or foreign, intruding into the realm of the sacred was an abomination that resulted in defilement. Thus the abomination that makes desolate may be described as a union of the secular and the religious—the state and the church—in which the religious aspect is defiled by its merging with the functions of the state. In the history of Christendom, such a union came about as a result of state support for the church, a situation which led to the development of the medieval papacy. It was the church's use of state secular power that led to the crusades as described above. It was also the church's use of state power that was involved earlier in the Arian wars of the sixth century with the result that the Arian churches and peoples were brought under the control of the Roman Church. The same combined state-church power continued on into the Inquisition of later times. That brings us to the subject of persecution, the next topic on which the prophecy focuses.

PERSECUTION OF THE SAINTS

The third activity of the king of the north/little horn power mentioned in the prophecy is persecution. Persecution of the saints is mentioned in Daniel 11:32–34, the only place in chapter 11 where such a persecution is mentioned. Based on the amount of text devoted to the topic, the prophecy seems to anticipate that this persecution will be particularly severe. Jesus makes the same point in His description of it in Matthew 24:21, 22. This same persecution is brought to view in Daniel 12:7 where the prophet is told that it will last for "at time, times, and half a time." The same time period with its accompanying persecution is also mentioned in Daniel 7:25. Thus all three of these texts, Daniel 7:25; 11:32–34; and 12:7, refer to the same great persecution carried out by the papal power during the Middle Ages. In our study of Daniel 7 (see pp. 209–211), we set the demarcating dates for this persecution at A.D. 538 and A.D. 1798. That same time span can be applied to Daniel 11:32–34 and to Daniel 12:7. Of course the severity of this persecution waxed and waned throughout the period.

SELF-EXALTATION

Verses 36–39 constitute the final passage of this section of chapter 11 and the fourth activity of the king of the north/little horn power. In these verses this power expresses its dominion and authority in a final way by exalting itself. The opening sentences of verse 36 set the tone for this passage: "The king will do as he pleases. He will exalt and magnify himself above every god and will say unheard-of things against the God of gods."

We find here two charges against this power: (1) self-exaltation; and (2) blasphemy. These charges correspond to the characteristics of the little horn as revealed in both Daniel 7 and 8. Daniel 8 specifically states that the little horn will exalt itself, and Daniel 7 directly implies the same. Daniel 7 refers to the blasphemy that the little horn speaks as his "great words against the most High" (vs. 25, KJV). Speaking of its self-exaltation, chapter 8 states that the little horn "grew until it reached the host of the heavens," and it "set itself up to be as great as the Prince of the host" (vss. 10, 11).

The object of all this blasphemy and self-exaltation is clearly God. Not only does this power exalt itself over all of the other gods, it sets itself up as a rival to the true God Himself. The word for "god" is rarely used in Daniel 11 because much of its description is couched in political and military terms. Occasionally there are references to the king of the north taking away the gods of the south, or vice versa, but these references are not common. Here in 11:36–39, however, the word or name for "god" is used nine times, showing the distinctly religious character of this power at this point and emphasizing the type of religious conflict into which it has entered by this time in the flow of history. Historically, all this rivalry against the God of heaven was manifested by the titles which this earthly power assumed and the claims that it made for itself. The power that this power claimed over earthly potentates was sometimes demonstrated by the humility it required of earthly rulers and the use it made of such threats as excommunication and the interdict. A famous example of this humbling of earthly powers is Gregory VII's action in forcing Henry IV of Germany to do penance by standing in the snow at Canossa, Italy, for three days in A.D. 1077 before he would give him a hearing.

This self-exaltation and blasphemy mark the fourth and final activity carried out by the power of papal Rome as described in this chapter. These can be summarized as follows:

1. Vss. 23–30 Military activity; the Crusades
2. Vs. 31 Intervention in the heavenly ministry of Christ
3. Vss. 32–35 Persecution
4. Vss. 36–39 Self-exaltation and blasphemy against God

The self-exaltation of this power culminates and brings together all of its other activities. All that has gone before is ultimately an expression of self-exaltation. This attitude, expressed at the end of this passage, opens the way to the next section of the prophecy.

THE TIME OF THE END

The next-to-the-last section of the prophecy of Daniel 10–12 begins with a statement about its location in time. Daniel 11:40a says that the events which follow will occur "at the time of the end." This point in the prophecy marks the transition from all that has gone on before, beginning in the prophet's own time, down to this final section of history. The distinction between the time of the end and the end of time should be noted carefully. The "time of the end" is a period of time, a segment of history in which certain events will happen. Those events are narrated in the next five verses. The "end of time" is a point in time; it is the end of human history as we know it. That point comes at the end of this section.

MODERN EQUIVALENTS FOR THE KINGS OF THE NORTH AND SOUTH

The prophecy declares that in the time of the end, yet another conflict will occur between the king of the north and the king of the south. We have now come to a point in history long after the Seleucids of Syria and the Ptolemies of Egypt have vanished from the scene of action. So we must be dealing with new powers that have taken their places. What are these new powers that make their appearance here?

Quite a number of possibilities have been suggested, but no final answer on this question has emerged. The question was debated hotly among the Adventist pioneers and by Adventist teachers in more modern times. Perhaps the best we can say is that since these events are still future, we will recognize them when they take place before our eyes.

The last actions of the king of the north/little horn power took place in 1798, when the papal power was temporarily deposed through the capture of the pope by General Berthier (see the discussion of Daniel 7 above). Therefore, it is reasonable to assume that the time of the end began at that point. In other words, we are now living in the time of the end. We have seen the historical fulfillment of all of Daniel 11 in the rise and fall of the nations from Daniel's day up to A.D. 1798. From that point onward, we may expect the fulfillment of the events prophesied in 11:40–45. Since they have not been recognized yet, they must still lie in the future. We must await that future fulfillment to understand just how these details will work out. For the present, therefore, we must be content with some estimates of which powers are involved here and how their actions and fate will work out.

One major question to consider is how much continuity exists between this passage and what has gone on before. A direct continuity would suggest that the king of the north in this final passage is the same papal power that we have seen featured prominently in verses 23–39. If the connection is not quite so direct, then some other power could be involved. This volume takes the position that the connection between this final passage and the rest of the prophecy is quite direct. Therefore, we should identify the king of the north in verses 40–45 with the papal phase of Rome—the same power that has been the central focus of the preceding section of the prophecy.

The king of the south appears briefly at the beginning of this section, but then takes a back seat as a more minor actor. Earlier in this chapter, the title, "king of the south," referred to Egypt from which the Ptolemies came. But here at the end of chapter 11 the identification seems to be more spiritual than political. Thus just as the king of the north has become the papacy and is no longer a territorial king in the literal sense in which chapter 11 presents him at its beginning, so the king of the south is also a spiritual entity here in these last verses of the chapter. Although in the twentieth century, the papacy does own a small piece of territory—Vatican City—its principal influence is spiritual. That comparison leads us to the conclusion that the king of the south should be seen here more as a philosophical force than a political or territorial power.

Thus we need to ask, What characteristic of ancient Egypt makes its reappearance here at the time of the end? One characteristic ancient Egypt demonstrated toward the people of God was to reject their God, Yahweh. "Who is the Lord, that I should obey him and let Israel go? I do not know the Lord and I will not let Israel go" Pharaoh declared (Exodus 5:2). In more modern times, this "Egyptian" attitude is expressed in rationalism which in the area of religion has led to atheism or agnosticism. There was a major eruption of this kind of thought in the French Revolution, right at the time when history came to the prophetic "time of the end" in 1798. The atheism expressed in Marxist communism is a direct descendant of the philosophy developed at the time of the French Revolution. It is interesting to note in this setting that the book of Revelation, too, appears to make just such a connection with its symbols. Revelation 11 talks about the two witnesses of God—the Law and the Prophets, or the Old and the New Testaments—who prophesied throughout the long 1,260 day-years period of the Middle Ages. Then at the end of that period, a new power was to arise that would put the witnesses to death, and their slaughtered bodies would lie in the streets of the city for three and a half day-years. This fits very well with the antibiblical actions and sentiments expressed at the height of the French Revolution (1789–1793) in which the Bible was rejected in favor of the goddess of reason. However, we need not limit our understanding of the king of the south in Daniel 11:40–45 to revolutionary France. It might rather be identified as rationalistic humanism—the major philosophical upheaval the French Revolution bequeathed to the modern world. That spirit has lived on in communism and in many other aspects of modern society. And it has been in conflict with the church. Witness the fate of the Catholic Church in communist countries, especially those behind the previously existing Iron Curtain. As a result, for a time the Soviet Union was the most popular nominee for the end-time king of the south. But with the collapse of communism there has been waning support for that idea.

We need not see the king of the south in this passage as a literal, territorial France or Russia. Rather, we can view it as embodying the same ideas on the subject of religion as presented in the philosophy of those powers. Rationalistic humanism, leading to atheism or agnosticism, would fit well the actions and attitudes of the king of the south. Revelation 11:8 provides a figurative connection between these ancient and modern attitudes by stating that the bodies of the biblical witnesses would lie "in the street of the great city, which is figuratively called Sodom and Egypt, where also their Lord was crucified." Jesus was crucified again in the philosophical terms and religious expressions of this Egyptianlike ideology that has been perpetrated by revolutionary France and Russia.

In summary, the king of the north in the time of the end probably should be connected with the preceding dominant power in the prophecy—the papacy of the Middle Ages, now in its final phase. The king of the south, modeled upon the anti-Yahwistic attitudes of ancient Egypt, fits well with the modern movement of rationalistic humanism that leads to atheism or agnosticism. In the modern world, revolutionary France and the former Soviet Union have been the special propagators of those ideas. Even though the power and position of these nations have declined somewhat, the spirit of the age which they fostered persists in many places and continues to present a major challenge to the church.

THE HISTORICAL MODEL OF THE END-TIME STRUGGLE

It appears that Daniel 11:40–45 utilizes an actual historical incident in Persian history as a model, or type, for the spiritual battle between good and evil that will take place in the time of the end. The example comes from the Egyptian campaign of the Persian king Cambyses in 525 B.C. Invaders of Judah and Egypt from the north had to come through Syria which lay to the north, and thus from Judah's viewpoint, conquerors from that direction ultimately came through Syria. In order to engage the king of the south in Egypt, "the king of the North will storm out against him with chariots and cavalry and a great fleet of ships" (vs. 40a). Cambyses was approaching Egypt by both sea and land, a course that is described in these words, "He will invade many countries and sweep through them like a flood" (vs. 40b). Among these countries would be Judah. "He will also invade the Beautiful Land" (vs. 41a).

Continuing his course southward toward Egypt, Cambyses bypassed Trans-Jordan and did not attack it as he passed thorough Judah. As Daniel 11:41b puts it: "Many countries will fall, but Edom, Moab, and the leaders of Ammon will be delivered from his hand." Cambyses did not bother with these nations as he traveled down the coastal road to the west.

Cambyses continued on his way to Egypt and conquered it. This victory is brought to view in verse 42: "He will extend his power over many countries; Egypt will not escape. He will gain control of the treasures of gold and silver and all the riches of Egypt." But Cambyses did not plan to stop with his conquest of Egypt, for the end of verse 43 says that he was going to obtain submission from the Libyans to the west of

Egypt and the Nubians to the south of Egypt (the modern Sudan).

Having gone this far, however, he was to receive dire news from the rear—from the east and the north (vs. 44). This means that the news from the east has traveled west and then has been brought down through Syria and Palestine to reach the king while he was in Egypt. Although historians don't know what this news was, it clearly upset Cambyses greatly. He set out with his forces in great anger to rectify the situation (vs. 44). As he retraced his road north, he came through Judah again. While passing through that territory, he encamped on his way. The location is given as "between the seas toward the beautiful holy mountain" (vs. 45). He did not come up to the holy mountain, Mount Zion in Jerusalem; he only pitched his tents toward it. His actual campsite location was down on the coastal plain of Sharon "between the seas and the beautiful holy mountain." His target was not Jerusalem; he was intent on returning to the north where he had come from and from whence his bad news originated. But while encamped in Judea he was to be overtaken by his end. It would come without human intervention. It was not to be brought about by battle, and no one could help him avert this personal tragedy (vs. 45).

While Cambyses was camped in the plain of Sharon, he died as the result of a self-inflicted wound, stabbing himself in the thigh with his sword. Among modern historians, interpretations of this event differ. Some say it was a suicide attempt; others say it was an accident. Whatever the cause, Cambyses died after twenty days, and none of the troops in his mighty army could help him. Paraphrasing the words of Daniel, he came to his end, but none could help him (vs. 45). The ancients saw this as a punishment from God. Cambyses was seen as a mad man by the people of his time, and one of his more mad acts was to kill the sacred Apis bull when he entered Egypt by stabbing it in the thigh. Thus when he struck himself in the same location, whether by accident or intent, this was seen as retributive justice.

THE END-TIME STRUGGLE

Thus all the events described in Daniel 11:40–45 took place in a literal way in the life, experience, and death of Cambyses the Persian king. But at this point in the course of the prophecy, we are not dealing any longer with ancient times. We are dealing here with "the time of the end" (11:40). The powers involved are no longer a literal Persian king and a literal king of Egypt. They have become symbols for the powers at the time of the end. Those powers we have identified as the papacy (the king of the north) and atheism (the king of the south). In some way, the religious power of the Roman church will gain some sort of victory over the forces of atheism before the end of time (vs. 43). But while this power is enjoying the fruits of that short-lived victory, more serious challenges will arise in the east (vs. 44), for the kings of the east will march forth, according to the book of Revelation (Revelation 16:12). The book of Revelation also speaks of that final spiritual battle in literal terms, locating it at Armageddon (16:16), or "the mount of Megiddo." Megiddo is also located between the seas and the glorious holy mountain. The papacy is one of the spiritual powers that will be involved in that final spiritual battle.

The plain of Sharon is located just south of Megiddo, and that plain leads up to the mountain range of Mount Carmel which intersects Megiddo and the plain of Sharon. It was on that literal, geographical plain of Megiddo that Cambyses was encamped when he died. It was on the mount itself where, in earlier biblical times, the contest between the true God and the false gods of Baal took place (1 Kings 18). That kind of spiritual struggle will be repeated in modern times, but it will not be a literal, physical struggle upon that geographical mountain (vs. 45). That ancient contest symbolizes the final spiritual conflict that will take place on a worldwide basis. From this final battle, Christ and His heavenly army will emerge victorious. Satan and all his hosts will be defeated in this final great spiritual battle on earth. That battle is described in Revelation 19:11–21. Revelation 16 describes only the preparations for the battle of Armageddon. Revelation 19 describes the actual battle of the great day of God Almighty, and Christ wins! By borrowing from the ancient experience of Cambyses, the course of that battle has been described. This modern Cambyses will fail too, just as the ancient one did. At this point, the powers of earth and their kingdoms will become the kingdoms of our God and of His Christ. This brings us to the last scene of this prophecy, the one that is found in the first four verses of Daniel 12.

The Final Message—Part 2

THE END OF TIME

Daniel 12:1–4 actually comprises the end of the prophecy of Daniel 11. The later addition of chapter divisions has made an awkward and unnecessary break here. This section is God's answer to what the king of the north does in the time of the end, as prophesied in Daniel 11:40–45. The phrase, "at that time," (12:1) connects chapter 12 to the last of the events narrated in the prophecy of Daniel 11. When the king of the north comes to his end and no one is able to assist him, that is the time when Michael stands up.

As can be seen from various places in Daniel 11, "to stand up," or "to arise," refers to taking up the kingship. The Hebrew verb used in Daniel 11:2, 3, 4, 7, 16, 20, 21 means "to stand up" "arise," or "appear," and in all of these instances it refers to a new king coming on the scene of action at the time that he ascends to the throne and becomes the new ruler (see also Daniel 7:24; 8:23). That is what Michael, God's representative, now does. Thus in Daniel 12:1 Michael comes on the scene of action to assume rulership in answer to what has been done in the name of all the previous kings that have arisen in Daniel 11. They were earthly rulers, but now the ruler from heaven will take over, and He will make up a very different type of kingdom, one that is ruled upon the principles of righteousness.

Michael is the "great prince," (12:1) who rules over all the heavenly host and who cares for God's earthly people. As we know from Jude 9 and Revelation 12:7, Michael is Christ. He appears in many places in the Bible, both Old and New Testaments, with various titles that express His various functions in the plan of salvation. The name, Michael, is used particularly in situations where there is conflict over the people of God. Michael comes to fight for them and protect them and deliver them. That is also His function here in Daniel 12:1–4. Things are going to get worse before they become better. "There will be a time of distress such as has not happened from the beginning of nations until then" (12:1). As the great controversy between Christ and Satan comes to its conclusion, Satan will exert all possible force to divert and destroy the people of God, but he will not be successful. Michael, who fights for His people, will step in to deliver them. "At that time your people—everyone whose name is found written in the book—will be delivered" (12:1).

The reference to this heavenly book is interesting. When the judgment was taken up in Daniel 7, "the court was seated, and the books were opened" (vs. 10). The reference there is in the plural—books. Here (12:1) the reference is singular. The examination of the books in the judgment of Daniel 7 has led to the roster of the names present in the book brought to view in chapter 12. This book is none other than the book referred to in Revelation 17:8 and 21:27 as the Lamb's book of Life. God does know His people, and He looks out for them with tender regard. He will deliver them out of the troublous times to come.

Two groups of people are identified in 12:2—the righteous and the wicked. The righteous who sleep in the dust will be resurrected to everlasting life. The wicked will also be resurrected, but to everlasting contempt, not to everlasting life. When they are finally destroyed in the lake of fire described by Revelation 20:14, 15, it will be seen by all that their sentence and punishment were just (Philippians 2:10, 11). Seventh-day Adventists have taken Daniel 12:2 as reference to a special resurrection that will take place just before Jesus comes. This special resurrection has been suggested because of the wicked who come up at this time also. The general resurrection of the wicked comes at the end of the millennium (Revelation 20:5–10) rather than at the second advent. But there is a special class of wicked, identified as those who pierced Him (Revelation 1:7), who will arise just before the advent (Daniel 12:2). This will be a special group who have opposed Christ personally. Along with this special class of wicked are the special class of righteous who are resurrected at the same time. This will fulfill the special blessing pronounced upon those who have died during the giving of the three angels' messages (Revelation 14:13). So the resurrection promise of this prophecy can be taken in both a special sense and a general sense.

The results are also clear. They are stated in beautiful Hebrew poetic parallelism in Daniel 12:3: "Those who are wise will shine like the brightness of the heavens, and those who lead many to righteousness, like the stars for ever and ever."

The first line of this poetic couplet refers to the intensity with which the saints will be glorified. The second line refers to the duration for which they will radiate this glory—"for ever and ever." Earlier in the prophecy, there were those earthly powers which attempted to lead many away from the covenant and righteousness (Daniel 11:32–35), but now those who were working in the opposite direction will come to the fore, and their opponents will fade into insignificance. The book of Daniel never describes the future kingdom of God in detail, as does the book of Revelation (chapters 21; 22). Here, however, one gets some inkling of the glory that will overtake the saints of the Most High when they finally enter His long-promised and long-prophesied kingdom.

The ruler of this great future kingdom is identified as Michael, for he is the one who stands up to take the kingship of that kingdom (12:1). This symbolism can be compared with Daniel 7:13, 14 where the figure who takes the kingship of that future kingdom is "one like a son of man". In our discussion of that chapter, we identified the Son of man as Jesus Christ. The book of Revelation says that there will be two rulers in that future kingdom, for the Lord God Almighty will be seated upon the throne along with the Lamb (Revelation 22:3). God the Father and God the Son will both sit on the throne. Where does that leave Michael who stands up here to take the kingship? It makes him equal to the Son of man. The ruler of that future kingdom is the Son of man, and that Son of man is Michael, according to the parallelism in the book of Daniel.

That brings up the comparison between Michael in Daniel 10:13, 21 and Michael in Daniel 12:1. They are the same individual, and Michael acts in similar ways in these two narratives. But the two narratives are set at far different times. Daniel 10 is set in the local time of Persia and deals with a local problem for the people of God at the time of the prophet. In Daniel 12, we see a view of Michael at the end of time and the part that He will play in those final events. His function is similar; He was struggling for and protecting the people God back then, and He will do the same sort of thing for the people of God at the end of time. No wonder that He is given kingship over the saints for eternity, for He has struggled with them and for them during their earthly pilgrimage here and now.

It is important to note at this point that 12:4 claims that the book of Daniel would be sealed "until the time of the end." We will return to that sealing and unsealing after our discussion of verses 5–12.

MORE PROPHETIC TIME PERIODS AND THE SEALING OF THE BOOK

Daniel 12:5–13 is an epilogue, or an appendix, to the prophecy of 11:2–12:4. What we have here is the time calibration for the body of the prophecy that has gone on before. This is a common way Daniel treats this matter elsewhere in the book. For example, the time element in Daniel 7 does not come until verse 25 even though the description of the vision is complete by verse 14. The same thing occurs in Daniel 8. The vision is complete by verse 12, but the conversation between the two angels regarding the time element of the 2,300 days comes in verses 13, 14. The same sort of thing takes place here in Daniel 11 and 12. The body of the prophecy is given in Daniel 11, but the times that go with those events are given in Daniel 12. These times are also connected by the events that they describe. They are not dating new events; they are dating events that have already been described in Daniel 11.

THE THREE AND A HALF TIMES (1260 DAYS)

The setting of Daniel 12 returns to that of Daniel 10. Once again God Himself is seen over the river, and He is described in some of the same terms that are used of His appearance in Daniel 10:4, 5. In addition to "the man clothed in linen, who was above the waters of the river," in 12:7, there were also two angels standing by, one on each side of the river, according to verse 5. One of them asked the being above the river, "How long will it be before these astonishing things are fulfilled?" The answer came back to him in the form of a solemn oath, for He lifted His two hands toward heaven and swore by the name of God that it would be "a time, times and half a time. When the power of the holy people has been finally broken, all these things will be fulfilled." This breaking of the power of the holy people refers to a time of persecution, and it must have been a prolonged and intense time of persecution to have worked this result. The only time of persecution that is described in any detail in the preceding chapter is the one given in verses 11:32–35. These three and a half times must, therefore, be connected with that persecution. The same three and a half times are also mentioned in Daniel 7:25 where they are also connected with persecution. We have a parallel equation therefore:

Daniel 7:25	=	Daniel 11:32-35	=	Daniel 12:7
3 1/2 times of persecution	=	a time of intense persecution	=	3 1/2 times of persecution

Daniel 11 helps us place that persecution in its historical setting. In the flow of events in chapter 11, persecution comes during what is known as the Middle Ages of the Christian Era. The three and one-half times are using time symbols in which each "time" equals a year (Daniel 4:16, 23, 25, 32; Revelation 12:6, 14; 13:5). Each prophetic year contains 360 days, having been rounded off from the irregular lunar calendar year of the Jews. Thus the book of Revelation equates the three and a half times (Revelation 12:14) with 1,260 days (12:6) or forty-two months (13:5). In apocalyptic prophecies, a day of symbolic, prophetic time equals a historical year (Ezekiel 4:6; Numbers 14:34). That means we are dealing with a historical period of 1,260 years here in Daniel 12:7. In our earlier discussion of Daniel 7, we dated that period from A.D. 538, when the city of Rome and the bishop of Rome were freed from pagan interference, to A.D. 1798 when the bishop of Rome was deposed by the forces of France. That prophetic period is reconfirmed here in this final chapter of Daniel, so that it stands as a prophetic landmark both in this book and also in Revelation where it is reused.

There is also an indication in Daniel 11 as to when, in general, this prophetic time period was to occur. In that chapter, the "time of the end" does not begin until verse 40. Thus, the persecution of verses 32–35 must occur before the time of the end. That locates it right in the heart of the Middle Ages, which is where this persecution dated from 538 to A.D. 1798 occurred.

THE 1290 DAYS

The second time period mentioned in Daniel 12 is found in verse 11: "From the time that the daily sacrifice is abolished and the abomination that causes desolation is set up, there will be 1,290 days." Thus we have progressed mathematically from the 1,260 days to the 1,290 days. The events of this time period are also described in Daniel 11:31. Once again, therefore, we have the event described in Daniel 11 and the date that is given to it presented in Daniel 12. The events described in both Daniel 11:31 and Daniel 12:11 include the taking away of the "daily" (Hebrew, *tamid*) and the setting up the "abomination that causes desolation." The same power is in view here that was present in the previously described episode of persecution. The little horn, the persecuting power of Daniel 7:25 and 8:10, reappears in Daniel 11 under the title of the king of the north. In all these verses the same power is brought to view, doing the same work.

How should the 1,290 days be marked off? Because of the nature of the events that occurred in A.D. 1798 when the papacy, the little horn, received its temporary "deadly wound" (Revelation 13:3, KJV) and was removed from the scene of action for a time, that date must mark the end of the 1,290 days as well as of the 1,260 days. It was at this time that the Medieval substitution for Christ's heavenly ministry received a serious blow through the papacy's temporary loss of power and prestige. Thus, we must extend the 1,290 days backward from that date so that the 1,290 days commence thirty day-years prior to the beginning of the 1,260 days. A.D. 538 minus thirty years takes us to the date of A.D. 508. What significant event occurred at that time to mark the beginning of the 1,290 day-years?

In Europe, one of the major events that year was the conclusion of the war between Clovis, king of the Franks (later France), and the Visigoths, whom he defeated and pushed into Spain. Clovis' other conquests covered the two previous decades with the defeat of the Visigoths being the last of these. Then Clovis was baptized and like Constantine, he marched his troops down to the river and through the river and had the bishop pronounce them Christians. These wars of Clovis also had religious overtones because some of the powers defeated, like the Visigoths, were Arian Christians. The Arians believed that Christ was a created being, and this view was anathema to the bishop in Rome. Thus when Clovis and the Franks defeated the Arian Visigoths and drove them into Spain, it was also a theological victory for the bishop in Rome. The relationship was cemented by the baptism of Clovis and his troops. In that way Clovis became, as it were, a new Constantine.

Two major elements come together here (1) the blending of the political arm of the state and the religious arm of the church; and (2) the use of the arms of the state to accomplish the ends of the church. With the defeat of the Visigoths as heretical Arian Christians, the church came to use the military power of the state to enforce its dogma. In this connection the three horns which the papal little horn plucked from the head of the beast representing imperial Rome (Daniel 7:8) can be seen as the following three powers: the Vandals in 534, the Visigoths in 508, and the Ostrogoths in 538. These were victories for the Frankish and Roman emperors, but they were also theological victories for the bishop of Rome. The first of these horns was plucked up in 508 at the beginning of the 1,290 days; the last of the three was plucked up in 538 at the beginning of the 1,260 days.

Thus the setting up of the abomination of desolation of Daniel 12:11 can be seen as the union of church and state and what the church set out to accomplish through the power of the state. This had the effect of eclipsing the true ministry of Christ as our High Priest in the heavenly sanctuary (cf. 11:31; 8:11–13). The eyes of humanity had been turned from heaven to earth to focus upon an earthly religious power that now stood in place of the great High Priest in heaven. For that reason titles such as "Vicar of the Son of God" that had been assumed by this earthly power take on great theological importance; they have obscured the truth about the plan of salvation carried on in the heavenly sanctuary. In this way the "daily," the continual heavenly ministry of Christ, was taken away by being put out of mankind's view by this earthly religious power after its consolidation of power in A.D. 508.

But this deflection of the view of mankind from the true heavenly Priest was not to last forever. It was to come to an end after 1,290 years as predicted by the time prophecy in Daniel 12:11. The date for that transition came to pass with the deposing of the pope by the French troops in Rome in February of 1798. It is interesting to see in this connection that the same power that started this process of the 1,290 days, the Franks, was also the power (France) that brought that process to an end at the close of the 1,290 day-years. When France descended into the revolution in 1789, the papacy lost its major supporter in Europe. Not long afterwards this former supporter turned upon the institution that it had formerly supported and brought it to a temporary end.

THE 1,335 DAYS

The last time period of Daniel 12—the 1,335 days in verse 12—belongs to a different realm. This time period is not related to the work of the little horn. The little horn had brought about persecution and an obscuring of the heavenly ministry Christ, but the 1,335 days have a different point of reference. A blessing is pronounced upon the persons who came to the end of this prophetic time period. This is a work of a different sort, the work of God, for He is the one who gives such blessings to mankind. What blessing was this, and when did it take place or begin?

Since we have a succession of prophetic time periods in this chapter, the 1,260 days (three and a half times), the 1,290 days, and the 1,335 days, it is logical to view their beginning points as related to each other. The 1,260 days began in A.D. 538. The beginning of the 1,290 days extends thirty years prior to that time, to A.D. 508. Since the next time period to appear is the 1,335 days, it is logical to correlate its beginning date with commencement of the previous time prophecy in A.D. 508. If we add the 1,335 day-years to A.D. 508, we come to the year 1843. In early Adventist writings, this date was taken to represent the time of the Millerite preaching when those giving this message announced that the end of the 2,300 day-years of Daniel 8:14 would come in 1843/1844 and eventually settled on October 22, 1844, as the date of fulfillment. Here in Daniel 12:12 we have a prophetic time period that came to an end in 1843. Thus the two events were very close in time.

As a matter of fact, these two prophetic time periods overlap. The last year of the 2,300-year prophecy of Daniel 8:14 extended from the fall of 1843 to the fall of 1844, according to the Jewish fall-to-fall calendar which the Jews utilized for their chronological reckoning. But we have calculated the 1,260 and 1,290 day-years according to the Roman calendar because that was the power that exercised dominion and authority at that time. These Roman years (Julian-Gregorian) begin in January and extend until December. This means that the last four months (October to December) of the 1,335th year overlapped the first four months of the Jewish calendar that year. In other words, these two prophetic time periods end very closely together, within the same twelve-month period—the twelve months leading up to October 22, 1844.

This is another way of saying that the 1,335 days actually take us to the end of the 2,300 days and that they should be seen as overlapping or coinciding with the 2,300 days in coming to that final ending point. The great event taking place at that time was the judgment that began in heaven (Daniel 7:9, 10; 8:14a, see especially the commentary above on 8:14). The blessing then comes upon those who come to that important event in the history of salvation.

A similar blessing is found at a similar point in time in the book of Revelation. "Then I heard a voice from heaven say, 'Write: Blessed are the dead who die in the Lord from now on' " (Revelation 14:13). The context of this blessing should be noted. It is preceded immediately by the three angels' messages. We know that these are end-time messages because they result in the second coming of Christ in Revelation 14:14–18. The first of these three end-time messages announces the judgment of God (Revelation 14:6, 7). That was the judgment that began at the end of the 2,300 days according to Daniel 8:14. Daniel 12:12 pronounces a blessing upon the persons who come to that great event, and Revelation 14:13 pronounces a blessing upon the people who live and die for God during the time of that judgment. The two blessings of these two books are related to each other and are historically continuous with each other. The ultimate blessing that God's people will receive has already been described by Daniel 12:1–3; it is deliverance from the troubles of the end time by Michael and an abundant and glorious entrance into His kingdom thereafter.

CONCLUDING REMARKS

Before mentioning the final fate of Daniel in the last verse in the book, some mention of the fate of the book itself should be made. Daniel 12:4 gives final instructions to Daniel regarding the prophecy of chapter 11. Daniel is told to seal up the book until the time of the end. Thus there was a special sense in which the content of this book was not to be known or made clear until a considerable amount of time had passed from Daniel's own day. L. E. Froom's study of historical interpretations of Daniel and Revelation, *The Prophetic Faith of Our Fathers,* notes that the individual prophecies of the book of Daniel were not well understood until the time of their fulfillment had come. Thus Daniel 9 pointing to the Messiah was the first of the prophecies to be understood. However, it was not until the Middle Ages and the Reformation that the other prophecies of the book came to be understood better. The final phase of this intense study of Daniel's book came in the late eighteenth century and the first half of the nineteenth century when the fulfillment of the 1,260 days came to its completion with the fall of the papacy in 1798. This event also marked the beginning of the "time of the end" in Daniel. It was also in this period that the end of the 2,300-day prophecy was noted by the Millerite movement and other students of Daniel's writings.

In the wake of the French Revolution (which looked like the beginning of the end of the world to many people), the first half of the nineteenth century was a time of intense study of the prophecies. The Albury Park Conference in England in 1826 marked one high point of that interest. The Millerite camp meetings of North America focused intensively upon those same apocalyptic prophecies of Daniel and Revelation. They were seen as having almost reached their final end. In that sense, the book of Daniel was unsealed at that very time, in the time of the end (12:4). Bits and pieces of the puzzle had been put together before, but now the prophecies of Daniel stood forth in their resplendent glory as a revelation of the foreknowledge of the true God reaching down to the time of the end.

The book closes with the promise to Daniel that he will be among those to arise at the last day to receive his part in the inheritance of God's people (12:13). That is a blessed promise that is offered to all who give their allegiance to Michael, the Son of man, God's Christ.

CHAPTER THIRTEEN

Daniel's Walk With God

Our study of the book of Daniel has taken us through a considerable amount of history and prophecy—often intertwined. We have looked at the history in which Daniel participated or which he observed in the sixth century B.C. We have also looked at prophecies which started in his time and have reached from that day down to our time—and beyond.

But there is another side to the book of Daniel and his experiences which are recorded there—the personal spiritual side. What was Daniel's own spiritual relationship with God? We know that it was strong and solid, or God would not have chosen him to be a prophet. But can we say anything more about it than that? Is there anything that we can learn from Daniel's own personal spiritual walk with God? I would suggest that there is. When we study the progression of the revelations about God in the book and in Daniel's experience, we can see a gradual unfolding of God's purpose for the prophet. That progression in revelation and spiritual experience provides a model for our own walk with God.

DANIEL 1

It must have been quite dreary trudging more than four hundred miles on foot from Jerusalem to Babylon as prisoners of Nebuchadnezzar's troops. There must have been many times along the way that Daniel and his friends asked, "Where is God in all of this? Why did this happen to us?" It would have been easy to have become discouraged and demoralized, but they didn't yield to this temptation. Even after they arrived in Babylon and were enrolled in school there, they were still willing to stand up for truth and the true God. They were still willing to make their faith manifest regardless of the consequences. In all of this, however, God was hidden from them. They did not have any direct visions or dreams at this time to encourage them along the way during their captivity and their studies in Babylon. Nevertheless, God was still with them even though He was unseen. Three times in Daniel 1 the text says that Daniel and his companions were blessed. God blessed them with favor in the sight of the Babylonian officials who were attending them, and thus they were able to obtain the diet that they preferred (vs. 9). This resulted in their appearing and performing in a manner superior to their fellow students. (Incidentally, do you think that Daniel and his three friends were the only Hebrew captives enrolled in this school?)

God also blessed them with knowledge and understanding in all of the material they studied (vs. 17). Finally, God gave them grace to demonstrate these qualities when they stood before the king (vs. 18). Even though God did not give them a direct revelation during this period, He still was with them, though hidden.

DANIEL 2

The first major revelation of the book came during the events described in chapter 2. This revelation, however, was not given directly to Daniel or his friends. It was given to Nebuchadnezzar, the pagan king whom they served. This made matters difficult for Daniel and his friends. By now they had come to be classified with the wise men of Babylon, and since these wise men had failed to provide either the dream or its interpretation to the king, the lives of Daniel and his friends were threatened along with the other wise men. The four Hebrews went to God in prayer, and what an earnest prayer meeting it must have been! Seldom have we had to pray as if our lives depended upon it. God was gracious and gave to Daniel just the knowledge that the king wanted. He and his friends and all of the wise men of Babylon were saved. It should be noted here, however, that when the revelations of the book of Daniel began, that the first was given directly to the king. Daniel served as the inspired wise man who interpreted the dream for the king through God's aid. As far as Daniel was concerned, the revelation was indirect. God did give him the knowledge to interpret the dream, but ultimately the vision was for the king; Daniel served as the conduit to present that knowledge to the king.

DANIEL 4

Since Daniel was not part of the experience described in Daniel 3, we need not comment on the mode of revelation employed there. The prophetic revelations take up again in chapter 4. There we have the same situation as in Daniel 2. The king had a dream, and Daniel ultimately came in to interpret it for the king. The king's dream was of a great tree which represented Nebuchadnezzar himself. It was cut down, representing Nebuchadnezzar's period of madness. Eventually he was to be restored and would recognize that the God of heaven is in control of earthly affairs—even those concerning Nebuchadnezzar's kingdom and his life. Daniel's part, again, was to serve as the inspired wise man who interpreted the king's dream for him. It was a direct revelation to Nebuchadnezzar; it was indirect to Daniel. The case is directly parallel to what happened in Daniel 2. Thus far in the book, we have chapter 1 in which God was hidden but still active, and chapters 2 and 4 in which the king received the primary revelation and Daniel served as the inspired wise man who interpreted the king's dreams for him.

DANIEL 7

This prophecy came to Daniel in the first year of Belshazzar or about 550 B.C. This was some time before the events of Daniel 5 and 6 which we can date to 539 B.C. and 538 B.C. respectively. Belshazzar was still one of the kings of the Neo-Babylonian Empire before it fell to the Persians. But in this case, the dream did not come to Belshazzar. It came directly to Daniel. It came to him exactly as the dreams had come to Nebuchadnezzar previously. Nebuchadnezzar had had dreams at night while he was lying on his bed asleep. The next morning when he awoke, he could not remember the dream; Daniel had to supply the dream itself as well as the interpretation. In this case, however, the dream came directly to Daniel as he lay asleep upon his bed. And he did not forget the content of the dream. He woke up the next morning ready to write down what he had seen in the dream. The mode of revelation was the same, a night dream, but the target recipient was different. In the two previous cases, the dream was given to the pagan king and Daniel had to go in to the king to interpret the dream for him. Now the dream came directly to Daniel with no intermediary.

One can say that Daniel became a prophet in his own right on this occasion. Previously he had served as an inspired wise man at court; now he stood free and independent as a prophet. The vision of chapter 7 was, in essence, his call to the office of a prophet. Another aspect of this prophetic dream was that within it, while in vision, Daniel was given an angel interpreter. He had not had such an interpreter previously. In 7:9–14, his view was lifted up to the heavenly court, and while he was watching, he "approached one of those standing there and asked him the true meaning of all this" (vs. 16). In vision, the angel spoke to him and gave him the explanation. This marks an advance in Daniel's experience over the two previous cases. Now the revelation was directed especially to Daniel himself, and he was given an angel interpreter within the night dream to interpret the symbols of the vision for him.

DANIEL 8

The vision in this chapter was of a different nature. Daniel was not given a dream while lying on his bed. Instead, he was taken out of his daily activities and transported in vision to the province of Elam east of Babylon. There he watched the rise of Persia through the symbol of the ram, followed by the rise of Greece through the symbol of the goat that came from the opposite direction. Then came the four horns and the little horn and finally the promise of the two angels who talked about the 2,300 days. In this vision, Daniel was transported east to Elam just as Ezekiel was transported west to Jerusalem. This does not mean that either of them were transported bodily; they were transported in vision. After Daniel had seen and heard the vision of Daniel 8, an angel interpreter was sent to him. In this case, however, the angel did not appear to him within the vision itself as had the two angels in the earlier vision who talked to him about the 2,300 days. Instead, Gabriel was sent to him personally, bodily, and audibly. While Daniel was in a deep sleep, having been overcome by the majesty and events of the vision, Gabriel touched him and gave him strength so that he could stand up and listen to the angel's explanation. In this case, therefore, the mode of presentation of the vision is becoming more and more direct. Daniel was the direct recipient of the vision and an angel is sent directly to him to interpret it for him. God is coming closer and closer to Daniel as the prophet continues His faithful walk with Him.

DANIEL 5

In terms of the order of the book, we need to drop back to chapter 5 in order to pick up the transition from the Babylonian kingdom to the Persian kingdom. Daniel 5 depicts the very night in which Babylon was overthrown by the Persians and tells us what happened in the palace at that time. A disembodied hand appeared and wrote on the wall of the palace throne room a message for the king and the people in attendance at the banquet. Only Daniel was able to interpret the writing. The writing on the wall signified that the kingdom of Belshazzar, the Neo-Babylonian empire, had come to an end and that the Persians were going to take over.

In this case, the mode of revelation was visible to all of the participants present. They saw the hand writing and the message it wrote, even though they could not read or understand it. This was a message sent directly from God through one of His angel servants. It was the direct presence of an angel that put the message on the wall. The revelation did not come through a dream or vision; it came through a personal appearance by the angel. This is very much like the second half of Daniel 8, where an angel came directly to Daniel to interpret the vision for him. In chapter 5, Daniel served as the interpreter of the writing which predicted the downfall of the kingdom that very night.

DANIEL 9

In the chronological order of the book, the events of chapter 9 follow next after those of chapter 5. Daniel's prayer and Gabriel's prophecy as recorded in this chapter occurred sometime during the first year of Darius the Mede, or 538 B.C., which was also the first year after the fall of Babylon to the Persians. What happened here bears considerable similarity to both the last half of Daniel 8 and the revelation in Daniel 5. In both of those cases, there was a personal appearance by an angel. The same thing occurred here in chapter 9. But there are a few differences. In Daniel 8 a vision preceded the angel's interpretation. In chapter 9, there was no immediately preceding vision, although the angel began his interpretive prophecy by referring back to the vision of Daniel 8. In Daniel 5, the writing of the angel was addressed to the whole audience present in the banquet hall. In chapter 9, the prophecy was directed only to Daniel himself, to be given by him to his own and later generations. Thus chapters 5, 8, and 9 all contain the same type of revelation—the personal appearance of an angel—but the circumstances were different in each case. In chapter 9 the focus comes down more directly to Daniel himself; here is a prophetic message delivered directly to Daniel orally and without any other audience present.

In Daniel 1 there was no direct disclosure of God Himself, He remained hidden, though active behind the scenes. In Daniel 2 and 4, God worked indirectly through the dreams of a pagan king which Daniel interpreted as an inspired wise man. Now in Daniel 5, 8, and 9, there is the personal appearance of an angel—once with writing, once with a day vision, and once directly with oral communication. Thus we see a progression in God's mode of revelation as He comes to Daniel more and more directly and personally. But an angel is not God, he is only a servant of God. Will Daniel ever see God Himself before his prophetic ministry is finished? That great climax comes in the last prophecy of the book.

DANIEL 10

Chapters 10, 11, 12 form a unit. Chapter 10 is the introduction to the prophecy given by the angel Gabriel; chapter 11 is the body of the prophecy; and chapter 12 is the epilogue. Daniel 10 carries the date of the third year of Cyrus, or 536 B.C. Daniel was an old man by this time. He had been carried into captivity in 605 B.C., so he himself had lived out the seventy years of Jeremiah's prophecy (Jeremiah 25:11, 12) in Babylonian captivity. Since he was about eighteen to twenty years of age when he was taken into captivity, Daniel must have been about ninety years of age at the time this final revelation came to him. The body of the prophecy in Daniel 11 was delivered orally by Gabriel to Daniel just as he had done in Daniel 9. But the introduction to the prophecy in Daniel 10 is something new that has not been seen before in the book of Daniel.

At the time of this vision, Daniel was out by the Tigris River. He was praying, mourning, and fasting about the interruption in the efforts of God's people to rebuild the temple. Now as Daniel is out by the river agonizing over this situation, something dramatic happened.

> I looked up and there before me was a man dressed in linen, with a belt of the finest gold around his waist. His body was like chrysolite, his face like lightning, his eyes like flaming torches, his arms and legs like the gleam of burnished bronze, and his voice like the sound of a multitude (Daniel 10:5–7).

Daniel was overwhelmed with the majestic theophany. This was a vision, but the English word, "vision" does not convey the full meaning of the original word used here. This was a *mareh* vision, or an appearance vision. It means that this Being had put in a personal appearance before the prophet. Daniel had been overwhelmed by previous visions, Daniel 8 in particular. But this appearance was far more powerful than anything he had ever received previously. This is a theophany—an appearance of God Himself.

There are two other passages in the Bible that present descriptions closely aligned with the appearance of this Being that is described here in chapter 10. Those two visions are found in Ezekiel 1 and Revelation 1. In Ezekiel 1, the prophet recognized that the Being that he saw was "the appearance of the likeness of the glory of the Lord" (Ezekiel 1:28). In Revelation 1, John turned to see who was speaking to him, and recognized that he was looking directly at his Lord, Jesus Christ. By means of these parallels, therefore, we know who appeared to Daniel when he was out by the Tigris River. On the basis of the parallel with Ezekiel 1, we know that this was God, and on the basis of the parallel with Revelation 1, we know that this particular manifestation of God was Jesus Christ. It was He who appeared to Daniel on the plain of the Tigris on that spring day in 536 B.C.

This was the same God who had been with Daniel all of the seventy years the prophet had been in Babylon. God had been working with him, working for him, inspiring him, and protecting him. He had been walking at his side all the time Daniel ministered there. Little by little, more and more, God opened Himself up to Daniel in terms of the revelations that He gave to Him. The mode of these revelations demonstrates the way in which God came closer and closer and closer to Daniel. First there was no revelation at all. Then the revelations came through a pagan king and his night dreams; then they came through a night vision given to Daniel himself. Following that, came a day vision and an angel, Gabriel, who began appearing to Daniel and communicating the prophetic word to him. Finally, near the end of Daniel's life and prophetic ministry, God Himself appeared to Daniel and said in essence, "Here I am, Daniel. We have been walking together for these past seventy years. Now I want you to see the One you have been walking with." Daniel met his Lord personally. God had been coming closer and closer to Him until He finally revealed His personal being to Him in all of His glory.

When Daniel lay down to rest in death, as the angel told him he soon would, He could do so with a smile on his face, for he had finally met his Lord personally. The next thing Daniel will know is awaking on the resurrection morning. His resurrection from the dead was also promised to him by the angel (12:13). Daniel will see that same glorious, radiant, smiling face beaming down upon him; he will listen to the Lifegiver's voice, "Awake, awake, you that sleep in the dust and arise." And Daniel will come forth to walk with his Lord anew in a walk that will take him into eternity.

Enoch's case is somewhat similar to that of Daniel in this regard, but Enoch was translated alive, while Daniel will have to wait a bit longer for that experience. Nevertheless, their spiritual experience has parallels. Ellen White has described Enoch's walk with God in very poignant terms that could well apply to Daniel:

> For three hundred years Enoch had been seeking purity of soul, that he might be in harmony with Heaven. For three centuries he had walked with God. Day by day he had longed for a

> closer union; nearer and nearer had grown the communion, until God took him to Himself. He had stood at the threshold of the eternal world, only a step between him and the land of the blest; and now the portals opened, the walk with God, so long pursued on earth, continued, and he passed through the gates of the Holy City—the first from among men to enter there (*Patriarchs and Prophets,* 87).

This type of experience is not just for Enoch, and it is not just for Daniel. It is also for us today. Granted, we may not have prophetic revelations as Daniel did. However, we may have a walk with God in which we come closer and closer to Him each day. That should be the course of progress in our spiritual lives as it was for Daniel. As we come closer to God in this way, we will understand His will for our lives better. We will also learn more of His character and come to reflect it more fully. As we become more and more like Him, people will take knowledge of us, as they did of the disciples, that we have been with Jesus.

Daniel would be happy to see this taking place in our lives. When he comes up in the resurrection, Daniel will be pleased to know that his book, which God gave to him, has provided such hope and comfort and inspiration to us in the final generation of those things predicted in it. In God's eternal kingdom, we will be able to continue the walk with God that we have begun here on this earth. At the head of that great throng will be our Lord Jesus Christ, leading us onward.